La Meri and Her Life in Dance

UNIVERSITY PRESS OF FLORIDA

Florida A&M University, Tallahassee
Florida Atlantic University, Boca Raton
Florida Gulf Coast University, Ft. Myers
Florida International University, Miami
Florida State University, Tallahassee
New College of Florida, Sarasota
University of Central Florida, Orlando
University of Florida, Gainesville
University of North Florida, Jacksonville
University of South Florida, Tampa
University of West Florida, Pensacola

La Meri

and Her Life in Dance

Performing the World

Nancy Lee Chalfa Ruyter

UNIVERSITY PRESS OF FLORIDA

Gainesville / Tallahassee / Tampa / Boca Raton

Pensacola / Orlando / Miami / Jacksonville / Ft. Myers / Sarasota

This book may be available in an electronic edition.

24 23 22 21 20 19   6 5 4 3 2 1

Library of Congress Cataloging-in-Publication Data
Names: Ruyter, Nancy Lee Chalfa, author.
Title: La Meri and her life in dance : performing the world / Nancy Lee
    Chalfa Ruyter.
Description: Gainesville : University Press of Florida, 2019. | Includes
    bibliographical references and index.
Identifiers: LCCN 2018059617 | ISBN 9780813066097 (cloth : alk. paper)
Subjects: LCSH: La Meri, 1898–1988. | Dancers—United States—
Biography. |
    Choreographers—United States—Biography.
Classification: LCC GV1785.H77 R89 2019 | DDC 792.802/8092 [B]—dc23
LC record available at https://lccn.loc.gov/2018059617

The University Press of Florida is the scholarly publishing agency for the
State University System of Florida, comprising Florida A&M University,
Florida Atlantic University, Florida Gulf Coast University, Florida
International University, Florida State University, New College of Florida,
University of Central Florida, University of Florida, University of North
Florida, University of South Florida, and University of West Florida.

University Press of Florida
2046 Northeast Waldo Road
Suite 2100
Gainesville, FL 32609
http://upress.ufl.edu

Dedicated to:

Selma Treviño

Phoenix Alexander

Frank Xavier Zacharias

Contents

Figures

Preface

I first met La Meri at Jacob's Pillow in the summer of 1953. After years of training in ballet, the only dance form about which I had any knowledge or appreciation, I left home to continue my dance studies—first in this noted summer dance program founded and directed by Ted Shawn, and then in New York City. At the Pillow, in line with Shawn's commitment to promoting a broad range of world dance, all students were required to take classes in ballet, modern dance, and what was termed "ethnic dance"—traditional dance arts connected with cultures from around the world. In 1953, those classes were Spanish and East Indian dance taught by La Meri, her partner Peter di Falco, and her sister Lilian Newcomer. Being introduced to these genres changed my life. After settling in New York City in the fall, I continued ballet training and worked in modern dance with the legendary faculty of the New Dance Group, but I was pulled ever more inexorably in the direction offered by La Meri and her staff. I was a student at her Ethnologic Dance Center (EDC) on East 59th Street and eventually became a member of di Falco's company for which La Meri served as artistic director. I maintained contact with her until her death in 1988.

At the EDC we were required to study the historical and cultural contexts of the dance arts being taught along with developing proficiency in the movement techniques. This started me on the path of reading more and more about dance and led eventually to my becoming a dance historian. Several years ago, while writing an article on La Meri for the *American National Biography* (published 1999), my memories of this revered and beloved mentor were renewed. I decided that someone—maybe I—should examine in depth her life; her career as a performing artist, teacher, and writer; and her significance in the history of dance.

After beginning this project, I learned that it was not the first attempt to investigate La Meri's life and contributions. In 1984, Josephine (Josie) Neal (1938–2001), a former dancer and noted critic in San Antonio, Texas, had begun intensive preparation for a biography of La Meri. The research included interviews with her subject from 1984 to 1987 and continuing work with a large collection of documents that were provided. She also contacted and questioned students, dancers, and others who had worked with La Meri. Sadly, however, Neal contracted lung cancer, and, in 2001, at the age of 63, she died before being able to get beyond her research for the book.

The documents that Neal had received from La Meri included letters, programs, articles, reviews, pictures, and personal statements that provide in-depth and detailed knowledge about La Meri's life and career that is unavailable elsewhere. Their very existence had been forgotten for a time, but then the late William J. Adams Jr. began searching and found that they were in a storage area at the home of Neal's daughter, Hannah. I am very grateful that, through the efforts of Adams and Hannah Neal, I received the collection in 2014. After making copies, I sent the originals to the La Meri archive at Jacob's Pillow. Adams had been involved with La Meri in Cape Cod as student, teacher, performer, and administrative assistant—and then he cared for her during the final years of her life. He was thus able to provide much information and insights into La Meri's life and work in the 1970s and 1980s. I visited him three times during his last years and I greatly appreciated our contact and all that I learned from him.

Others have also contributed significantly to this project. Insights and information have been provided by Mariano Parra, Jerane Michel (Costanza), and the late Peter di Falco—who began as La Meri's students and developed into professional colleagues (information about each is provided in the text). As research assistants, two close friends have accomplished a great deal in the gathering and organization of information. One is Selma Treviño who, over several years, helped with investigating the materials on La Meri in the New York Public Library for the Performing Arts. The other is Dr. Phoenix Alexander, who has spent years working with me here in California. With technical expertise and indefatigable perseverance, she ferreted out obscure information and clarifications that I had little hope of finding on my own. In addition, she has carefully organized and logged every item I obtained; and this information along with the original documents is also in the La Meri archive at Jacob's Pillow. Others who contributed to the research include Kana Benz and Marion Hart while they were both students at the University of California, Irvine. Important assistance was also provided by the staffs of the Jerome Robbins Dance Division of the New York Public Library for the Performing Arts, the San Antonio Public Library, Jacob's Pillow Dance Festival, and the Duquesne University Tamburitzans.[1] Each of these institutions has rich archival materials on La Meri and her life and work. Finally, I am very grateful to Frank Xavier Zacharias for his help with translations and with preparing the photographs for publication.

Most of these illustrations are from a collection of more than 600 photographs sent to me by William Adams, the Executor of La Meri's estate. None had any identification, but information as to dates, places, photographers, etc. has been found for some.

Introduction

Who owns a culture? Who inherits it? . . . Nobody, of course. For when
one inherits, one inherits a global collective web, a web not concentric or
symmetrical, but connected in all its parts . . . , a web which one is meant,
indeed bound, to reweave. . . . [C]ultural representations . . . can be borrowed
without anyone missing them or attempting to retrieve them at gunpoint;
they have the grace (like human beings) to be fruitful and multiply . . . , and
they have the good sense (also like human beings) to transform themselves
in the process.

(JULIE STONE PETERS 1995, 210–11)

The subject of this book is La Meri, an international dance artist whose work
represents the kind of cultural borrowing and integration that Peters defends. La Meri built her career on the practice of dance from many world
cultures before issues such as appropriation, commodification, orientalism,
voyeurism, and the like became concerns within academic studies. During
La Meri's extensive international touring from 1926 to 1939, she would study
with teachers of local dance genres, acquire recordings of the music and traditional costumes, and add the new works to her concert repertoire. Eventually her programs consisted solely of traditional dances from various world
cultures and, later, also original works she created using one or another of
those dance languages. La Meri performed her repertoire in Latin America,
Europe, Asia, the Pacific area, and the United States. She also taught in Europe and the United States, and her writings set forth her conceptions, un-

derstandings, goals, and methodology. This book is both a biography of La Meri and an analysis of her work, including her performance, choreography, writings, and teaching. What is her legacy and significance in the contexts of dance as an art form, dance studies, and dance theory?

In the twenty-first century, people in urban centers have access to a rich variety of world art forms. One can view Japanese Kabuki in Paris, Bolivian theater in Cádiz, Mexican art in New York City, Western contemporary dance in Beijing—and the list goes on. Dance companies specializing in theatrical adaptations of traditional folk, social, or ritual dance from their own cultures tour extensively, and artists from an array of traditions perform and teach internationally. Dance genres originating in one culture have come to be practiced all over the world—for example, Western ballet, modern dance, and jazz; Spanish flamenco; Bharatanatyam and other forms from India; and Latin American social dances. Through books and articles, films, television, audio recordings, and the internet—not to mention actual as well as virtual travel—one can choose to explore the myriad forms of expression across the globe. Not only does this provide the opportunity for people to become acquainted with more or less traditional practices from many cultures but also with the development of various kinds of adaptations and fusions. The latter have included the mixing of elements from two or more traditions to create new forms such as Indo-jazz or Bulgarian hip hop or works such as innovative theater director Peter Brook's controversial 1985 production of the Sanskrit *Mahabharata*. Inevitably, there is also a growing body of literature—both pro and con—on such phenomena (see, for example, Balme 2007, Foster 2009, Gainor 1995, Lengel 2005, Marranca and Dasgupta 1991, and Pavis 1996).

La Meri's work represents one stage in the progression of interculturalism in Western dance that can be traced back several centuries. In Europe, at least from the Renaissance on, and in the Western Hemisphere from the early days of colonization, there has been a history of intercultural appropriation, sharing and/or imposition. Typically, the exchange has been between more powerful and less powerful political or social entities.

In dance, intercultural manifestations in Europe can be seen from the early Renaissance dance treatises written to serve an international court culture that shared social dances and entertainment forms. The pan-European social dance repertoire included the pavan (Italy, Spain, and France, sixteenth–seventeenth centuries), the sarabande (Spain and Latin America, sixteenth century, and then throughout Europe), the minuet (seventeenth–nineteenth centuries), and the allemande (fifteenth–nineteenth centuries). Such dances were taught and spread by members of an increasing cadre of professional and often itinerant dance masters. The early social dances were incorporated into court ballets, masques, and other entertainments and began to develop into what eventually became the ballet tradition. A crucial event in the internationalization of performance forms was the 1533 marriage of Catherine de Medici (1519–1589), from the prominent Italian family, to the French prince who would become King Henry II in 1547. Catherine brought Italian performing and plastic arts to the French court, where they became established. As the power of France increased, French culture, including the elements that had developed from borrowed or appropriated practices, influenced court cultures throughout Europe (see, for example, Kant 2007; McGowan 2008; Sorell 1986).

Western interest in other cultures and in the appropriation of selected elements from them for incorporation into hegemonic art forms such as opera and ballet continued into the Baroque era and beyond. Dance historian Deborah Jowitt writes of the "decorative Orientalism of the eighteenth century: the nobility-in-turbans dances—as in Jean Philippe Rameau's *Les Indes Galantes*—or cavorting Siamese 'grotesques' or the porcelain figures come to life in Jean Georges Noverre's *Les Fêtes Chinoises*" (49). In referring to these manifestations and others from the later Romantic era, she notes that "Authenticity was never an issue," that, for the most part, the term "'The Orient' has designated a pleasure garden for the imagination—an Orient restructured to fire European longings and justify European conquest" (50). In addition to the Middle East and Asia (usually conflated under the term "Orient"), librettists and choreographers also drew from the Western Hemisphere (the so-called New World) and the Pacific area; and there was a range of borrowing—from merely decorative elements to actual dances, dance styles, and dance movements.

European interest in the actual dances of various cultures can be documented from the eighteenth century. Dance historians Lisa C. Arkin and Marian Smith note that "many ballet theoreticians of the late eighteenth and nineteenth centuries expressed a keen interest in the authentic, 'true' and 'natural' folk expressions of various nations" (30), and cite as evidence treatises by Giovanni-Andrea Gallini (1772), Gennaro Magri (1779), and Carlo Blasis (1820, 1828, 1847) (30–34). They also write of choreographers such as August Bournonville and dancers such as Fanny Elssler seeking instruction in dances outside their own ballet traditions (34–35), although any such material would have been adapted for the ballet stage (35–45). One might investigate how the process of such nineteenth-century ballet practitioners differed (if it did) from that of Igor Moiseyev or Amalia Hernández in their adaptations of Russian or Mexican folk dances for twentieth-century "folk ballet" performances, or from that of La Meri in her presentation of world dance traditions on the concert stage.

Interest in the exotic "other" continued into the twentieth century. Pioneering nonballetic dance artists such as Maud Allan (1873–1956) and Loie Fuller (1862–1928) borrowed themes from the Middle East in exotic depictions of, for example, the biblical dance of Salome, a favorite theme on both sides of the Atlantic (Cherniavsky 1991, 141; Garelick 1995, 85; see also Albright 2007 and Garelick 2007). They developed their choreography on popular images and conceptions of the "Orient" rather than on any kind of historical or ethnographic research. Loie Fuller, best known for her innovations in theatrical lighting effects in combination with voluminous swirling silk fabrics, stepped into the exotic East with *Dance of the Seven Veils* (first performed 1895 and then enormously successful at the 1900 Paris Exposition) and with her presentation of the Japanese dancer Sada Yakko, also at the 1900 Exposition (Current and Current 1997, 80–85, 141–44). In the field of ballet, the Ballets Russes of Diaghilev had explored various exotic themes, and some of the solo works of the incomparable ballerina Anna Pavlova (1881–1931) incorporated actual movements as well as images and themes from Mexican, East Indian, and other cultures (Lazzarini 1980, 1998; La Meri 1977a, 67).

Two innovative and highly influential dance artists, Ruth St. Denis (1879–1968) and Ted Shawn (1891–1972), researched to some extent the elements of foreign cultures that interested them. They studied art works and texts to understand spiritual concepts as they developed their dance vocabularies, choreography, costuming, and stage design, and they did learn some actual dances during their tour of Asia in 1925–26 (see Shelton 1981; Ruyter 1979, 64–65, and 2000b, 25–26). For the most part, however, St. Denis and Shawn were not attempting to either learn or present actual dances or dance languages from other cultures. Allan, Fuller, and St. Denis, who had begun their lives and careers twenty to thirty years earlier than La Meri, became established professionally during the orientalist mania of the late nineteenth and early twentieth centuries that raged on both sides of the Atlantic.[1] St. Denis, Allan, and others sought to capture a Westernized concept of some mysterious oriental "essence" in their dancing, or as expressed by the dance historian Susan Manning, they presented "Western stereotypes of the East" (161).

While La Meri was the first twentieth-century American dancer to actually pursue the study of foreign dance languages—their movements, choreographic forms, styles, and cultural components—she developed that interest and commitment only gradually. In the early years of her training and her performance, her repertoire was an eclectic mix of ballet, proto-modern (or interpretive) dance, and impressions (à la Denishawn) of the dances of non-Western cultures, accompanied by Western piano or orchestral music. It was her extensive international touring in the 1920s and 1930s that brought her into contact with a wide variety of traditional world dance forms. Beginning with her first foreign engagement in Mexico, she became interested in learning some of the dances and movement techniques that were native to the culture she was visiting. While in the course of her life, she became most knowledgeable about the dance arts of Spain and India, she also learned, performed, and wrote about dances from other parts of Asia, from the Pacific area, and from Latin America.

Chapters 1 through 8 are devoted to La Meri's biography from her childhood to her last years, covering her development as a performing artist, choreographer, teacher, and writer—and her personal relationships. Chapter 9 focuses on her writings, and chapter 10 on the significance of her work in general and in relation to theoretical and ethical issues that have become important in academic studies in recent years.

1

Russell Meriwether Hughes

The Early Years, 1899–1920s

The woman who became known as La Meri was born May 13, 1899, in Louisville, Kentucky, and named after her father, Russell Meriwether Hughes.[1] As she developed her amateur and later professional performing activities, she used various versions of her birth name, and among family and friends, from childhood on, she was called "Dickie," a nickname that stayed with her for the rest of her life. Since it was in the mid-1920s that she adopted "La Meri" as her professional name, I'll use her birth name, Russell, up to that point, except when referring to her later writings.

Russ Hughes, as her father was known, lived from 1857 or 1860 until 1914.[2] His family of wealthy plantation owners had lost everything after the American Civil War of 1861–65; and as Russ matured, he worked as a journalist, a musician, and a music teacher. He then turned to business, establishing a company in Louisville that produced vinegar and cider and eventually had branches in San Antonio, Texas, and Middleport, New York. By the early 1890s, Hughes had achieved the financial stability he deemed necessary to embark on marriage and the creation of a family. La Meri describes her father as almost six feet tall, slim, with blue eyes and wavy dark brown hair, and notes his interest in the sports of golf and tennis as well as in music. Russ had known (and reportedly loved) his future wife, Lily Belle Allen (or Allan; c. 1855–1927),[3] since grade school, but waited to marry her until 1891 when they were both in their thirties and his financial situation was secure and growing.

Writing decades later in her autobiography, La Meri characterized Lily as "a woman of great beauty with a strong streak of Scottish moral stubbornness" (1977a, 1). In the section of her autobiography the publisher chose not to include, she states that her mother "always stood in my mind as sort of a faraway princess, a beautiful creature in sparkling satins and marvelous perfumes" (*Draft* 1977, 4). In many passages of this manuscript, La Meri discusses Lily's character and refinement, her commitment to what she deemed proper education for Russell and her older sister Lilian (1892–1965), and her strategies as a mother. La Meri also discusses her feelings for her sister and father and aspects of the family's life together. For example, she writes:

> My sister Lilian was my ideal and my Pappy was my "pardner." I copied everything they did. Pappy played the fiddle, Lilian was taking violin lessons, so nothing would do but that Pappy had to buy me a violin. When he and Lil would get out their instruments, set the inexpert but willing Lily down at the piano to read through simple chamber music, I would sit too with a piece of completely undecipherable music before me and contribute my personal bedlam. (ibid.)

This passage refers to a time when Russell was approaching six years of age, before she had begun her first formal violin lessons.

The Hughes company turned out to be so successful that the family enjoyed a luxurious lifestyle for years. They spent summers in the Virginia mountains and made trips to Florida, New Jersey, New York, and Texas. Despite the rigors and challenges of train travel, the young Russell loved it and was happy to be a part of what she called her "peripatetic" family. In her autobiography she writes: "I still love the sound of a train whistle, for those coal-run monsters that belched cinders over one all day and night were the open sesame to new worlds" (1977a, 1). These early experiences must have primed her for the extensive touring on which she thrived during her career as a dance artist. She frequently wrote of how much she enjoyed travel and how she missed it when settled in one place for a time. In 1973, for example, she characterizes the last years of her international touring (1936–1939) as "the best of all the years . . . from a ship's deck watching the sun come up over an exotic harbor . . . a string of hotels, a string of theaters, sometimes elegant, sometimes primitive, a string of ocean-liners and coast-wise cargo boats" (*Chronology 1973*, 6).

It was probably in 1899, when Lilian was seven and Russell still an infant, that the family first visited San Antonio, Texas, and around 1900, they bought a house there at 321 West Laurel Street. Russ Hughes was suffering from a bronchial problem (he was a smoker, so perhaps it was emphysema), and his doctor had recommended that he live in a climate drier than that of Louisville. The whole family began to spend part of each year in Texas, but Lily, Russell, and Lilian would return to Louisville for the girls' schooling. Around 1906, they decided to move permanently back to Louisville, probably because of Lily's reluctance to live and raise her daughters in what she saw as a wild and unrefined culture. In 1910, however, they changed their minds and settled in San Antonio. There the two girls spent the remainder of their formative years, and La Meri the final years of her life. While their mother had doubts about this western city and its culture, La Meri has written that she and Lilian "loved San Antonio from the start." They were enrolled in the Mulholland School (a private girl's school), and to get there each day, Lilian rode one of the family's carriage horses and Russell her own "Mexican burro," which her "Pappy" had bought for her when she was about six (*Draft 1977*, 3–4; *Letter 1979*, 15).

Whether in Louisville or San Antonio, the family lived in elegant houses with servants, stables for the horses and carriages, and, eventually, space for the new automobiles that were becoming popular among the wealthy. La Meri has written that as soon as the autos first appeared, her father "became a buff" and "was the proud owner of one of the first Oldsmobiles" (*Letter 1979*, 7). Later, in San Antonio, the family experienced a terrible accident in "an electric Victoria" that Hughes had bought. One day, the French chauffeur he had hired to drive the family on outings ran the car into a telephone pole. While the two girls were not hurt, Lily suffered an injury to her kneecap, and the doctor predicted that she would never walk again. Many years later, La Meri writes, "How little did they know Lily, or understand her stubborn Scottish spirit! To the end of her days she walked with a limp, but walk she did" (*Draft 1977*, 6–7). While the first autos in the family were driven by Russ and then also by Lilian, for Christmas 1912, Hughes gave the thirteen-year-old Russell her own "small gray-and-black roadster, bedecked with Christmas ribbons, and with initialing on its doors, *RMH, Jr*" (ibid., 15; see also 1977a, 2). This was a good story for the society pages that thrived on news of families such as the Hughes—and a photograph of Russell and the car was published in the *San Antonio Express* of December 29, 1912 (*Draft 1977*, 15).

At some point after 1910, Russ's health began to seriously decline. Nevertheless, he took on the task of having a new home built for the family in Laurel Heights (312 West Courtland Place). During its construction, Russ and Russell would travel by horse and buggy to oversee the progress since Russ no longer felt safe driving a car. Designed by an architect to the family's specifications, the house was in "Mission" style and had fifteen large rooms, a tennis court, and a two-car garage. Russ was determined to have the house finished, and as La Meri writes, "The building was becoming his heartbreakingly gallant race with Death. A race to house his 'three girls' safely and solidly before he was forced to leave them forever" (*Draft 1977*, 22–23). The family moved into the house sometime before Russ died in mid-May 1914 (ibid., 27).

Years later, La Meri wrote about the experience of watching her father become more and more ill and finally leave them. She realized that he "must have felt a despairing terror and aloneness toward the end," but for his family he always had "laughter, love, and endless patience" (*Draft 1977*, 22). She writes that even after her father suffered a stroke and "was confined permanently to his room, . . . [his] indomitable will kept him alive for a year." And she continues, "My Pardner, tired from a lifetime of grueling work, and old before his time, still listened to all my problems, teasing me intermittently as usual with gay rhymes and sketches" (ibid., 27). He died shortly after Russell's fifteenth birthday; and many years later, she wrote: "Pappy, my ideal, my pardner, who had been the core of my existence, was gone. I began to be accountable for my future. From wherever he was, he would see. The drive to make something of myself was born within me. I must do something to make him proud of me" (ibid., 30). And she certainly accomplished that, in many different ways.

In the house in Laurel Heights, each girl had her own bedroom, Russell's with "a little study attached." The basement was turned into a "dancing-club room" and the top floor into a billiard room. On Sundays, Russell and Lilian would host an open house in the basement room for the "Phi Alpha Sigmas," a girls' club organized by the mother of one of their classmates. Lily did not permit dancing on Sundays, but on Fridays and Saturdays the two sisters would host dances for their teenage friends—both boys and girls—hiring a pianist for two dollars to provide music. The dancing-club room was also used for other social events and for rehearsals (*Draft 1977*, 12, 23–25, 27). By

1984, when La Meri returned to San Antonio, the house had been made into a Catholic Student Center near the San Antonio College campus (Igo, 1984).

During the years that the United States was involved in World War I (1917–1918), the family participated in support activities for the troops. Some seven "war-time camps" had been established in the San Antonio area, and La Meri writes that "the city teemed with them [the soldiers]. Each camp bulged with lonely, uprooted young men" (1977a, 12). Russell, Lilian, and their mother held open house on Sunday afternoons for some of the homesick troops stationed in the camps. The women also contributed to the war effort by knitting socks and sweaters and rolling bandages; and Russell, Lilian, and their young friends gave performances at the camps and attended dances for the soldiers. Looking back on that time from 1977, La Meri writes: "Weekly I fell in and out of love with young men from all over the country, and from a few distant countries as well. I danced miles and miles with soldiers and for soldiers, and when entertainment programs were insufficient, as they often were, I could be depended on to dash forth, carrying the biggest Tri-color this side of France, to sing 'La Marseillaise' in a willing but wobbly soprano" (1977a, 12). Such activities continued until the war ended on November 11, 1918.

Russell and Lilian discovered that the war was over when they were awakened by "a distant, bewildering sort of roar, punctuated by gunshots." Through the window, they saw "a strange pink glare" in the sky and realized that the end had finally come. They were eager to rush to the town center to join the celebrants, but Lily did not consider that safe, would not permit it, and insisted that they return to their beds—which they did. Lilian at twenty-seven and Russell at nineteen were still very obedient daughters. Later, at the end of World War II (V-E Day, May 8, 1945) when La Meri "traipsed the whole screaming length of Broadway in New York City," she realized that their mother had been wise in keeping them from the crowd so many years before (1977a, 13–14).

In 1918–1919, an influenza pandemic infected millions internationally—killing approximately 675,000 in the United States alone.[4] Sometime after celebrating Thanksgiving on November 28, 1918, Russell and Lilian contracted this flu, and their doctor predicted that Russell would not survive it. They were bedridden for a month, but both fortunately did slowly recover. Many years later, La Meri had memories of her first outing after the illness—

a New Year's "tea dance" at a local hotel where, in the beginning, she "sat at the table, too weak to dance." Soon, however, she was approached by an attractive captain with whom she fell instantly in love, and she writes that, as they danced, she "returned to full strength." She then describes their relationship, which continued for the next four years (1977a, 12–13; *Draft 1977*, 43–46). One cannot know if the sudden recovery she describes actually happened that way or was a fantasy. In any case, both Russell and Lilian did recover completely and were able to return to their normal life and regular activities.

From an early age, the Hughes daughters were exposed to a broad range of experiences in dance, music, acting, and painting. In her autobiography, La Meri writes that at age six, she began what would be eight years of violin lessons; at twelve, classes in ballet; and in high school, singing, acting, and painting. The amount of arts education provided to the sisters was probably way beyond what wealthy families of that era usually provided for their daughters (or their sons). Sometime during high school, Russell briefly became a member of the local symphony orchestra (*Draft 1977*, 13; 1977a, 2). By her twentieth year, she had published her first two books of poetry (of a total of six); sung, danced, and acted in amateur venues; written plays; composed songs; and exhibited her paintings. The range of her education and experience in the arts constituted a unique preparation for her subsequent life and career and helped her to achieve international acclaim as a performing artist, an innovative choreographer, a dance educator, and a writer and theorist.

Lilian had similar experiences during her youth, and throughout her life, she often collaborated with her sister—dancing and playing the violin in San Antonio; dancing in performances in New York and on tour; and performing and teaching at La Meri's school in New York and at Jacob's Pillow. Involvement in the arts was not the center of her life after September 1920, when she married David Newcomer (1899–1944), a lieutenant in the army (*Letter 1979*, 27), but she remained active in dance. Newcomer was generously supportive of the performance activities of both his wife and her sister. He frequently offered financial assistance to La Meri and agreed for Lilian to sometimes tour with her. The marriage ended tragically with Newcomer's death in the war zone in Europe in August 1944 ("David Albert Newcomer," Arlington National Cemetery website).

According to her own memories, Russell's early attempts at dance were not encouraging, and her earliest teachers, Professor Bellessa at White Sulphur Springs, Virginia (when she was three or four), and a Miss Collins at the Kentucky Home School for Girls (when she was about ten), found her "hopelessly awkward" (*Chronology 1973*, 1). Her next teacher was Mollie M. Moore in San Antonio, with whom she studied social dance forms, ballet, and other genres. La Meri writes that when she began the social dance classes she was twelve, vulnerable to passionate crushes and self-conscious about her "plumpness." At first, she suffered through the agonies of dealing with boys while trying to learn the patterns of cotillions, waltzes, and two-steps. The situation improved, however, as the boys discovered that she was not a bad partner to have as they faced their own dance challenges. And when she celebrated her fourteenth birthday with a formal dance in the ballroom of a local hotel, she enjoyed the pleasure of having her dance card "initialed to overflowing" (*Draft 1977*, 11–12, 15).

What La Meri remembered as her first performance of dancing was in a Sunday school pageant at the Travis Park Methodist Church in San Antonio (probably around 1910)—a program that was not planned to include that art at all. In one part of the pageant, several girls "dressed in flowing Grecian robes, stood in a semi-circle and pantomimed, a la Delsarte" while one girl read a poem.[5] In another section, Russell and three other girls were each to sing an ode to a flower. Her poem was "Poppy," and she sang the first verse as she had rehearsed it but shocked and amazed the pianist and everyone else when she performed a dance she had prepared as the second verse (*Draft 1977*, 16–18). This seems to have been the beginning of Russell's amateur dance performance, which would continue into the 1920s. Apparently the family were active Methodist Church members—initially at the Travis Park Church, and then at the Laurel Heights Methodist Church—and there are frequent references to Russell's performances or other involvement in church events.

A major venue for dance in San Antonio was the annual Carnival Week Fiesta sponsored by the Battle of Flowers Association. It featured an actual "battle of flowers" in which "long lines of carriages drove around and around Alamo Plaza, the occupants pelting each other with real flowers" (*Draft 1977*, 4). The Carnival Week also included a "Fiesta Fete," remembered by La Meri as a "presentation event" in which "everyone from three-year olds to young

lieutenants from Ft. Sam [took] part in the ballets or other dancing special-
ties" (ibid., 16). From 1913 to at least 1917, Russell and Lilian danced in this
Fiesta Fete, which, beginning in 1914, was staged by Mollie Moore. The sisters also appeared in recitals presented by Moore; in shows to entertain the
army troops; on programs for charities, churches, and organizations such
as the Elks Club, Lions Club, American Legion, and San Antonio Musical
Club; and, on September 8, 1915, in an independently staged program in the
dancing-club room of their own home.

In addition to their regular schooling, their studies of various art forms,
and their performing, Russell and Lilian attended concerts and plays by established artists of dance, drama, and music who passed through Texas on
cross-country tours. In this way, Anna Pavlova, Denishawn, La Argentina,
and Diaghilev's Ballets Russes provided models for the future La Meri, inspiring in her a passion for world dance cultures that would dictate the direction of the rest of her life.

It was probably in 1913 that Russell attended a performance of the famous ballerina Anna Pavlova (1881–1931), although, in her autobiography,
La Meri says it was 1912.[6] In any case, seeing Pavlova's art apparently resulted
in the young woman eagerly embracing the art of ballet. Decades later, La
Meri wrote that as she watched this noted artist, "Everything else faded away.
Young as I was, I could feel in the marrow of my bones a beauty of movement
that the world has yet to see surpassed." And she realized that she "might
aspire to it, perhaps even attain it" (1977a, 2).

Russell might have already begun her ballet classes with Mollie Moore
before seeing Pavlova, and she was very soon performing. She writes that
two months after beginning the training, she made "a brief appearance" in
a benefit program arranged by Moore and presented at the San Antonio
Grand Opera House. This was on March 25, 1913. One of the "Dance Poems"
staged by Moore for this program was "Dance of the Hours," and years later,
La Meri remembered herself as "the rotund, but starry-eyed youngster in
the last row at the darkest moment, the chorus of 'Night'" (1977a, 2–3; Program). Soon after that debut, she was regularly performing group and solo
dances in local amateur events. Many of these were ballet-based, with titles
such as "Butterfly," "Ballet of Narcissus," "Zingara," and "The Shepherd Boy's
Dream." The repertoire also included ballroom and historical dances such
as the minuet, Spanish and "Oriental" dances, a Russian dance, and some-

thing called "Egyptian Frieze Dance" (Programs). In 1914, Russell performed her first solo *en pointe* (in ballet toe shoes), and she would continue to do *pointe* work well into the years of her professional touring (*Chronology 1973*, 1; Programs).

It was probably in November 1914 that Russell saw Denishawn, the innovative dance company that existed from 1914 to 1931 and toured extensively. Its creators and leading performers, Ruth St. Denis (1879–1968) and Ted Shawn (1891–1972), presented concerts of experimental dance works that reflected aspects of different international cultures.[7] Seeing Denishawn—and especially Ruth St. Denis's "Dance of the Five Senses"—inspired the young Russell to explore many aspects of "oriental" culture. She began what she calls a reading "spree" on everything she could find related to the subject: "poetry, travel [literature], history, even philosophy," and she founded an all-girls club, "The Alhambra of Tooba," devoted to the study of the "orient" and "oriental" dancing. She writes of that time: "In my abysmal ignorance 'Oriental' was all of a piece . . . I casually mixed Moorish, Indian, Turkish, Armenian, and what have you" (1977a, 6; *Draft 1977*, 38). The club, usually referred to as "Alhambra Tooba," consisted of Russell, Lilian, and six other young women, all of whom took on exotic names, dressed in "oriental" costumes, and met in the Hughes dancing-club room, which had been decorated to reflect the same theme. They performed at the annual San Antonio "Fiesta Fete" and for charity, fraternity, and other events. A somewhat tongue-in-cheek feature article about the group, illustrated with photographs of its members in costume, appeared in the society news of the *San Antonio Express* (November 21, 1915).

Russell's interest in Spanish dance was similarly inspired by one of the great dance artists of the era—La Argentina (Antonia Mercé y Luque, 1890–1936) whom she saw perform in the Mexican quarter of San Antonio (probably in 1916)—for a 25-cent ticket.[8] This made her crave to do Spanish dance, and, fortunately, Moore knew something about that and agreed to teach her. In a few weeks, La Meri writes, she was performing a fandango with castanets (1977a, 6, 8). Eventually, she would study Spanish dance in New York City and Spain, perform its various genres, teach it, and write about it. It would become one of her major areas of specialization.

Dance, however, was just one of Russell's many interests. In addition to the variety of art activities she pursued, she also became proficient in the sports of riding, shooting, swimming, and tennis; she enrolled in college courses; and she enjoyed the attention of many young swains. She could have followed any of a number of paths in her life, from an early marriage to various careers. After graduating from Mulholland High School (May 14, 1915), she had decided that she should commit in some direction—it was time to "get at it." But, she writes, "to get at what? Therein lay my problem" (1977a, 9). In her autobiography, she uses the image of beautiful, vari-colored horses on a carousel to illustrate her dilemma and imagines leaping on and off one and another in indecision. There were so many options: the pink horse of the social whirl; the red horse of sports; the pale horse of music; the dapple horse of a career in Western films, which would involve both acting and riding; the dark horse of dance; and the pinto—her poetry (ibid., 17–22).

For one academic year, September 1916 to June 1917, Russell attended the College of Industrial Arts (CIA) in Denton, Texas, and there she continued to be involved in the arts: she wrote more poetry; performed music, drama, and dance; went on field trips to attend performing arts events, including the Diaghilev Ballets Russes; and, with a friend, ran what they termed the "Dance Department" of the college (1977a, 9–10; *Draft 1977*, 39–40). Her next foray into higher education would be in New York City.

As demonstrated by her imaginary "horse carousel," Russell became immersed in many areas and activities besides those related to education and dance. In her autobiography, she relates that, at the end of the spring 1917 term at CIA, she was invited to visit the ranch of her roommate's father in South Texas. Russell accepted and had a wonderful time there, participating in what was for her an entirely new world. She enjoyed nature, riding horses, helping to herd the cattle—and socializing in a new environment. Many years later she remembered that: "Sunrises and sunsets were pageants of glory. Mocking birds sang all night under the brilliant summer moon. Here was the Texas I had loved yet scarcely known yet." And she relates that "For long hours at a time I hung around the cowboys, swapping yarns while they squatted on their heels in the shadow of the bunkhouse" (1977a, 10). After more details about her experiences there, she concludes: "On the ranch I discovered the cowboy who could become the means of my coping with Euterpe, who had proven somewhat indifferent to my Oriental flights. Under my typing fingers, 'Silver Cy' and 'Whiskey Pete' came to life. Pages flew, bristling with valorous cattle, six-guns, and fight-provoking senoritas" (ibid., 11). As her reference to Euterpe, ancient Greek muse of lyric poetry, demonstrates, her experiences on the ranch provided inspiration and content for more of her own poetry—which will be discussed in chapter 9.

After Russ Hughes's death in 1914, the financial situation of the family seems to have remained stable for a while, although not as strong as it had been while he was still alive. La Meri writes that her mother received a "salary" of $100 each month as "president of R. M. Hughes & Co." and that she saved much of that to use for travel related to Russell's training and education. The two women traveled to New York City, probably in September 1919, for Russell to go to Columbia University for "guidance in the art of versification" (1977a, 15). However, in her *Chronology 1973*, La Meri says that during this time in New York, she studied poetry at Barnard College, journalism at Columbia, music at Damrosch Conservatory, and ballet "(briefly) with Kosloff" (1). She writes that she saw Martha Graham in *The Greenwich Village Follies* performing "a sort of Javanese dance" (1977a, 16), but I have found no record of Graham in the *Follies* until 1923. In March 1920, when "the money gave out," the two women returned to San Antonio (1977a, 16). In 1922, Russell and Lily were again able to spend time in New York City, probably beginning in late April or early May, and La Meri writes that while there, she studied singing with Louis Simmions[9] and ballet with Ottokar Bartik[10] (*Chronology 1973*, 1).

The two women also traveled to Europe in 1922. They left New York City by ship on or around July 1 and returned in late September. For her Christmas 1924 gift to her mother, Russell created a three-volume chronology of the trip with more than 100 pages of typewritten text and about 180 illustrations—postcards, clippings, and photographs that they had taken. It includes a full narration of their itinerary—France, Belgium, England, Scotland, Spain, Italy, and Switzerland; descriptions of the cities and sites they visited in each country; and remembrances of their experiences along the way (*Travel 1924*). That Russell would take on the compiling of this elaborate and lengthy history of their three months in Europe foreshadows the detailed and probing research and writing that she would do in the future. And it is interesting that at this early stage, she was already well aware of the standards of writing. In her opening statement, "Apology," she tells her motivation for creating the work—to help her mother remember the details of their travel. She spends a paragraph explaining that this is a "first draft" that needs more work and ends by writing: "I humbly apologize for all the most obvious errors; for the bad grammar; worse rhetoric; and 'worser' . . . spelling! It is written expressly for you, Mother, and I hope its only critic and entire public will be very lenient with it. For no matter how many errors have gone into it, you can be sure that, along with them has gone just twice as much love." This passage demonstrates both her close attachment to her mother—and her awareness of Lily's concern with doing things properly.

One phase of their 1922 trip that would be very important in the development of the future dance artist was their visit to Spain (August 22 to September 3). After staying overnight in the border city of Irun, they took the train to Madrid (an all-day trip), where they visited the Prado Museum and other sites. On August 26, they traveled to Barcelona, where they stayed for about a week. While there, Russell took classes in Spanish dance with an elderly teacher, Doña Paulina,[11] who was perhaps in her seventies by then and teaching "in a dingy room over the Lyric Theater." La Meri writes that despite her age and heavy weight, she would occasionally demonstrate for her students, and then "[s]he was the embodiment of 'salero' (pep) and femininity. . . . Age had not dimmed the luster of her great black eyes and she knew how to express everything with them, with her castañuelas, and with the tilt of her head and shoulders" (1967, 129). While they could not afford to stay long in Spain, Russell acquired at least some direct experience with the culture and some further training in castanet playing and Spanish dance forms. In the fall they returned to San Antonio, and Russell enrolled in Lady of the Lake, a Catholic college in San Antonio, where she studied history and literature (*Chronology 1973*, 1; 1977a, 22).

Although this young, multitalented woman finally committed to the dance, her early life with its broad and eclectic range of experiences contributed significantly to the development of the artist and teacher we know as La Meri. Her parents were unusual in the way they brought up their daughters. Far from limiting their training and activities to what would prepare them for traditional marriage and child-raising, Russ and Lily encouraged their daughters to explore a range of arts, education, and physical training—and they had the economic means to support that and to encourage them to take on any challenge. In her autobiography, La Meri has written, "From childhood my parents had impressed upon me that I could set my hand to whatever I liked so long as I always finished the job, recognizing that the real reward comes in the joy of accomplishment" (1977a, 14). Both girls were attracted to the arts, and their experience with a variety of expressive genres gave them knowledge of spatial and temporal forms, trained them in various techniques, developed their aesthetic sensibilities, and taught them the value of hard work and discipline—and the satisfaction of accomplishment.

2

Early Professional Work and Touring, 1920s

In the early 1920s, while Russell was still performing for nonprofessional events, she also began the transition from amateur to professional.[1] And, while dance eventually became her sole focus, in her early engagements she continued acting, singing, and playing the violin. Several of Russell's first paid appearances were in "prologues," a form that developed as part of the silent movie culture. These were live performances staged with music and dance that would reflect or elaborate on some aspect of the theme or characters of the motion picture being shown. Before the introduction of sound films in 1927, the larger movie houses engaged professional musicians, singers, dancers, and other performing artists to provide musical accompaniment for the film and a prologue as integral parts of each presentation. A typical program would consist of a musical overture, current newsreels, the prologue, the film and a musical closure.

Russell's first prologue engagement was probably in June 1920 at the Empire Theater, a well-known movie palace in San Antonio. Titled "Garden of Roses," it accompanied the film, *The Dancin' Fool* and featured Russell acting, dancing, and playing the violin. It was identified in the *San Antonio Evening News* as the "first of a series of prologues to be used as introductory presentations to photoplays at the Empire." While giving no indication of the content of the work, the reviewer praised Russell's performance, writing that she "distinguished herself in a role which called for a display of not only considerable histrionic ability, but a thorough knowledge of the terpsichorean art and understanding of the violin" and concluding that she "displayed a versatility that any footlight star of prominence might well be proud of" ("Prologue feature of bill at Empire—'Garden of Roses' presented as introductory to Wallace Reid picture," June 14, 1920). Such praise would continue throughout her career.

In her autobiography, La Meri writes that she was encouraged by a theater manager to enter the 1921 "Ince Girl" contest. A newspaper article, probably from the *San Antonio Evening News,* identified the competition as the "EVE-NING NEWS Beauty Contest launched by Thomas H. Ince" and announced its opening. Ince (1880–1924) was an extremely important silent film producer and innovator with more than 800 films to his credit (Wikipedia). The un-dated article identifies Russell, "a talented society girl," as one of the first two contestants and includes a picture of her and information about her studies in New York and her abilities as musician, dancer, and poet ("First Entrants in Big Beauty Contest"). Russell was one of two winners who were invited to Hollywood to embark on film careers. She chose not to take that offer, but perhaps as a result of winning this competition, she obtained some small roles in Western-themed films that were shot in Texas—roles that involved her horse-riding skills as well as her acting abilities. It is interesting that years later in New York, when she went to see a major film starring Douglas Fairbanks, the second feature was one of those "horse-operas" (1977a, 20–21; "To dance before royal court," *Waco Daily,* October 23, 1921).

Another important engagement in Russell's developing career was that of the "Premier Entertainer" for the prestigious "Queen's Ball" at the Texas Cotton Palace in Waco on October 25, 1921. She had danced for this event the previous year (according to the "First Entrants" article referred to above) but in 1921, she was its star. The Texas Cotton Palace, a single exhibition hall in 1894–95, was rebuilt, expanded, and reestablished in 1910 as a very large site with "a 10,000 seat coliseum, a racetrack, a football field, livestock fields, an auditorium . . . , carnival grounds . . . , a small zoo, and buildings to display automobiles and poultry." Each year, from 1910 until 1930, there was an autumn exposition that included many events, exhibitions, perfor-mances, and the "Queen's Ball," a major social occasion.[2] Two unidentified Waco newspaper announcements, each with a picture of Russell in Spanish costume, give embellished (and incorrect) accounts of her dance training and accomplishments—a publicity practice that became usual during her later international touring.

In her autobiography, La Meri writes that she "received a 'royal command' to dance for San Antonio's 'queen' of the Court of Birds" (1977a, 21) during the Carnival Week Fiesta in which she and Lilian had previously performed with Mollie Moore (see chapter 1). Every year, a woman from a prominent family was elected Queen of the Order of the Alamo to "reign" over the Fiesta, and her coronation ceremony and the accompanying program would be attended by the wealthiest and most prestigious people of the city. Each year's court had a different theme—such as the Court of Flowers (1909), the Court of Fairies (1916), the Court of the Sea (1922).[3] The Court of Birds was in April 1920, and La Meri writes that the dance she composed and performed for this event was *The White Peacock* to music of Delibes, which "ultimately evolved into an interpretation of Griffes beautiful *White Peacock* composition" (ibid.). This work, in its early or later form, was a major attraction in La Meri's repertoire for many years—until at least the mid-1940s.

As noted in chapter 1, Russell and her mother traveled to New York in April 1922; were in Europe from July to September; and after their return to San Antonio, Russell enrolled in another college program. Despite her studies, however, she continued performing and choreographing. Some of this was still for organizations such as the Laurel Heights Methodist Church, the San Antonio lodge of the B.P.O.E. (Elks Club), the Women's Club of San Antonio, and others, but her focus was increasingly on professional work.

An indication of the growing appreciation of Russell's talents was her inclusion in programs of the prestigious San Antonio Tuesday Musical Club, an organization that has existed from 1901 to the present. She performed in at least two of the meetings in their 1922–23 season. On February 12, a presentation, "Behind the Scenes at the Opera" by noted musicologist Sigmund Spaeth (1885–1965), included Russell illustrating three major opera roles through dance: Madame Butterfly, Carmen, and Salome. Then on April 23, "famous paintings" were depicted through music, dance, and "posing." A *San Antonio Express* article focuses on "Meri Russell Hughes, premiere danseuse," and provides a list of her dances, information about them and their sources, and a paragraph about her February performance with Spaeth. In addition to Russell's dances, the April program included nine "poses" in which the performers depicted different art works and four solo songs by sopranos and a tenor that also referred to specific paintings. The pianist Catherine Clarke, with whom Russell frequently collaborated, accompanied all her dances on this program. Four were to music by well-known composers: "Salome" (Richard Strauss), "Hungarian Dance No. 6" (Johannes Brahms) and "La Cygne (After Pavlova)" and "Danse Macabre (both by

Camille Saint-Saëns). Russell also performed two Spanish dances and "Katinka, the Wooden Doll from Russia," which was identified as being "from" a European revue company, the "Chauve-Souris" (The Bat), which toured in the United States from 1922 to 1931. The choice of dances on this program was, of course, a result of the theme of the event, but it also illustrates the continuing expansion of Russell's interest in a broad and international spectrum of music and dance—something that would develop further and further as time went on.[4]

Russell continued doing prologue performances, and particularly important in that area was her relationship with the Philippinis of the Empire Theater in San Antonio. Don Philippini was the theater's symphony orchestra conductor and presentation director, and his wife worked with him in its administration and on productions. She was involved in staging many of the prologues in which Russell performed. La Meri writes that in 1924 "Mme. Philippini" had contracted her for eight weeks of dancing, singing, and acting in the Empire prologues—four shows a day during the week and five on Saturdays and Sundays. This might have started in 1924, but it is more likely that the contract was made late in 1924 for work in 1925. The earliest assignment with the Philippinis might have been that announced in the *Empire Close-Up* program for the week of January 31, 1925—her performance in "Days of 49," an "atmospheric prologue" that preceded the film *The Devil's Cargo*. In La Meri's archives there are also notices of other presentations at the Empire that spring. For the week of March 21, for example, the feature film was *The Thief of Bagdad*, and the prologue, with the same title as the film, was "conceived and staged by Don Philippini with Russell Hughes playing the Slave Girl"—what she termed her "Oriental" number; and during the week of April 4, with the film *Too Many Kisses*, the prologue was "'A Kiss from Old Castile' with Mexico's Premier Baritone, Federico M. Flores, and San Antonio's Dance Delight, Russell Hughes." As La Meri recalled many years later, "One week I would be in my Pola Negri aspect, doing a Spanish dance; the next I would be an 'emoting' Alice Terry, complete with blond wig. Or I would be doing an Oriental number for *The Thief of Bagdad*" (1977a, 22–23; Empire Theater announcements).

In early May 1925, the Empire's feature film was *The Charmer* starring the famous silent film actress Pola Negri (1897–1987). A short article announced that the prologue would include Mexican dance by Adelia Hidalgo from Mexico and Spanish dance by "Miss Hughes," who had "studied in Spain for several years," and whose "interpretation will be pure Castilian and Catalonian in nature" ("In Prologue at Empire," *San Antonio Express,* May 3, 1925). As noted before, such fabrication was usual in newspaper articles about performers—at that time and throughout La Meri's touring years. It is interesting that the article includes "Catalonian" in the description, since nothing that Russell was performing came from that northern Spanish culture. The picture accompanying the article was typically tantalizing, showing her as a glamorous lady in a revealing bodice and Spanish hat—and holding a cigarette. In those days, smoking was apparently considered essential to the image of a budding or established performer.

The three Hughes women were devoted letter writers, and in the Jacob's Pillow Archive, there are nine letters from this period that Lily wrote to Lilian, who was in Honolulu where her husband, David, was stationed. Dating from October 1924 to December 1925, they include reports on Russell's performing and particularly on her great success in the prologues at the Empire. Lily also wrote that when Russell sang for Federico Flores (mentioned above), he was so enthusiastic about her talent that he suggested she should sing in opera and invited her to do a duet with him (letter of April 4, 1925). From the letters, it also appears that Lily always accompanied Russell to the theaters for rehearsals or performances.

Russell's professional engagements also began to include work outside San Antonio. Sometime in 1923, she and pianist Catherine Clarke toured Texas with a production advertised as an "Unusual program of Costume Songs and Ballet Dances; All Numbers Rendered in Costume." Besides playing the piano, Clarke, dressed as a sailor, related stories of travels around the world that "Meri Russell Hughes, Character Artist" illustrated through dance. This was presented in movie houses as a prologue and in other contexts. Another foray outside San Antonio occurred in 1925, sometime after Russell's eight-week Empire engagement. In the final week of that contract, she had been performing a dance on pointe to the singing of "Flower from an Old Bouquet" by a baritone named MacDonald (perhaps the Canadian H. Ruthven MacDonald). The production was such a success that it was held over for another week. Then MacDonald invited her to join him on what was known as "the prologue circuit." She accepted, and properly accompanied by her mother, performed in New Orleans, Atlanta, and other cities until they finally reached New York City. She has written that it was "late spring" when they arrived (1977a, 23; *Chronology 1973*, 3). It had to be later than that, however, since there are records of her performing in San Antonio until mid-June. The first evidence of their being in New York is a telegram of July 30, 1925, addressed to "Miss Russell Hughes" at the Hotel Walcott [Wolcott], 31 5th Avenue.

New York City (1925–1926)

In her autobiography, La Meri writes that by the time she and her mother reached New York, she knew that she wanted to commit to theater, but she does not specify if she meant singing and acting as well as dance. Her family (mother, sister, and brother-in-law) were all supportive and ready to help financially. Lily could not afford to stay in New York, so she returned to San Antonio and sent Russell $20 each week to help with expenses. La Meri then goes on to say that her sister's husband would pay her expenses to come to their home in West Point each weekend for three days of food and lodging without cost (1977a, 23–24). La Meri gives no time frame for this period of family support, but it was probably in the beginning of 1926 or later. Among the nine Lily-Lilian letters referred to above, three provide proof that Lily was in New York with Russell and the Newcomers were still in Hawaii until after mid-December 1925. Two letters from November and one from December 20 or 21 of that year were sent by Lily from the New York address where she and Russell lived (319 West 82nd Street) and were addressed to Lilian in Honolulu, where David was still stationed.

In New York, Russell continued developing her dance techniques and repertoire. She writes that she studied ballet, tap dance, and some Spanish dance and that her expenses were $8 a week for her room, $4 for the four days' food when she was not with the Newcomers and $8 for dance classes and subway fares (1977a, 23). At some point, her mother rejoined her in New York City, and they "settled down in a theatrical hotel just off Broadway" (ibid., 24). Russell was now 26 years old, but even at this age, it seemed important both to her and to Lily that she have the companionship and perhaps protection of her mother. This period, 1925–26, would be a turning point in her life as she obtained more professional engagements, acquired an agent, and prepared for her first experience in international touring.

As is true of much of the chronology of La Meri's life, when, where, and with whom she was studying or performing is often unclear, with conflicting dates given in different sources. It was probably in late 1925 or early 1926 that she was introduced to Maria Montero who, she writes, was "at that time . . . the finest Spanish dancer in America" (1977a, 25). Prior to that she had had some training in Spanish dance with her San Antonio teacher, Mollie Moore, with Doña Paulina (or Rosa) in Barcelona, and with some teachers in New York City. Now, the chance to work with Montero and her Spanish dance company was an opportunity to gain more experience, technique, and repertoire.[5] La Meri writes in the second edition of *Spanish Dancing* that she performed in the Montero group without pay "on the agreement that I could steal everything from her I could get" (1967, 130); and in her autobiography, that Montero "was a wonderful friend to us all. Between shows she taught me several dances and gave me endless, good, professional advice. With her act I traveled the best of the subway circuit.[6] When we closed, I was far richer in technical experience and knowledge of the stage and its ways" (1977a, 25). Russell continued developing her Spanish dance technique and castanet playing and rehearsing the dances she had learned in Spain and from Montero.

With her earnings from prologues and other performing, Russell was eventually able to rent a studio and accompanist for her work, and even an agent. She writes that, in the studio, she "worked and worked and worked" and explains:

> However ethereal a dancer may appear onstage, her preparation will have been anything but glamorous. Studio practice is all dust, sweat, tears, and aching muscles. I defy any but that fanatical, brave race known as dancers to survive the two to five hours of daily brute labor that goes into kindling that three-minute spiritual fire that you, out front in the audience, survey and possibly admire from a comfortable seat. (1977a, 25)

Throughout her career and touring she would continue such grueling (but satisfying) work, not only in practicing the dances in her repertoire, but also in creating new dances and mastering the many world dance techniques and choreographies that she learned.

It was probably in December 1925 that Russell met Guido Carreras,[7] an experienced impresario who would become her manager and eventually her husband. By the time they met, Russell's focus was Spanish dance. Since her "current agent" felt that he didn't know enough about that, he arranged an audition with Carreras, whom he incorrectly identified as a "native of Spain." Russell sang and played the violin as well as performing a Spanish dance at this first meeting, and, while Carreras apparently saw promise in her work, he wanted the advice of specialists in each field before making a commitment. The violinist and the singing coach he consulted were not impressed by her performance. The Spanish dance specialist, Amalia Molina (1881–1956), whom La Meri identifies as "Queen of the Castanets," was somewhat more positive although not really enthusiastic. For Molina, Russell danced a "Jota" she had learned in Barcelona and Maria Montero's "Mirando a España." Molina expressed the opinion that the young woman "has *something*," an encouragement that apparently led to Russell's decision to focus totally on dance and Carreras's decision to manage her (1977a, 26–28; 1967, 130).

Very little information is available about the life and career of Carreras before or after his time with La Meri. He left no writings about himself, and in her autobiography La Meri generally writes about him in an impersonal way. It is known that in 1903 he had married his first wife, Maria, an Italian concert pianist who died in New York City in 1966, long after their marriage had ended; and that they had one daughter, Consuelo, a musician and dancer who died in 1932, also in New York (obituaries, *New York Times*, April 18, 1966; June 21, 1932). Some of La Meri's undated notes in the San Antonio Public Library archive provide information about Carreras and their life together in Italy. She writes that he was born in Leghorn [Livorno], Italy, of an Italian father and an English mother and that his "advanced education" was in France and England. In comparison to her own limited knowledge of Italian, Spanish, and French, she writes that her husband was fluent in English, Italian, Spanish, French, German, Portuguese, Swedish, and Danish. A bit more information about him can be found in one of the few published articles that focuses on Carreras rather than La Meri. Titled "Bosom Pal of World Famous Artists," it relates that he was born in Italy, and after various kinds of work including teaching languages and translating, plunged into the career of managing artists (*Smith's Weekly*, Sydney, Australia, July 18, 1936). While La Meri writes that he had "worked for" Pavlova and Nijinsky (1977a, 27), that seems unlikely. The Sydney article only mentions Fritz Kreisler and Eleanora Duse. As with nearly all of the promotional articles, however, information far from the truth—such as a romanticized story about how he and La Meri met in Texas!—is included to entice prospective audience members, so one needs to question everything. Carreras probably did know several languages, however, judging from the apparent ease with which he seemed able to negotiate bookings and publicity for his star in many different countries—as well as his ability to present the lecture part of their frequent "lecture-demonstrations."

Among the many unanswerable questions about Carreras, however, is what made him decide to take on this beginning artist, Russell Hughes, as his focused project for the next several years. Was it that he truly felt she had the talent to become a major performing artist? That he was attracted to her? Or a combination of the two? Their romantic relationship had to have begun sometime before May 26, 1926, as that is the date of a loving letter she wrote to him while he was in Mexico managing a concert pianist. She opens the letter with "Dear My-Heart" and includes in it a poem that begins:

My heart is dumb for the sound of your voice
My eyes are blind for your smile.
Yet, somehow, my fingers can feel your hair
And touch your cheek awhile.

At that time, her mother, Lily, was still alive and accompanying Russell everywhere, so one may ask if, when, and where Russell and Carreras were able to be alone together as their relationship developed. One can also wonder about Carreras's financial situation, what source of income he might have had as he prepared La Meri for her first concert tour—perhaps it was from continuing work with other clients such as the concert pianist mentioned above.

La Meri writes that as she worked with Carreras she became aware of "the economics of my calling." She had to rehearse, which required space and music; she had to develop a workable program of dances; and she had to acquire costumes for them—which her mother made on a rented sewing machine. Russell created her repertoire based on her studies up to that time, including dances she had learned from others. By spring, she had five dances ready to perform, and Carreras began finding work for her "on the subway circuit to pay studio rent and buy costume fabrics" (1977a, 28). Throughout the nearly twenty years that La Meri worked with Carreras, there were financial ups and downs, but he was an experienced manager and always found some way to raise money for their artistic endeavors and living expenses, and to book engagements locally as well as internationally.

Mexico City (1926)

La Meri's first foreign appearances were in Mexico City in 1926. She traveled there with Carreras and Lily (1977a, 28) and, according to an unidentified article in the Jacob's Pillow archive, seven trunks and their dog! She writes that she spent three months in Mexico City (ibid., 31), but it was actually about six weeks—from June 11 or earlier to July 22. The announcements of her arrival introduced her with statements such as "Una de las más bellas y aplaudidas bailarinas de Broadway" [One of the most beautiful and applauded dancers of Broadway] (*El Universal Gráfico*, June 11, 1926). As was typical of promotional material, exaggeration was the rule. It is interesting that on this and subsequent tours in Latin America, the fact that she wrote and published poetry was noted and praised, and sometimes articles included one or more of her verses.

Later, La Meri would write that it was on this first trip to Mexico that she had acquired the professional name she kept for the rest of her life—that an interviewer for a Mexico City weekly referred to her as "La Meri" instead of Meri Hughes, which she had previously been using (1977a, 29–30; 1978, Part I: 62). However, prior to this tour, the name "La Meri" had already appeared in an article in the *Morning Telegraph* of New York (March 18, 1926), was on her stationery letterhead by the time she wrote the May 26 letter to Carreras (see above) and was also used in the June 11, 1926, newspaper announcements of her performance at the Hotel Regis in Mexico City.

La Meri's initial engagement was in the cabaret of the Hotel Regis and opened on Saturday, June 12—with a memorable incident. As she relates in *Spanish Dancing*,

> My debut at the St. Regis was very swell, and starred with social and political celebrities. I entered in a white "mantilla" (lace head-scarf) and a white lace Spanish costume with a cascade of natural flowers

adorning it. I did my paseo di gracia [*sic*] to polite applause. I made a quick turn to begin "Miranda [*sic*] a España." Then both feet went up and I sat down with such a thud that natives suspected an earthquake. My "peineta" (comb) dropped over one eye, and I broke off a heel and ruined my castañuelas. (1948, 142; see also 1967, 130–31; and 1977a, 29)

The audience was sympathetic, and after they and she had shared a startled laugh, La Meri went to change her shoes and broken castanets, reappeared, and this time with great caution, finished her program (1967, 130–31; 1977a, 29). It is surprising if she had not had a rehearsal or at least a "walk-through" in the space and with the orchestra before she performed—or perhaps the floor had been waxed at the last moment. How long her season lasted at the Regis is unclear, but it must have ended sometime in early July.

On Saturday, July 3, La Meri appeared at the Teatro Iris with other performing artists in a benefit concert for the "damnificados [victims] de León," who had suffered a disastrous flood in that central Mexican city (program announcement in *El Universal,* July 2, 1926). And beginning on Saturday, July 10, she was a featured entertainer at the Teatro Nacional, site of a grand "Exposición de Automoviles."[8] At the theater's cabaret bar and restaurant, performances for families were given from 5:00 to 7:00 p.m. and a "Gran Cabaret" show from 9:00 p.m. to midnight. An article announced that the last performance of "la mejor atracción del Teatro Nacional durante estas últimas noches" [the major attraction at the National Theater during these last nights] would be on July 21 since La Meri was leaving Mexico the next day to return to San Antonio for the inauguration there of a new auditorium ("La despedida de 'La Meri,'" *El Universal Gráfico,* July 21, 1926).

On this first journey outside the United States, La Meri established what would become her habitual practice—seeking instruction in dances and movement vocabularies of the culture she was visiting. She writes that in Mexico, she took lessons in Mexican regional dance, in movements of the *torero* (bullfighter), and in Spanish dance, and that she also attended performances of visiting Spanish dance artists (1967, 131; 1977a, 30–31). Her lessons in bullfighting movements as well as her observation of actual bullfights led to dances she choreographed such as "The Toreador" and "La Corrida," which she performed for years.

One of the popular traditional dances of Mexico became another important addition to La Meri's concert repertoire. This was the *jarabe tapatío* (known in English as the "Mexican Hat Dance"), which dates from the late nineteenth century. In an article, "Nueva Visión de México," attributed to "la Poetisa y Bailarina 'La Meri,'" she discusses her learning of this dance as well as other experiences in Mexico and her enthusiasm for being there. She writes about studying the *jarabe* with two teachers, Pedro Valdez and Rafael Díaz, and also claims that her mastery of the dance was confirmed by a number of notable figures including a general named Roberto Cruz, Montenegro, Covarrubias, and Torreblanca.[9]

Regarding the teachers she names, I have found no information about Pedro Valdes, but the other one was probably Rafael Díez, who later taught at the Escuela Nacional de Danza (National School of Dance). Of those she claims praised her performance, Roberto Montenegro was an established artist and designer with an interest in Mexican folklore; Torreblanca was probably Nepomuceno Torreblanca, violinist and director of a well-known "orquesta típica" rather than his son, Marcelo Torreblanca, who became important in Mexico as a dancer, choreographer, teacher, and researcher; and Miguel Covarrubias was an artist and scenic designer who became director of the dance department of the Instituto Nacional de Bellas Artes (INBA) in the early 1950s. Why the general, Roberto Cruz, was included in the list is not clear. The approval that La Meri, or more likely, Carreras, sought—and which may or may not have been actually obtained from known figures such as these—would hopefully add to her prestige and credibility as a dance artist venturing into new areas.

In her autobiography, La Meri credits Pedro Valdez with teaching her the *jarabe tapatío* and identifies him as "Mexico's finest native dancer, who had taught Pavlova and helped her with the staging of her well-known *Mexican Dances* ballet" (1977a, 30). However, Mexican dance historian, Alberto Dallal, writes that it was Eva Pérez, a specialist in Mexican dances, who had worked with Pavlova to develop her *jarabe* on pointe (Dallal 1995, 69; 1997, 69–70. See also Lavalle 2002). La Meri also writes that she was engaged to perform solo dances and the *jarabe tapatío* with Valdez on a program of the National Symphony Orchestra of Mexico but gives no place or date. She says that this performance led to an invitation to participate in a charity show at the Mexico City bullring. She was to enter the ring on horseback and perform the *jarabe* (1977a, 30). The only clipping referring to the charity show, however, places it sometime after her season at the Regis and says that this was to be La Meri's first performance of the *jarabe*.

Looking back after many years, La Meri writes that her experiences and the enthusiastic reception she enjoyed on this first venture into the great world outside the United States was overwhelming: "Mexico City began to supply me with a glamour I had hungered for all my life. My suite was stupefyingly crowded with gigantic baskets of flowers; my days were a whirligig of photographers and interviews" (1977a, 29). Carreras must have also felt the thrill of success. He had groomed this budding artist to appear in various venues, and, except for the initial fall at her first performance, everything worked out well.

While the response in Mexico to La Meri's developing art was generally very enthusiastic, there was at least one negative review. In a long article, the critic Jorge Buset writes that La Meri's poetry sounds like it comes from "una 'society girl' del Boston," rather than someone who is from Texas, and he mockingly concludes that

en todo, en sus aficiones artísticas, en su refinado "diletanttismo," [*sic*] aun en su gusto por la equitación, y en medio del cabaret, ejecutando las danzas de la antigua Hesperia, sigue siendo la damita americana de sociedad, un poquito frívola y un poquito sentimental. [in everything, in her artistic inclinations, in her refined dilettantism, even in her taste for riding, and in the medium of the cabaret, executing the dances of the ancient Hesperides, she continues being the American lady of society, a bit frivolous and a bit sentimental.] ("'Meri,' la Bailaora Americana," *Revista de Revistas*, June 20, 1926, 21)

He may have had a prejudice against Americans, or perhaps he was evaluating La Meri's performance in comparison with that of more mature and established foreign dance artists, such as Anna Pavlova, and felt that the adulation she was receiving was unwarranted.

Return to New York City (1926–1927)

It is likely that La Meri and her mother spent some time in San Antonio after leaving Mexico City, but there is no record of any performances there in connection with a new auditorium or otherwise. An unidentified clipping reports that Olivia Baldessarelli, her friend of many years, gave a tea in honor of this artist who had "just returned" with her mother from Mexico after great success there. La Meri writes that they were "back in New York by late August"; and once there, Carreras wasted no time arranging publicity and performances. As she notes, "he was inconceivably astute where publicity was concerned" (1977a, 31).

Probably by late November 1926, La Meri was performing in what she describes as a "'flash act'—a showy vaudeville specialty—titled *Sevilla*, which Carreras had built around two singers," one of whom paid for the sets and costumes. La Meri writes that, as "Queen of the Spanish Shawl," she performed one dance with castanets and another in which she manipulated a large, heavily embroidered Spanish shawl (*mantón*) using movements like those of the bullfighter with his cape (1977a. 31). For the latter, she was dressed in tight-fitting shorts, long hose, heeled shoes, and a wide-brimmed male hat— far from anything a Spanish lady—or traditional Spanish dancer—would have dreamed of wearing. This fourteen-minute production, set as a Spanish street scene, appeared first on the Keith–Albee vaudeville circuit. In a short article on the production, press agent and journalist Walter J. Kingsley (1876–1929) includes the usual kind of promotional misinformation previously mentioned. Besides writing about Carreras as a producer, he identifies La Meri as "an American girl of famous family who has lived long in Spain and saturated herself with the traditions and folklore of the nation. She has so completely gone Spanish that she passes for a native and in Seville they call her 'Queen of the Spanish Shawl'" ("La Meri" in column "The Playboy of Broadway," *Vaudeville News and New York Star*, November 26, 1927). Of course, she had only been in Spain for a couple of weeks in the summer of 1922 (see chapter 1).

After the Keith–Albee performances, *Sevilla* was booked into the huge 5,300-seat Hippodrome Theater. In a review of its performance there, a critic identified as "Fred" notes that the act included three vocalists and four musicians and that La Meri performed three, not two, dances. From the description, it sounds like the third was her "Jarabe Tapatío" with another dancer (probably Lilian) as the male partner ("New Acts This Week," unidentified publication, December 8, 1926). Apparently, at this time, neither La Meri nor Carreras saw any problem with presenting a Mexican dance as part of a

Spanish scene. *Sevilla* ended when the lead singer, resenting the amount of publicity La Meri was getting, left the production, taking the sets and costumes with her (1977a, 31–32).

Carreras found other engagements for La Meri in theaters and nightclubs and, finally, a major part in *A Night in Spain*, presented by the Shubert brothers. This revue featured three dance troupes: the Gertrude Hoffman Girls, the Allan K. Foster Girls and the Casino de Paris Girls. It was staged by Gertrude Hoffman (1886–1966), a leading vaudeville dancer and choreographer, and Charles Judels (1881–1969), a well-known actor. After opening January 11, 1927, at the Majestic Theater in Brooklyn, it toured for fourteen weeks to Baltimore, Philadelphia, and other cities before its Broadway debut in early May. In the original version, La Meri sang, acted, and performed her "Shawl Dance." However, programs in the NYPL archive as well as her own memories attest to the constant changing of the show. She writes:

> A rehearsal was called after the show practically every night, and nearly every rehearsal turned up a new part for me to play. . . . I was only too happy that Mr. Shubert judged me capable of the many things he told me to do. I changed costume in the revue thirteen times; I spoke the prologue in Spanish; I sang songs with the chorus line behind me; I played *torero* to Grace Hayes' song; I appeared in comedy skits with George Price. And my *Shawl Dance* was prepared as a special feature, complete with gold costumes and full stage set. (1977a, 32)

A reviewer in Baltimore, commented on the "strikingly beautiful La Meri" as a "center of attention" when on stage, but he also criticized the production as a whole for having too many "thinly clad beauties," which lowered its quality (J.D., "'A Night in Spain,' Shubert Revue, On Auditorium Stage." *Baltimore Sun*, February 1, 1927).

Lily usually traveled with La Meri and would wait at the stage door each evening to accompany her daughter to their lodging. In early March 1927, however, she became ill and returned to New York City for consultation with her physician. It turned out that she had pneumonia, and, after a slight recovery, it became worse and worse. La Meri then left the company to be with her mother, who died March 13, 1927 (1977a, 33–34; Manhattan County death certificate #6666, Soundex H220).

Before her return to *A Night in Spain*, a prologue engagement at the Mark

Strand Theater (April 16–22) resulted in what was probably La Meri's first contact with Michio Itō (1892–1961), the noted Japanese dancer and choreographer who combined elements of Eastern and Western dance in what he termed his "dance poems" (see Caldwell, 1977). The program included La Meri in her castanet and Spanish shawl dances, and Itō's "Easter Greetings," performed by the Mark Strand Corps de Ballet. It was perhaps later in 1927 that La Meri began to study with Itō and learn some of his dances.[10] Most of these first appeared on her 1927 Caribbean tour and several stayed in her repertoire for years (programs 1927 and beyond). And, in her autobiography, she writes that she worked with him on repertoire in preparation for her 1928–29 Latin American tour (1977a, 46). La Meri must have had Itō's permission to perform his compositions, but at this time in her professional life, she (and/or Carreras) apparently had no sense that there should be acknowledgment on the printed program of who had choreographed a work—perhaps that was not a part of the dance concert culture in those days. While La Meri mentions working with Itō in her autobiography (1977a, 46) and names the dances she had learned from him in a short article in *Arabesqué* (1986, 12), there is rarely mention of him in either her printed concert programs or the many articles that Carreras was able to get published worldwide to promote her performances.

La Meri apparently returned to *A Night in Spain* for its opening at the 44th Street Theater in New York City on May 2 (*The World*, Color Gravure Section, May 1, 1927) and performed during some of its run there, but soon she left again to prepare for a Caribbean tour that Carreras was arranging for the summer.

The Caribbean: Cuba and Puerto Rico (1927)

During the spring of 1927, Carreras began putting together the music and dance company he would present as "Teatro de las Artes" on a summer tour to Cuba and Puerto Rico. It featured La Meri, of course, and a pair of Russian ballet dancers, Lora Shadurskaya and W. Kuderoff, who had settled in the United States. Also performing were La Meri's sister, Lilian, and Billy Vine, a young woman La Meri had met in one of her movie theater engagements. Lilian's husband, David, had agreed to her spending some time with La Meri after their mother's death in March, and Lilian was with La Meri during the entire tour (1977a, 35; programs). In the company were also three musicians (pianist, violinist, and cellist) and two singers (soprano and baritone). Five different programs were prepared, with each divided into two parts—the first consisting of classical songs and instrumental music and the second of dances. On the printed programs, the dancers and musicians were named for each piece, so Lilian and Billy had the same visibility and recognition as La Meri and the other artists. This contrasts with future programs in which Lilian participated but, for some reason, was not often named. Several of the dances on this tour were Itō's choreography, although they were not identified as such.

The debut performance of the group was at the Stratton Theater in Middletown, New York, on June 7, 1927. It included a broad range of music and songs and the following dances: La Meri's solos ("Tango," "Anitra's Dance," "Dance of the Spanish Shawl," and "Prelude"), Lilian and Billy ("Egyptian Frieze Dance" and "Golliwog's Cake Walk"), Shadurskaya and Kuderoff ("Arlequin and Colombine" and "Slave Dance"), and Shadurskaya's solo ("Valse Bluette"). The program ended with a group work, "In a Java Temple," danced by La Meri as the Idol, Kuderoff as the Thief, and Lilian and Billy as Priestesses. The total repertoire of the company also included many more dance works: solos by La Meri and others, duets with various pairings, and group works for three or four of the dancers. A look at the entire repertoire shows the wide range of dance presented: ballet, Spanish, "interpretive," humorous—and, of course, impressions of the mysterious and exotic "East."

The company left New York for the Caribbean on June 11 (*Daily Herald,* Middletown, New York, June 8, 1927). Remembering that time from decades later, La Meri writes: "The trip down was beautiful—at least I think it was, for I was in a dream beyond dreaming. First dancer in a company en route to foreign climes! I was blissfully unaware of frictions and undercurrents already beginning to flow among other members of the company" (1977a, 35). She then gives details about problems encountered during the tour: poor hotel accommodations, an episode when she was being aggressively followed by men she characterizes as "the Cuban equivalent of drugstore cowboy," minimal audiences at the performances, "peepholes" in the dressing rooms that had to be filled or covered to deter "peeping toms," robberies of their costume pieces, and so on (ibid., 36–38).

From June 30 until close to mid-August, Teatro de los Artes gave around thirty concerts in cities of Cuba (Havana, Santiago, Cienfuegos, and Santa Clara) and Puerto Rico (San Juan, Guayana and Ponce). The Caribbean debut was Thursday, June 30, at the Teatro Payret in Havana, and there were ten more performances there through July 10. On at least two of the Havana programs (July 8 and 9), the stage was shared with the Mexican "Orquesta Típica" led by Don Nepomuceno Torreblanca, whom La Meri and Carreras had probably met in Mexico City. These joint concerts, which must have been exceedingly long, were divided into three sections, with the Mexican musicians performing in the first and third parts and Teatro de las Artes in the second. After one performance in Cienfuegos and three in Santiago de Cuba, the group traveled to Puerto Rico. There, from July 28 to August 6, they gave at least seven performances at the Teatro Municipal[11] in San Juan; then one in Guayama (August 9) and two in Ponce (August 11 and 12).

Reviews of the concerts in Havana and Puerto Rico were generally very positive, and many lavished exceptionally high praise on La Meri. Soon after the company's first appearance in Havana, for example, the Cuban critic Carlos Rocha wrote:

> Bellísima y original bailarina es la Mary [sic]. En su cuerpo donde predomina la línea escultórica impecable hay extraña fascinación. Sus danzas exóticas y finísimas, de un exotismo y finura, que llegaron con enorme facilidad al público, la convirtieron sin dificultad en una favorita. [La Meri is a beautiful and original ballerina. An impeccable sculptural line predominates in her body and is fascinating. Her exotic and delicate dances, with an exoticism and refinement that come to the public with great facility, turn her with no difficulty into a favorite.] (*Union Nacionalista*, July 2, 1927)

And then, on August 6, the day of the group's last performance in San Juan, the poet and newspaper contributor Vincente Palés Matos (1898–1959) wrote a long article published most likely in *El Mundo*, one of the city's major newspapers at that time. He discusses dance in general, La Meri's accomplishments in the field, and her poetry—which, of course, held special interest for him. About one moment in her performance he writes:

sus ojos nos encendia en un divino éxtasis. De repente, todo su cuerpo, elástico y fino, parecía una llama viva, encendíase en ella ese "fulgor psicológico" que daba la luz viva del espiritu del pueblo y que era, como en el poema de Samain:—"Ya llama ya flor, ya mariposa." [her eyes turned on us in a divine ecstasy. Suddenly, her whole body, elastic and fine, seemed like a living flame, ignited with the psychological spirit of the people and that, as in the poem of Samain, already calls up the flower and the butterfly.] ("La Meri," *El Mundo* [?] San Juan, Puerto Rico, August 6, 1927)

While there were a few negative reviews during the tour, most were enthusiastically positive like the two examples given.

Sometime around mid-August, the Teatro de las Artes ceased to exist. As La Meri writes, "Our company fell on evil days. What with money running low and the calendar drawing toward the fall, the musicians and singers announced they were leaving us, sailing for New York." And, after an argument over salary, the two Russian ballet dancers also left (1977a, 39). The entire group performed together for the last times August 11 and 12 in the Teatro Broadway in Ponce. On August 13, La Meri, Lilian, and Billy gave a final performance at San Juan's Teatro Municipal. Its announcement said that the three dancers would be in collaboration with local young ladies and a well-known poet, and the evening was advertised as "Despedida definitiva de la gran Compañia" [Final farewell of the grand Company]—even though the total "company" was no longer together.

The four who were left in San Juan found themselves in a dire financial situation. La Meri writes that she, Lilian, and Billy shared one room and small amounts of food that they prepared on a gas burner. Carreras, of course, had his own room. To cover their living expenses and eventually have enough money for travel back to the mainland, he was able to get them engagements in movie house prologues in September and October, but the pay was very little. Assuming that much of the concert repertoire would not have "popular appeal," for such performances, La Meri and Lilian "revived" some of "the songs and ukulele numbers" that they had performed for soldiers in the war years, and Billy created a "tap routine" (1977a, 39–40). According to an advertisement for their appearances at San Juan's Gran Teatro Olimpo in early October, they also performed some of their exotic concert dances. One can wonder what sources of music they had available. The income from such engagements, minimal as it was, became totally unattainable when first Billy, then La Meri, became ill with an unspecified tropical fever. Fortunately, Lilian was able, through her husband's military connections, to get treatment for them at the local U.S. Army hospital (ibid., 40). And, somehow, the four remaining partners of Teatro de las Artes managed to continue living and planning for their return to the mainland.

Eventually, Carreras was able to book transportation for the three dancers on what La Meri remembered as "the cheapest freighter bound for the United States." Since there was not enough cash to pay for a fourth passenger, it was decided that he would remain in Puerto Rico until La Meri and Lilian arrived in San Antonio and could borrow money and wire it to him. One can only wonder what Carreras lived on during that time, since there was no income from performances. La Meri relates that she, Lilian, and Billy were the only passengers on the "SS Lake Fairport," which she describes as a "rusty, wallowing old freighter" with a captain who was "seldom, if ever, sober" (1977a, 41). In the complete letter to Carreras discussed below, she tells about drunkenness among the rest of the crew also and their harassment of the three women. From Puerto Rico, the ship went to Santo Domingo in the Dominican Republic; to Sagua, Havana, and Puerto de Vita in Cuba; and finally to Mobile, Alabama.

During this twenty-day journey, La Meri wrote two or more diary-like letters to Carreras with the same kind of daily reporting that she would send to Lilian when they were not together. In her autobiography, she writes that during the first part of the trip, they "stopped at every port around the entire island of Puerto Rico" (41); and there are two pages from a letter that describe three of those stops between October 15 and 17. Carreras saw them off at the first departure, which may have been on October 14 or 15; then, when they were in the port of Aguadilla on Tuesday, October 18, he was there to bid good-bye again. The second letter, which is complete (16 pages), was written from October 19 to 26, and begins with La Meri's heart-rending description of her second farewell to Carreras. In Aguadilla, as the ship was pulling away from the harbor, he was continually lighting matches, and those flares allowed her to be aware of his presence as long as possible.

There is so much information in this letter—about the journey, the ship's captain and crew, frightening events that occurred as a result of the crew's drunkenness and their attitude toward females, the different ports where they stopped, and the women's activities on and off board. Regarding their dance work, La Meri writes that they practiced "every morning before sun-up" to avoid being watched by the men, and this gave them the pleasure of seeing "gorgeous sunrises." She also writes about ideas she was considering for a San Antonio concert after their arrival there (15). La Meri seemed to function to some extent as a mother figure or advisor both to Billy and Lilian, who were apparently being adventurous (or reckless?) in socializing with crew members and wandering on shore with them while the ship was in a port. After one such worrisome episode, La Meri writes that she talked with the two "girls" for thirty minutes about their long absence from the ship, and that they "were much chastened," but she describes Lilian as "pathetically man-crazy" (3–4). Later in this letter, she asks why Lilian lacks "self-respect" and "dignity"; why she cares more about the feelings of the crewman she is seeing than those of her sister; and "why a hundred things?" (10–11). Even though Lilian was in her mid-thirties by then and had been married since 1920, she apparently saw no problem with socializing (and perhaps more) with strange men. However, despite La Meri's disapproval of this behavior, the two sisters always had a close relationship throughout their years together.

Most notable in this letter are the sections where La Meri expresses her passionate feelings for Carreras and their collaboration. For example, she writes, "Oh, my dear! You are all my hope in life; all my fulfillment of love & beauty; all my happiness of soul; all my everything! It was so good of God to give me the wonderful strength of your love just when I needed it most— just when I lost Mother" (2). And further on, she expresses her elation both about the tour and about being with Carreras:

I am so satisfied. I can hardly realize that I've *really* been to the beautiful tropics—& with you. . . . I have been to the land of poets & sailors; of double rainbows & singing lizards; . . . of dreams & love. For just myself it has been worth *anything*, & I shall never cease to dream & sing about it. I hope it isn't just a dream! It is real, isn't it? Real that I have danced through the Antilles, & been sad and happy there—& have belonged gloriously to you. (3)

Later, at the end of a section referring to her experience of their intimacy, she writes:

> I love you! I love you! God bless you &, if we have sinned, forgive us. Yet I have tried to play the game square with Him, too. I have not told you for fear you'd laugh—or feel sad—but the night you took me—in that hot, little room you are in now, I knelt down & promised Him that "for better or worse" I would "cleave only unto" you "til Death do us part."—I hope Mother & Daddy understand! (13–14)

Apparently, the religion with which she had grown up was still with her, although there is no evidence that she attended church services. From her statement about her feelings on the night he "took" her, in the hotel room in San Juan, it sounds like this was the first time they were intimate. Although she had been expressing passionate love for him from as early as her May 9, 1926, letter, the relationship was probably not consummated until this time in the Caribbean.

The ship arrived in Havana on October 26, and the next day, La Meri mailed her long letter to Carreras in San Juan.[12] After Havana, the ship continued to Puerto de Vita and then on to Mobile where the three dance artists had an unexpectedly pleasurable experience going through customs. As La Meri remembered it years later:

> The customs officials welcomed a little break in monotony. Never having been called upon to handle anything like our trunkfuls [sic] of costumes, they were delighted, even donning our hula skirts to give an impromptu dance, which we applauded, not without an eye to the practical. We had been afraid there would be trouble, red tape, duty we could not pay—and we got hula dancers! (1977a, 41)

Another fortunate occurrence in Mobile was contact with the Philippinis, who were associated with one of the movie houses there. Mrs. Philippini offered to pay in advance for a future two-week prologue engagement, and this provided the funds necessary for the three women's train fare to San Antonio. The engagement was fulfilled by Lilian and Billy early in 1928, on their way back to New York (ibid., 42).

It was probably in late October that La Meri, Lilian, and Billy arrived in

San Antonio, where they first had to find a place to live and then "get Carreras out of bondage." The house in Laurel Heights was still in the Hughes family's possession, so they opened that up, gave it what La Meri terms "a lick-and-a-promise cleaning," and moved in. She writes that their "spirits revived" and they "plunged into a round of rollicking homecoming parties." To rescue Carreras, La Meri and Lilian were able to borrow money from a "longtime banker friend" and wire it to their "manager" (1977a, 42). It is interesting that, as usual in her autobiography, La Meri refers to Carreras in a very impersonal way.

It was probably around the middle of November when Carreras arrived in San Antonio, and he immediately began to work with La Meri on a concert scheduled for December 8 at the prestigious Beethoven Hall.[13] In her long letter mailed from Havana, La Meri had discussed ideas for a San Antonio concert, particularly for organizing the program in a new way: instead of two sections—one for music and the other for dance—there would be three, all focused on dance, and titled "Oriental," "Interpretive" and "Spanish and Latin American." Apparently Carreras approved of this plan, and the three-part form, sometimes with different categories, was used frequently for future concerts.

The December 8 program included twenty-two dance numbers, and the music was provided by an orchestra under the direction of Edgar Rogers and by Catherine Clarke, the pianist with whom La Meri had toured through Texas in the early 1920s. La Meri performed nine solos—four or five of which were dances she had learned from Itō—and she also appeared in five other works. Lilian danced in eleven of the numbers, Billy in ten, and two other dancers, only identified as "Thelma" and "Reynolds" were part of the cast of "In a Java Temple" and performed one duet together. La Meri had choreographed two of her solos, "Morgiana Dances" and "The Pale Dancer," to poems of those names by William Rose Benét (1886–1950), which were read in the performance by La Meri's old friend, Olivia Baldesarelli. A review published the next day in *San Antonio Express* praised the performers, the dances, and the costumes, but found the program much too long and the orchestra weak ("'La Meri' Greeted with Enthusiasm," December 9, 1927).

Sometime—perhaps around December 20—Carreras returned to New York City, apparently to begin plans for the dancers' return and their future engagements. La Meri and her "girls" remained in San Antonio and were doing movie house performances until at least the end of December. In a letter to Carreras mailed December 27, she writes that their last group performance would be December 30, that she had been booked to sing somewhere on New Year's Day, that she and Lilian had been working to "straighten up Mother's estate & put the house in order for renting," and that they planned to leave San Antonio on January 3. At some point, Lilian's husband, David, had come to join them for the holidays, and in her Christmas Day letter, La Meri writes: "We have had a very happy Christmas. We spent the morning opening presents and then David served us a gorgeous dinner, after which we flew to the theater." According to her autobiography, after they all left San Antonio by train, Lilian and Billy stopped in Mobile to fulfill the contract with the Philippinis (1977a, 42). La Meri presumably went straight on to New York, and probably all three were together there by the third or fourth week of January.

Back in New York City (January to May 1928)

La Meri relates that early in 1928, "we" moved into a small "theatrical hotel," but she doesn't specify if the "we" included Carreras as well as her sister and Billy; she adds that at some point, David came to "retrieve his wife." By now, La Meri felt herself to be on the "way to becoming a concert dancer"; and, in relation to that, she writes: "We plunged into the training, not the least of which were more movie-house and nightclub engagements, to make the wherewithal for living" (1977a, 42–43). There is no information about their activities during the first weeks in New York City—or what she might have meant in the passage quoted above by "training." However, beginning in the middle of February, the archives are full of materials attesting to her continuing professional development and performances.

The first important engagement in the city, "La Meri and Her La Meri Girls" was produced by Carreras and booked at the "Little Club," a supper club in the basement of the 44th Street Theater. It opened February 14 and apparently ran nightly for at least a month. The "Girls" included Lilian, Billy, and someone named Edna, and in addition to performing, Billy had designed and made costumes for some of the works. La Meri sang as well as dancing, and music was provided by Joe Chance and his orchestra. The program included some of La Meri's Spanish dances, a "fantasy" titled "Asia and Africa," and a Hungarian dance, among other numbers. An unidentified critic for the *New York Evening Post* wrote: "La Meri is talented to a superlative degree and she emanates a charm that is rare in its efficacy. Her artistic manner of presenting each number, whether a song or a dance, bespeaks a delicate understanding . . . There are several ensemble numbers given by Miss La Meri and company which are colorful and artistically presented" ("Supper Clubs; . . . ," February 25, 1928). It is interesting that La Meri was still singing in performances in 1927 and 1928.

The major event for La Meri during this time was her concert debut in a matinee performance, Saturday, May 5,[14] at the John Golden Theater. Pianist Frederick Bristol, who would be part of the coming South American tour, accompanied her dances and played several solos, and Lilian partnered her in the "Jarabe Tapatío." La Meri performed dances identified as Arabic, Indian, Japanese, Spanish, and Mexican, as well as her interpretive solos—all still to western piano music. She had, of course, done some study of actual Spanish and Mexican dances by then, and the piece on a Japanese theme was from Itō, but the dances from other cultures were still in the area of "impressions." She also performed "The Pale Dancer" with the poem recited by guest artist Teresa Guerini and music by Chopin. No music had been mentioned for the December 8, 1927, performance of this piece in San Antonio. During the intermission of the concert, copies of La Meri's 1925 book of poetry, *The Star Roper*, were given without charge to the audience members.

The concert received serious reviews in at least five New York newspapers—some full of praise and others quite negative. Charles D. Isaacson (1882–1936), music critic for the *New York Morning Telegraph* and later, music editor for *Dance Magazine*, was equally charmed by La Meri's poetry and her dance. He had just finished reading *The Star Roper* before going to the concert, and in his review, he writes: "With the same skill she had shown in the selection of her poetical themes did she discover the range of the dance." Then he gives examples of her poems and dances to illustrate that point. Later in the review, he states, "La Meri is as full of fire and red blood as her songs of the open spaces." After more specific discussion, he concludes his review with praise of Bristol, rating his work as "the best piano accompaniment of a season of dance recitals" (*New York Morning Telegraph*, May 6,

1928). La Meri writes that the Isaacson review provided her with "a benison of encouragement as I went about preparing for a South American tour that was to begin on June 1" (1977a, 46).

Two mainly negative reviews noted the similarities between her work and that of Itō, one saying that about half of the dances were from his repertoire and finding nothing positive at all in the concert ("La Meri in Dance Debut: Prodigality in Evidence Throughout the Performance," *New York Times*, May 6, 1928). The other, while finding value in some aspects of her choreography and performance, felt that she "displayed no outstanding qualities that might set her apart from scores of other dancers." Regarding the Itō works, this reviewer wrote: "She must be a pupil of Michio Itow [*sic*], for her 'Empress of the Pagoda' was an exact duplicate of one of Itow's dances, and that she emulated the unique footwork so well and imitated his gestures and characteristics proves that she is a good pupil of a real dancing master" ("La Meri in a Dance Recital" by H.M., *Evening Post*, May 7, 1928). This critic also said that the performance "turned out to be a piano recital with some dancing thrown in" and that only the playing of "the untiring and accomplished Frederick Bristol" saved it from disaster (ibid.).

It is unknown when Carreras began organizing La Meri's long tour in Latin America, but his management was remarkable—not only in obtaining the numerous theater engagements, but in organizing all the travel, publicity, and production technology. This tour, lasting a little more than fourteen months, was a demanding and complicated endeavor. By the end of May, however, all was ready for the departure; and on May 30, 1928, La Meri, Carreras, Lilian, and Frederick Bristol set sail for Venezuela, where their first performances were scheduled. In her autobiography, La Meri notes that David had "again loaned" his wife to her (46).

Latin America (June 1928–August 1929)

La Meri devoted fifteen pages of her autobiography to this tour with details about their travels and experiences. Because the company had multiple engagements in some of the cities, they were prepared to present at least three different concerts. In addition to some thirty-six trunks of costumes, they traveled with sound equipment, a cyclorama, floor cloth, and spotlights, which, in each venue, would have to be adjusted to the layout of the theater. To help with that, Carreras hired a young Venezuelan man to work as their stage assistant (1977a, 46–48). In contrast to the printed programs for the Caribbean tour, which gave only names of the dances and performers, the programs for this tour provided information about the theme, narrative, and/or cultural tradition of each dance. However, despite performing on each program, Lilian was rarely named until they were in Panama—an omission that was commented on by some reviewers. To provide details about every part of this tour would take a book in itself, so I will discuss some, but not all, of the travel, performances, reviews, and experiences that were significant.

Sometime before June 14, the group arrived at La Guaira, the main port of Venezuela. In the harbor, while still on ship, they were met by a "reception committee" sent by the Venezuelan president, General Juan Vicente Gómez (1857–1935), to welcome "any artist bringing culture to his country." As La Meri describes it,

> a shining launch, filled with official looking men cut a spumed path from pier to ship. Gold-laced officers came aboard smartly—and asked for me! . . . So it was not without some pomp that I disembarked, surrounded by military "brass" and laden with flowers. All customs formalities were dispensed with, and we hurtled up the winding, dangerous road to the capital in a cavalcade of black Cadillacs. (1977a, 47)

Throughout their time in Caracas, the president also sent champagne for each of their dinners at the hotel and bouquets to the theater for each performance (ibid.).

The season in Caracas ran from June 14 to 26 and included six concerts. The opening at the Teatro Nacional featured thirteen dances or dance suites to Western piano music of the usual range of composers: Ravel, Delibes, Debussy, Strickland, Griffes, Poulenc, Ketelvey, Rameau, Rachmaninoff, Grunn, and Menéndez. It also included the "Jarabe Tapatío" and "Hula Hawaiiana" done to recorded traditional music and three sections of piano solos by Bristol. As noted above, the printed programs contain substantial information about each dance work—and the paragraph on "Empress of the Pagodas" when it was presented gives credit to Itō as the teacher from whom La Meri had learned it. Other dances from Itō, however, are not identified as such.

The reviews in Caracas were generally very positive. For example, referring to La Meri in the opening concert, an unidentified critic wrote:

Sus danzas, entretejidas y desenvueltas, en el marco de suntuoso deco-
rado, con la belleza típica de su fuente original son los poemas coreográficos de las razas, los ensueños de los genios de la música y los
ritos y leyendas de misteriosas y extrañas civilizaciones. [Her dances,
interwoven and unveiled in the framework of sumptuous decoration
with the beauty typical of her original sources are the choreographic
poems of the races, the dreams of the geniuses of music and the rites
and legends of mysterious and strange civilizations.] ("La Meri," *El
Heraldo*, June 15, 1928)

Such praise became very common throughout the tour.

During the group's season in the capital, the president invited them to give
a concert at what La Meri identifies as his "summer palace in Maracay," a
short distance from Caracas. Meeting him for the first time there, La Meri
found Gómez to be "an extraordinary man." After their arrival, he invited her
to have tea with him in his garden and "admire his collection of rare white
peacocks." One would assume that the rest of the company was also included,
as she then writes that "he showed us around"—apparently referring to the
palace and its grounds (1977a, 47). On the printed program, the location of
this performance on June 23 is identified as the Teatro Maracay, and ticket
prices are given, so it may or may not have been a part of the palace. La Meri
writes about severe problems there—the stage having "an unevenness rivaling
the brooding Andes" and the piano "so out of tune" that she was "never quite
sure what dance Fred Bristol was playing." Nevertheless, the audience seemed
to enjoy their performance, and Gómez, "enthusiastically pleased" presented
her with a check and a wristwatch as gifts (ibid., 48).

Throughout the tour, each program usually followed one of the set for-
mats, but at the June 26 farewell performance in Caracas, La Meri sang four
songs that had reportedly been requested by the public and the press. These
were "Heav'n" and "Curly Headed Baby" identified as songs of the Negros
of Alabama, and two Spanish songs from the repertoire of Raquel Meller
(program). Meller (1888–1962), was an internationally known Spanish film
and stage actress and singer who specialized in popular song forms such as
cuplé and *tonadilla* (Wikipedia).

After their resounding success in Caracas, the company went on to perform in Maracaibo, a city La Meri describes as "a mess." Besides the unpaved, muddy streets and the horrible conditions at the "best hotel in town," their performance venue, the Teatro Baralt, was in dreadful condition, not having been in use for some time. La Meri writes of the opening concert:

> I shared my solo program with a democratic collection of bats and rats, which scurried happily about the stage, ignoring the performance but causing consternation among the lily-livered foreign artists. There was an interesting added attraction. It was some saint's day and the governor, sitting attentively in the stage box, had to call out soldiers to stop the audience from shooting off firecrackers in the aisle. All in all, I think I gave the most courageous and least artistic performance of my life. (1977a, 48)

Despite all of this, the concert on July 5 was highly praised, with one critic writing of La Meri as "la estrella de la danza en la universalidad de sus formas" [the star of the dance in the universality of its forms] who gave to the audience the opportunity to enjoy "la majestuosidad de su arte voluptuoso, atrayente, exquisito, lleno de sugerentes emotividades" [the splendor of her voluptuous, attractive and exquisite art, full of suggestive emotions] (Benedicto, "Meri, La Gloriosa," unidentified publication, July 7, 1928). Two more concerts had been scheduled for July 7 and 8, and a fourth was added on July 11, a "Farewell Performance Dedicated to the American Colony of Maracaibo."

The tour continued. In late July and early August, they performed on the northern coast of Colombia, in Cartagena and Baranquilla, and, then, in Panama—at the Teatro Nacional in Panama City (August 17–23) and the Balboa Clubhouse in the Canal Zone (August 24–27). In Panama, there was a local orchestra directed by a Maestro Zozaya that was listed on the programs. And Lilian was given more recognition there than in the earlier engagements—her name appeared on the programs and her dancing was mentioned in some of the reviews. La Meri and the concerts elicited much interest and appreciation in two Panamanian English-language newspapers, the *Panama American* and the *Star and Herald*. Critics praised the performances in the Teatro Nacional but regretted that they had not drawn more interest among the public. One wrote, for example, "The audiences at the recitals have been disgracefully small and the lack of attendance is a regrettable indictment of the people here" ("La Meri Triumphant in National Recital," *Panama American*, August 20, 1928). However, the last Teatro Nacional performance on August 23 was packed (see "Predict Record Crowd for Last Show of La Meri, *Star and Herald,* August 23, 1928). This was probably due to the inclusion of fifteen dance students who were announced on the program as "varias señoras, señoritas, y niñas de las Sociedades de Panamá y de la Zona del Canal" [various ladies, young women, and young female children from the Societies of Panama and the Canal Zone]—and as "alumni" of local dance teacher Llona Sears and of Lilian, who trained them in the dances for this event. All the students, as well as Lilian, were named in the program and in the review "La Meri Captures House in Last of Panama Recitals" (*Panama American*, August 24, 1928).

Because she was expecting to give birth toward the end of the year, Lilian's husband, David, came to escort her back to the United States (1977a, 50). After only seven months of pregnancy, on or before October 30, Lilian gave birth to twins at the Walter Reed Hospital in Washington, D.C., but, tragically, both babies died—the first one soon after birth and the second somewhat later. Information about the births, deaths, burials, and Lilian's feelings about the loss of these children are in letters she wrote to La Meri between October 31 and November 19, 1928.

In early September, performances were scheduled in Costa Rica (San José and Cartago), and after that, there was a season in Lima, Peru, that ran from October 2 to 19. Sometime around mid-October, Bristol had to return to the United States to fulfill a contract, and he was replaced by an Argentine pianist and conductor, Ricardo Cendalli (1977a, 52–53). It is unclear from the programs whether he worked with them for the entire remainder of the tour or just parts of it.

The next country to be explored—and entranced by La Meri's performances—was Chile. From October 1928 until mid-January 1929, the company toured there, performing in Santiago and four other cities. On December 1, while they were in Valparaiso, a strong earthquake hit the coastal region and created much destruction and more than 200 deaths. On December 4, La Meri participated in a benefit performance for the victims, for which she received praise from Chilean and Peruvian government officials—and from the United States President-elect, Herbert Hoover (unidentified publication, "La Meri Now Good Will Bearer").

In February and March, the group gave performances in Brazil (São Paulo) and Uruguay (Montevideo and Salto), and between April and August, they had engagements in Buenos Aires and thirteen other cities in Argentina. They also traveled in June to Asunción, Paraguay, for three performances and in July to Salto, Uruguay, for two. In her autobiography, La Meri gives details about the travel, the theaters, and their financial problems—and also about their rehearsing and performing and about her learning of dances from the local cultures. She says nothing, however, about her relationship with Carreras.

Of the many letters that La Meri must have written during this time, there were only two in the materials given to Josie Neal. The earlier one, dated May 24, 1929, was sent to Lilian from Santa Fe, Argentina. In the beginning, La Meri writes that she has not been in one place long enough to get mail forwarded and thus has no current letter from her sister. Then she asks Lilian for a number of "favors," mostly requests for things to be sent through the mail. An important item was the March 1927 issue of the periodical *The Dance*, which includes one of La Meri's first published articles—"South of the Rio Grande; Where Dancing Is Unaffectedly Mexican." She relates that this was one of several items stolen by Ricardo Cendalli's wife, whom she had hired to do some sewing for her in the hotel room. When La Meri was not present, this woman apparently went through everything and took, in addition to that article, pictures, clippings, gloves, and bracelets. In this letter, La Meri also writes about the group's deteriorating financial situation since the briefcase in which Carreras carried all their money had disappeared on the trip from Costa Rica to Peru in September—and then what she terms their "flop in B.A." What she meant by the latter is unclear as the reviews for the performances in Buenos Aires, April 11–16, 1929, were very positive.

The other letter was sent from Uruguay, September 1, 1929, to Mrs. Clegg in San Antonio, and included a number of photographs taken during the tour. Apparently, at that time, typing rather than handwriting a personal letter was not considered "proper," since La Meri makes an excuse for doing that at the beginning, and at the end, writes: "Again I apologize for writing this on the machine, but let me not feel that there exists the need of formality between such good friends." She signs it "Most Affectionately, Russell." Mrs.

Clegg was probably Agnes Terrell Clegg (1904–1990), who seems to have been part of the circle of La Meri's San Antonio friends that included Olivia Baldessarelli. In the letter, La Meri expresses the hope that both of them might join her in Spain in the winter. The letter of course includes information about the group's touring and performing, but what is remarkable is La Meri's writing about her intense and passionate interest in the scenic and historical sites that she always found time to visit in her travels.

During the fifteen months of this tour, there were about 150 concerts given, and La Meri writes that, as they traveled, she was "steadily creating new dances, learning new dances and acquiring new costumes via buying and making" (1973 *Chronology*, 3). She also writes about the difficulties as well as the pleasure of touring:

> Although extremely happy, I was close to exhaustion a good part of the time. Performances ran for an hour and three quarters with only one intermission. I had made myself so expert at changing that I was never offstage more than three minutes between numbers. . . . An evening's performance was, therefore, grueling work; but I was sustained by my love of the theater, my dreams of the future, and that out-of-time-and-space catalysis every artist feels when the curtain goes up. (1977a, 53)

Her commitment to and love of her art continued throughout her life.

In her autobiography, La Meri noted that "at the end of every exhausting season, there would be a lazy boat trip to recharge my system" (54). However, the one at the end of this tour—in Paraguay before their departure for Italy—was quite an ordeal rather than a pleasant rest. This was a trip by boat from the city of Asunción to the region of Chaco—to go hunting! It turned out to be far from any kind of "lazy" escape from the rigors of performing. She writes that the group on the boat "consisted of Carreras, myself, Cendalli, three members of our local orchestra, and three hunting dogs," and that, in the middle of the journey, the boat began to leak, creating what was "the most frightening half-hour" of her life. Carreras, however, was apparently not frightened, just concerned about her gun—advising her that, if the boat should sink and she landed in the water, she should "be sure" to hold the gun high so it would not get wet and rust. Fortunately, they managed to reach the shore before that happened, and they found another boat to get to their destination (1977a, 58–59).

The organization and realization of a tour such as this must have been daunting. The constant travel would have been exhausting. Added to that were border crossings with all the stage equipment, costumes, and personal belongings having to pass customs; adjusting the equipment and performances to new theaters; arranging publicity, transportation, lodging, and so on. Not least in the work was taking care of the costumes, which, for each performance, had to be unpacked, ironed, and arranged for La Meri's quick changes. But under Carreras's direction, all seemed usually to go well.

As noted above, reviews throughout the tour were almost totally enthusiastic. And La Meri felt that she grew enormously as an artist through the experience. She writes: "The tremendous work and experience afforded me by that South American tour gave me my first real sense of being a recognized concert dancer. I felt artistically better armed, fortified to assimilate what lay ahead in new environments, to strengthen and extend my capacities" (1977a, 61). After this long time in Latin America, they left by ship sometime in late August or early September—and La Meri would next introduce her work to the Europeans.

3

Life in Italy and Beyond, 1929–1936

Around September 5, 1929, La Meri and Carreras left Latin America for Europe. They probably sailed from Montevideo, Uruguay, since the last performances were there. Writing many years later, La Meri remembered her enjoyment of this twenty-day journey on a "French liner." After so many months of strenuous touring, it provided her with what she felt was "a reward in the form of an unbrokenly beautiful voyage over the calm South Atlantic" (1977a, 61). Of course, she still practiced regularly, and she also gave a performance on board (September 18). The program for that identifies the ship as the "Paquebot Valdivia" and lists eight numbers: interpretive works and dances related to particular cultures. There is no indication as to the source of the music, which, as usual, included works of classical composers.

La Meri and Carreras arrived in Dakar, Senegal, on September 20 and six days later in Almeria, on the southern coast of Andalucía. There, they were met by Lilian, who would spend some time with them in Europe. From the various sources, it seems that they were in Granada, September 27 to 30, and in Seville until October 19. Then, after spending five days in Fez, French Morocco, they returned to Spain and made short visits to Malaga, Granada, Madrid, Toledo, and Barcelona (1977a, 61–64; *Chronology 1973*, 3; *Chronology Notebook*, 1929). On November 2, they left Spain for Italy. One wonders what happened to the stage equipment and the many trunks of costumes that they had had on tour. Were they carting all of this with them? Had it been left behind? Or shipped?

Spain

In Spain, La Meri, Carreras, and Lilian spent the longest time in the city of Seville, a major center for flamenco dance and music in the region of Andalucía. La Meri (and perhaps also Lilian?) took lessons in dance, and the three went to bullfights and to cafés where popular singers and dancers performed. And, of course, La Meri also had costumes made (1977a, 61–64; 1967a, 131–39). Most important for the development of her Spanish dance knowledge and proficiency were La Meri's private and class lessons at the studio of the well-known dance master José Otero Aranda (1860–1934)—and her acquisition of his 1912 publication, *Tratado de bailes* (Treatise of Dances).[1] In both editions of *Spanish Dancing* (1948 and 1967), La Meri draws heavily on her training at Otero's and the information in his treatise.

At the studio, much of the teaching was done by Otero's nephew under his aging uncle's supervision. By that time, José Otero was almost 70 and his nephew probably about 40. The younger Otero would demonstrate the movements and teach the steps and sequences of a dance. La Meri writes that, as the lesson progressed, Maestro José Otero would make comments and correct his nephew as well as the students. In addition to her appreciation of all she was learning from the Oteros, La Meri was fascinated by the teaching room, which she saw as "historic" and describes as follows: "The walls are covered with colored posters of the bullfight; the floor, filthy with three generations of taconeo [rhythmic footwork], sags and bounces when danced upon. Chaste wooden benches line the walls, and a wheezy piano stands in the corner" (1967a, 132). The private lessons in the morning were accompanied by piano and the evening classes by guitar and bandurria (ibid., 132–33). Having live music for such classes is an advantage to both the teacher and the students.

La Meri had already had some training in Spanish dance, so she could follow the instructions without difficulty. Years later, in discussing the teaching and learning of Spanish dance, she stated that "going to Spain to study Spanish dance is useless unless you have already a first class command of the technique given you by someone who has studied abroad long enough to know the importance of teaching technique before dances" (1967a, 133). And in her classes at Jacob's Pillow, the Ethnologic Dance Center in New York, and elsewhere, she demonstrated her commitment to that precept. While the traditional practice in many parts of the world is that students develop their technique in the process of learning complete dances, La Meri argued for the approach to dance pedagogy usual in training for ballet, modern dance, and other Western theater dance forms—first, develop mastery of the technique in repetitive exercises and short sequences, and then learn complete dances.

A major contribution to her growing knowledge about and experience in Spanish dance were the days La Meri spent in Granada (probably September 27 to 30, and again in late October). Her contacts and experiences there were very significant for her life, her learning, her writing, and her art. In that city, she and Carreras spent some time with the composer Manuel de Falla (1876–1946) and discussed his ballets *El Amor Brujo* (Love the Magician) and *El Sombrero de Tres Picos* (The Three-cornered Hat)—and his ideas about how they should be staged (1967a, 138–39; 1977a, 61). When she began to choreograph parts of *El Amor Brujo* in the early 1940s, then to mount a full production in New York in 1944, and a restaging of it for Jacob's Pillow in 1953, she was presumably following what she understood to be Falla's conception for the ballet.

Falla introduced La Meri and Carreras to Mariano Morcillo Laborda (1870–1954), a noted guitarist, singer, and dancer who had developed friendships with the local Roma (Gypsy) communities, could speak their language (Calo), and was accepted by them—an unusual situation for an outsider.[2] La Meri writes that before taking her to meet with a group in the Granada district of Albaicín, he instructed her in the best way to approach and interact with the Gypsies. During this visit, some members of the community sang and danced for them, and La Meri was particularly impressed with one young woman, La Bisca. To her delight, this dancer agreed to come into the city to help her learn some flamenco dance—but, of course, that had to be kept secret, since the community was typically against members sharing knowledge of their culture and practices with outsiders (1967a, 137; 1977a, 61–62).

La Meri describes one of those sessions, in the morning off-time of a cafe, to the accompaniment of an out-of-tune piano by a nearly blind pianist. She writes that La Bisca arrived "in a summer street dress and rolled stockings of the 'flapper,' her bobbed hair flying." Until the pianist arrived, La Bisca accompanied herself by whistling and snapping her fingers as she began to teach La Meri typical flamenco forms such as the *alegrías* and *bulerías*. The pianist eventually came in, and they began working together, with La Bisca demonstrating and La Meri following. As they continued, the dancing and music elicited *jaleo*—shouts of encouragement and rhythmic clapping—at first by the small group itself: La Bisca, La Meri, Lilian, Morcillo, and Carreras. Gradually, however, they were joined by people who lived in rooms along the balcony of the cafe and who had been wakened by the noise (1967a, 137–38). This all resulted in an experience that La Meri remembered as unique in her life:

> "Olé! Olé!" they shouted. La Bisca's eyes sparkled, and I think we were all slightly hysterical. She caught at my hand and pulled me up on the floor with her. I don't know what or how I danced, and I didn't care. Neither did anyone else, for it was perfectly clear to all how I felt, and it's the feeling that counts in gitano dancing. I know I have never danced the baile Flamenco so perfectly before, or since, because that was the one time in my life when I had to dance, when the fear of death itself could not have kept me off that floor! And that's just what gypsy dancing must be! (1967a, 138)

La Meri also refers to a concert she gave in Granada (1977a, 62; 1967a, 135), but there is no archival evidence of this.

Morocco and Middle Eastern Dance

In her amateur years, La Meri had performed what she termed "oriental" dances, and in her early professional work, there were also dances on Middle Eastern themes: "Danza Arabe" (Tchaikovsky), "Arabian Dance of Greeting" (Strickland), and "Dance of the Handkerchiefs" (to traditional music). Now, she wanted to learn actual techniques and dances of a Middle Eastern culture, partly to improve the existing pieces in her repertoire, but also to be able to perform more authentic works. She claimed—almost forty years later—that another reason for this study was her belief in the connection between the Moroccan and Gypsy cultures, writing: "The Moorish influence is so apparent in the art of the Granada gitanas that I felt I had to go to Morocco and see the 'grandmammy' of the 'baile gitano'" (1967a, 139).[3] But one can ask to what extent she could have known about either culture in 1929, or about the history of the Moors in Spain, the history of the Gypsies, or the current Moroccan culture.

During their five days in Fez, La Meri and Carreras attended performances, and La Meri was able to obtain instruction from a teacher named Fatma (or Fatima) that Carreras had found. La Meri writes that this "long-time favorite dancer of the sultan" was probably in her late thirties by then and had retired from performing. In addition to providing lessons, she also helped them find costume materials. There is no information about how the three communicated—if Fatma knew some English, or if Carreras had engaged a translator. In the lessons, with the accompaniment of three musicians, the teacher would demonstrate techniques and dances for her student to imitate (1977a, 64; 1984c). Decades later, La Meri recalled those lessons:

> In all my years of foreign study, I have seldom had such merry sessions. Foot movements were relatively easy, arm movements not difficult . . . But when it came to control of the belly muscles, instruction came to a halt on a wave of laughter.
>
> "Why do you all laugh?" I asked.
>
> "Because you are trying so hard, but have nothing there to move," replied Fatma, "Never mind. With hard work your belly will develop and grow larger." (1984c, 19)

And La Meri writes, "Having always considered myself a little too well-endowed in that area, I silently vowed to leave it as it was" (ibid.).

Under Fatma's supervision, La Meri revised her dance with the handkerchiefs. She titled this new version "Chethat-al-Maharma" (1984c, 19); and it stayed in her repertoire for many years. La Meri's enthusiasm for Middle Eastern dance was so stimulated by what she saw and learned in this short time in Fez that, when she and Carreras were in Paris, she searched for written sources on the dance genres of the region and sought out teachers. She knew some French but probably needed Carreras to translate for her. La Meri was particularly interested in what she termed "pantomimic dances" (in contrast to "belly dances") and worked with a group of Middle Eastern students who helped her develop the dance "Chethat-al-Selah" (Dance of Salutation) (ibid., 19, 32). This also became a regular offering on her concerts.

As noted above, after this short time in Fez, there was more travel in Spain—to various cities—and sometime in early November, the three departed for their next destination.

Italy and European Touring

By November 12, 1929, the travelers had arrived in Italy, Carreras's home country. They stayed in Florence for about two months, celebrating the holidays and preparing for future performances. To work with them, Carreras hired a young pianist, Luigi Dallapiccola (1904–1975), who went on to become well known as a composer and teacher. The new program was first presented in a matinee concert, January 11, 1930, at the Accademia dei Fidenti, where La Meri would be teaching after they settled in Italy in 1931 (see below). The program lists eleven dances, all requiring different costumes, and with no announced breaks except for one intermission. No pianist is named, but it must have been Dallapiccola as he played for their subsequent engagements in Vienna and Berlin.

The next performance was a matinee concert in Vienna on Sunday, January 19, 1930, at the Theater in der Josefstadt, which at that time was under the direction of noted theater and film director Max Reinhardt (1873–1943). La Meri and Carreras considered this to be her formal "European debut." Dallapiccola was listed as the pianist; and Lilian, who was still with them, probably performed here and in other European concerts, but the programs and reviews do not mention her. The dances presented in the Florence and Vienna concerts included both old and new works. Four were probably the same choreographies that she had learned from Michio Itō: "Passapied," "Three Preludes," "Empress of the Pagoda" and "Tango." She also performed "The White Peacock," "Introspection," "Nautch Dance," three dances from her Spanish repertoire, and "Hula Hawaiiana." And in the Vienna concert, as usual, the pianist performed solos as well as accompanying La Meri's dances. Both concerts had extensive publicity, thanks to the efforts of Carreras, and there were mostly very positive reviews—a few short ones in Florence and many more in Vienna. La Meri particularly appreciated the analytical evaluation of her work by Felix Cleve,[4] whom she identifies as "Europe's premier authority on dance, drama, and motion pictures" (1977a, 66). Cleve would continue to write articles and evaluations of her work into the 1940s. Sometime after the January 19 concert, La Meri and Dallapiccola also collaborated on a program for the American Woman's Club in Vienna. He played selections of Falla's music, and she read poems from her books *Mexican Moonlight* and *The Star Roper* (*Vienna Herald*, January 25, 1930).

The group was in Berlin from January 29 to February 26 (*Chronology Notebook*). Since there was only one concert scheduled (a matinee on February 9), La Meri had time to investigate the dance culture in this major city. She writes that there was great conflict between the local practitioners and supporters of ballet, on one hand, and modern dance, on the other—that they "were at each other's throats." But she continues: "As it happened, this worked out very well indeed for me. Paradoxically, my program, mixing both philosophies of movement, inspired both sides to roar that *this* was true dance in its purest form!" (1977a, 66). She notes that rather than taking sides, she "impartially" visited studios where the different genres were taught. She also had some contact with the well-known pioneer of German expressionist dance, Mary Wigman (1886–1973). While La Meri and Lilian knew nothing of the German language, they took "jaunts through the city," and when they needed it, they would receive kind help from the "Berliners" (ibid., 66–67). Presumably that was to find their way to various destinations.

After Berlin, the group was in Stockholm, February 27 to March 20 (*Chronology Notebook)*, with three concerts scheduled (March 6, 11, 19). Apparently Dallapiccola was no longer with them, so Carreras had to find and engage other musicians. The next part of the tour was in Norway where La Meri gave six performances in three different cities: Oslo (March 21, 24), Bergen (April 1, 3), and Stavanger (April 7, 8). They were in Copenhagen from April 11 to 17, but there is no record of any concert engagements in that city (*Chronology Notebook*; programs). At some point during or after this first Scandinavian tour, Lilian left the group.[5] By at least September 1930, she had joined her husband, David, in Nicaragua as shown by letters La Meri sent to her there during the fall months.

In her autobiography, La Meri tells about being "engaged for Dance Week in Oslo" and meeting Anna Pavlova, who, with her company, was in the evening concerts while La Meri was scheduled for the afternoons.[6] And she relates how, at the opening banquet for the visiting artists, she was thrilled to be sitting opposite this world-famous ballerina. She had seen Pavlova perform many years before in Texas (probably in 1913) and credited that experience with spurring her own early interest in ballet (1977a, 2). La Meri writes that she was overwhelmed when this great artist recognized her as a specialist in "ethnic dance arts"[7] and asked for her opinion of the Mexican ballet that Pavlova and her company were presenting (1977a, 67; 1984a, 17). In 1919, Pavlova had performed in Mexico and, while there, learned the *jarabe tapatío* and perhaps other traditional Mexican dances. She had adapted the *jarabe* for her ballet performances, dancing it *en pointe*. While La Meri did not remember how she answered Pavlova's question, she writes that through this interchange she was struck by a sudden sense of her own intellectual viability in relation to the art of dance: "I discovered I could discuss dancing objectively and intelligently, and that I felt, perhaps for the first time, that I had ideas on the subject that were definite and my own" (1977a, 67). Was this perhaps the first stimulus for what would become a significant corpus of writings on dance?

La Meri's work was so well received in Norway that she was contracted for another tour there in September. She and Carreras spent the summer in Paris where La Meri rehearsed, developed additional repertoire, performed, and attended "wonderful plays and concerts" (1977a, 68). As was true throughout her career, La Meri was busy preparing new dances for her concerts and collaborating with different musicians, who ranged from solo pianists to small ensembles to full orchestras. Of course, such changes in both program content and accompaniment required much work and rehearsal time.

While in Paris, La Meri gave a well-attended and, for the most part, enthusiastically reviewed concert at the Salle d'Iéna (May 26, 1930) with Boris Golschmann on the piano. It was almost the same program as those given in Florence and Vienna. Then, in June, she acted the role of the mute Cassandra in *La Tragédie de Kassandra* by André Stirling at the Théâtre de L'Oeuvre (1977a, 68; programs). Sometime after that, Carreras engaged a young man, Tony Gregory, to be La Meri's new "assisting artist."[8] Originally from Corsica, he had worked in various styles of dance, performed with different partners, taught dance, sang, and recited. In a 1932 article, he was described as "avant-garde" and "one of the oddest performers of today," but no details are given (Robinson, 164). La Meri writes that he was a "modern dancer" (1977a, 69); and in some of the concert programs he is identified as a "dancer-mime."

Gregory performed with La Meri during a week-long dance festival at the Château de Madrid, Bois de Boulogne, Paris (July 3–9); on the Norway tour in September and October; and in later performances in Paris. In addition to partnering her in a few pieces, Gregory also performed solos, which provided La Meri with time for her costume changes. In her correspondence with her sister, La Meri wrote about their collaboration and how much she enjoyed working with him. For example, in a letter from Oslo she writes: "We *all* wish you were here. Tony is *so* funny & I know you'd make a great team.

We laugh all the time! We did cut the program down—two numbers. Tony isn't strong enough to steal the show from me. It really is the best-balanced presentation we have ever had" (letter dated October 1, 1930, and mailed December 17). She gives more information about him and his work in other letters.

On the fall tour through Norway, the musicians were a piano team, Jacques Depiane [Jacques Paul-Boncour] and Denise Rossi [Mme. Denise Blottière] (1977a, 69; programs). In her letter of September 9, La Meri tells Lilian about them and praises their abilities as accompanists. There was obviously a good relationship between these musicians and La Meri as evidenced by a humorous packet, dated October 5, that they mailed from Oslo to Lilian. It includes a one-page letter from each and what they called the "Nit-wits Bulletin"—eleven pages of cartoons and humorous captions about the group's performances. In her message, Rossi mentions that "Dickie" has told her a lot about her sister and that she wishes Lilian was with them. In his, Depiane makes jokes about his poor English. What La Meri has written about the four performers having fun together illustrates that, while the touring was arduous and hard work for all, the members of the group also managed to enjoy life and each other—and to get relief from the pressure. In some of her letters to Lilian, La Meri mentions dinners and other social occasions that they also shared.

The tour was indeed arduous. From early September to about October 20, they gave more than twenty performances in Oslo and nine other Norwegian cities. In her September 20 letter to Lilian, La Meri includes part of their itinerary, which, at times, was very tightly scheduled. For example, on September 16, there was an evening concert in Kristiansund; the next day, from 8 a.m. to 2 p.m. they traveled from there to Molden, where they performed that evening; and the following morning, they departed at 7 a.m. for the next destination. This kind of scheduling would have been difficult even without the work needed for each concert: setting up the stage, ironing and arranging the costumes, and packing everything at the end. But La Meri, Carreras, and the others somehow managed it all, and the performances were well done and well received.

After this second Scandinavian tour, La Meri and Carreras returned to Paris where they spent Christmas. They were living in what she termed "a small pension" at 36, Rue Bonaparte, and La Meri continued her daily rehearsing and work on new pieces. During the first five months of 1931, there was one concert in Lyon on January 13, eight in Brussels from February 10 to 16, and one in Paris on May 4 (*Chronology 1973*, 3–4; programs). La Meri writes that Carreras wanted to include a second male dancer in the company; and, in Vienna, they had met a young artist who was interested in working with them: Willem van Loon (1911–1980), son of the Dutch-American historian and journalist, Hendrik van Loon (1882–1944).[9] They invited him to come to Paris to audition, hired him, and under the stage name Van Gerard, he participated in several of the concerts, sometimes along with Gregory (1977a, 70; programs). He later was a member of the Humphrey-Weidman modern dance company in New York City, and the archive of his extensive correspondence with German dancer and choreographer Harald Kreutzberg (1902–1968) and others is in the Jerome Robbins Dance Division of the New York Public Library for the Performing Arts. In 1972, he published a biography of his father, *The Story of Hendrik Willem van Loon* (Philadelphia: Lippincott). La Meri and Carreras became such good friends with the van Loon family that Hendrik was planning to attend their wedding, and his wife helped La Meri through the difficult times preceding that event (see below).

The Lyon program at the Salle Rameau on January 13 illustrates how La Meri and Carreras were developing a more and more richly varied repertoire for the concerts—with new works as well as established favorites. This Lyon performance featured La Meri in "The White Peacock," "Minstrel," "Empress of the Pagoda," and some of her Spanish dances, including the "Jota Aragonesa" (the latter with Gerard as partner). Gerard also performed solos: a Zuni ritual dance; an "American Tango"; and a piece he had probably created in which he caricatured the dancers Isadora Duncan, Mary Wigman, Josephine Baker, and Alexander Sakharoff (a Russian modern dancer and teacher who toured internationally). Another unusual offering on this concert was "L'Ame du Jazz" (The Soul of Jazz), danced by La Meri and Gerard to music arranged by Depiane and Rossi, and described in the program as "Vision chorégraphique cherchant à dépendre l'origine nègre des rythmes syncopés qui ont envahi la musique populaire sous la poussée frénétique de la vie moderne (Choreographic vision with the aim of depicting the Negro origin of the syncopated rhythms that have invaded popular music under the frenetic pressure of modern life). This piece and Gerard's portrayal of Josephine Baker were unusual elements in a La Meri concert. Up to this point, the only other examples of anything related to African or African diaspora cultures were the two songs of the "Negros of Alabama," which La Meri sang in Caracas on July 26, 1928, and the dance "Curandero Swahili," which was on her programs during the 1928–29 Latin American tour. Perhaps the new works were added as an acknowledgment of the growing popularity of jazz, which had begun to soar in Europe in the 1920s. In subsequent performances of "L'Ame du Jazz," La Meri was partnered by Gregory rather than Gerard.

One of La Meri's major concerts was that of May 4, 1931, at the Théâtre des Champs Élysées in Paris. This was a benefit for *Service Social de l'Enfance,* an organization for helping children in need or in danger, and according to the agreement, the organization would pay all the expenses and receive all the profits (letter to Lilian, May 6, 1931). Titled "Gala de Danses," the program consisted of three sections: "Five Free Interpretations," "Five Aspects of Spanish Dance," and "Five Ethnologic Dances"—the latter from India, Arabia, Mexico, Argentina, and Hawaii). Depiane and Rossi were the main musicians, but, since an international fair with musicians from many cultures was in Paris at the time, Carreras was able to also engage "native orchestras" from the Middle East, Mexico, Argentina, and Hawaii to accompany what by now La Meri was designating as "ethnologic" dances—and a flamenco guitarist for one or more of the Spanish dances. La Meri writes that she had been able to rehearse with all the musicians except those from the Middle East. That group saw no reason for preperformance rehearsals and insisted that she should just dance and they would follow her, which she found to be quite an unnerving experience (1977a, 70). There is no indication that Gregory or Gerard performed with La Meri in this concert.

Being in Europe gave La Meri the welcome opportunity to see the work of and even meet notable concert dance artists, two of whom she has credited as significant influences during her early years in dance. One of these, of course, was Pavlova (discussed above). Also very important was the opportunity to experience again the art of La Argentina—probably at a concert in May 1930 at the Opéra Comique (*Homenaje,* 183). Seeing La Argentina's performance in San Antonio around fifteen years earlier had stimulated the young Russell's first interest in Spanish dance, and the Paris concert included La Argentina's production of Falla's *El Amor Brujo,* which La Meri and Carreras had recently discussed with the composer during their time in Spain. So there were two reasons for La Meri to be particularly interested in seeing this artist's work in 1930.

A third major dance artist whose work La Meri experienced during this time in Europe was the innovative East Indian dancer and choreographer, Uday Shankar (1900–1977). According to Indian dance historian Joan L. Erdman, Shankar was "the founder of India's modern dance." He had worked with Anna Pavlova in the 1920s and left to form his own company of "Hindu dancers and musicians" (Erdman 1998, 580). Although this artist was not presenting Indian dance in its traditional forms, seeing him and his company provided La Meri with her first exposure to any actual Indian dance culture. She was familiar with choreographic works on Indian themes, such as those presented by Denishawn, and had performed her own "Nautch Dance" to Tchaikovsky music—but seeing Shankar's company, perhaps at their March 3, 1931, premiere performance in Paris, was a total revelation. She writes that she was so taken with his art that she wanted to study with him. He told her that he had given up teaching but invited her to watch his rehearsals and performances and make her own dances, which he would then look at and correct (an offer similar to that of Montero years before in New York). He also gave her a book on Indian dance by Ananda K. Coomaraswamy (perhaps the 1917 first edition of *The Mirror of Gesture*, or *The Dance of Shiva* of 1924) and some recordings of music. The result of this was her first "Hindu" dance, a creative work she titled "Lasyanatana" (1977a, 68–69; 1984d, 12–13; *Chronology 1973*, 4). In her May 6, 1931, letter to Lilian, she mentions taking "a few lessons" from Shankar, but that probably refers to his observing her dances and offering corrections. The contact with Shankar started La Meri on a path that she would pursue for the rest of her life. Along with Spanish dance, Indian dance became one of her two special areas of knowledge and virtuosity.

On June 24, 1931, La Meri and Carreras were married in London. Several newspapers had reported that the ceremony was to be in Paris, with Hendrik van Loon, a Baroness, and other notables in attendance—but unforeseen legal barriers prevented that. In her letters to Lilian from late 1930 to summer 1931, La Meri discussed their plans, the problems, and her extreme anxiety. On October 27, she wrote that Carreras had begun the process of divorcing his wife; and, on May 6, that the divorce proceedings were taking place in

Mexico, and that she and Carreras were engaged. By May 22, the divorce papers had arrived, and the ceremony was to be on June 4—if Carreras received his birth certificate from Livorno by then. However, their lawyer discovered that a divorced Italian could not marry in France because Italy did not recognize divorce and the French policy was to follow the laws of a person's home country. Carreras then found that they could marry in England if he would reside there a minimum of fifteen days prior to the ceremony, so he traveled to London on June 7. The residency requirement did not apply to the woman, but a visa was necessary, and La Meri's application for that was originally refused because she was a "theatrical person." Fortunately, the visa finally came, and she left for London on June 14.

In her letters to Lilian, La Meri tells about her suffering through this whole process—and also about the loving help she received from Hendrik van Loon's wife. For example, on June 11, she wrote: "I could not eat one bite all day yesterday. I have cried so much that I can hardly see, and today I could not finish my lunch. I certainly am one hell of a blushing bride. It would be funny if it wasn't so tragic." And remembering that time after she and Carreras were in Florence, she wrote that, after struggling to get the visa problem solved, she "went home and to bed and spent two of the most horrible days imaginable" but that Mrs. van Loon "was an angel. She didn't miss one day after Guy's departure coming to see me. And while I was sick she came and got me food and made me eat it, though goodness knows I didn't want to" (July 7 letter). Despite all the anxiety and suffering, however, La Meri had continued to pursue her interests such as attending performances, engaging in an unsuccessful search for a Cambodian dance group that she had heard was in Paris, and visiting a bookstore. And she survived all the trauma.

In her autobiography La Meri doesn't mention any of the difficulties prior to her marriage. She just writes that she and Carreras "popped over to London and got married. The ceremony took place in a dingy mid-Victorian registry presided over by a beaming, if rather seedy-looking civil clerk. However, glamour was provided by our two witnesses, Mr. Lord of the American consulate and the long-famous dancer Maude Allan [*sic*]" (1977a, 70–71). The marriage certificate verifies that the ceremony was in that city, and an unidentified clipping from London reports that while they were there, La Meri gave a private recital for a few friends at Maud Allan's home in Regents Park, performing dances of several different cultures to piano music. Some of the clippings about their marriage say that they planned to travel to the Orient in the fall, but this did not happen. Their relationship is discussed further in chapter 6.

Italy (1931–1936)

After their marriage, the couple returned to Carreras's native Italy. They apparently had no awareness of nor concern about the political situation there under the leadership of Benito Mussolini, founder of Italian Fascism. They spent the rest of the summer of 1931 in a Tuscan village, I Ronchi, reportedly on their "honeymoon" (1977a, 71; *San Antonio Evening News*, August 19, 1931). That was a strange way to identify it, however, since as La Meri writes, during this visit to Tuscany, Carreras "spent most of his time with the local menfolk while I turned to my typewriter and wrote my first full-length book on dancing" (1977a, 71). To stop touring was not a decision La Meri would have made on her own, and in her autobiography, she writes that "Carreras, twenty-five years my senior and with forty years of traveling behind him, longed to settle down in a home and be done with wandering. As obedient artist and faithful wife, I acquiesced. Nevertheless, I spent many hours staring through tear-dimmed eyes at the sea, weeping for the Orient I might never see" (1977a, 76). Fortunately, she would be on the road again eventually and experience that "Orient."

During their years in Italy, Carreras arranged various engagements for his wife that kept her somewhat active as a dancer, choreographer, and teacher— but his time and energy were clearly no longer devoted to her professional life. She taught some; had occasional solo concerts and other kinds of performances, mostly in Italy; choreographed works for herself and her students; and, as noted above, completed her first book on dance. The contract with A. S. Barnes and Company for publication of *Dance as an Art Form: Its History and Development* is dated May 12, 1933, and the book came out some time before November of that year when generally very positive reviews began to appear in daily newspapers in various cities and in special interest publications such as *The American Dancer* and *Research Quarterly* (see chapter 9).

La Meri writes that in the fall of 1931, they moved to Florence, and Carreras was able to get her a position teaching dance at the Accademia dei Fidenti, where she had performed her first European concert program the year before. The Accademia, a state-supported school of theater arts that dated from 1850, was located on the Via Laura in Florence and already had units devoted to experimental theater, acting, *Teatro della fiaba* (theater based on fables or fairy tales), something termed *consulenza musicale* (musical advice or consultation), scenography, and costume. A dance unit, Accademia dell'Arte della Danza, was created with La Meri and Carreras as its directors. The brochure for 1932–33 announces two sessions (November 15 to February 15; and February 15 to May 15) and a curriculum that included classes in "preparation" (training exercises for beginners), ballet (the Enrico Cecchetti method), free interpretation, Spanish dance, Indian dance, and dance for children. It is interesting that one of the offerings was Indian dance, as La Meri's experience of that was still very limited.[10]

In the summer of 1932—when the Accademia was not in session—Carreras and La Meri moved back to the Tuscan sea coast, to Viareggio, a small community north of Livorno. She writes that they had invited "two young artists" to come with them, not saying who they were or if they were dancers, and that she felt herself "happily surrounded by young people with whom [she] could swim, sail, and play tennis" while Carreras went "trap-shooting." Carreras invited her to join him in that sport, his favorite hobby, and he and La Meri got to know the attendant who operated the machine that sent the clay pigeon targets into the air (1977a, 71–72). He was an "ex-marble worker from Carrara," named Averardo Bertocchi, and he ended up working with them for years as light and sound technician. La Meri's writing suggests that this summer was purely vacation, but in Viareggio, on July 21, she gave a solo concert of "ethnologic" dances, and on August 7, performed at a literary event with a singer and two reciters.

From late August to late October 1932—before the winter session of the Accademia began—La Meri spent almost two months in the United States, visiting with Lilian and others, and collaborating in the arrangement of matters pertaining to their family estate. From letters written to Carreras, the itinerary seems to have been as follows. Her ship arrived in New York City on August 27, and from there, she traveled to Louisville and then San Antonio. Lilian was with her in both places and on September 2, they departed by train for Portland, Oregon, where David was stationed—and where the Newcomers now lived. They also traveled to other locations in the northwest and to Los Angeles. In Louisville, they had to settle legal matters associated with the closing of part of their father's company and also, perhaps, in relation to the farm, which was still in the family's possession. La Meri did not do much professionally on this trip, but in San Antonio, she did give what sounds like a mentoring lecture to a group of advanced dance students. Of course, both her visit and that session were grist for the mill of the local society pages.

After her time with Lilian, La Meri returned to Italy in late October, before the opening of the fall term at the Accademia. There, besides teaching, she developed a group of students to an advanced level and began to present them in performances. One major event was "Una Conferenza Storico-Didattica" (A historical-educational conference) with a lecture and dance demonstrations that were presented at the Accademia, February 10, 1933. A booklet was printed that contains both the twenty-nine-page lecture and the program of dances. The lecture briefly touches on the presumed origins of dance, discusses the art of dance in Europe, and then goes into the principles of ballet, "free dance," and "ethnologic dance"—the same subjects covered in La Meri's first published book. While the booklet credits La Meri with reading the lecture, it is more likely that Carreras did that since the text was, of course, in Italian. After the lecture, dances from the three categories that had been discussed were performed by La Meri and seven of her students. The music was directed by Mario Salerno, who was a major figure in the school's music unit and who played for or directed the music for many of La Meri's performances in Italy and later on tour. This particular program ended with a dance, purportedly from Africa, titled "Voodoo"—again an unusual offering on a La Meri concert (1977a, 71; brochures of R. Accademia dei Fidenti; lecture booklet). In her February 13, 1933, letter to Lilian, La Meri tells about this event, which she says was "a tremendous success" with more than 600 people in the hall (which was designed for only 350) and with great coverage in the press. She also describes some of the dance works that were presented.

Even though La Meri was teaching, choreographing, and performing during the years they lived in Italy, the engagements were much less intensive than when she had been on tour. She and Carreras would stay in Florence during the sessions of the Accademia and then find a place to live on the coast during the summer. Carreras, however, continually dreamed of obtaining a permanent residence of their own there, and probably in late 1933 or early 1934, they found what seemed like an ideal location and house on the

Tuscany coast, south of Livorno. They bought the property and renovated the house, adding a very large studio for La Meri's teaching and rehearsals. Their address was Villa Alegrias [Villa Happiness], Campolicciano, Castiglioncello (Livorno). It seems that she felt content there for some time—maybe as much as a year. She writes that "[t]he months sped by happily, spent in refurbishing, painting, and gardening," and that there were "many homely, bucolic joys" including "hunting in the fall and swimming from May to December." They were visited in their new home by Lilian and David, many friends, and some former pupils (1977a, 73).

In spring 1934, La Meri was invited to represent Italy at the ten-day International Dance Concourse and Folk Dance Congress in Vienna which opened May 26. Carreras did not want to travel to Vienna for this event, but she writes that he "allowed [her] to go alone." She felt nervous because she knew no German and little French, and for her performance she would not have the usual technical and moral support of her husband and their by now faithful assistant Bertocchi (1977a, 74). However, she decided to be brave and take on the challenge.

While there, La Meri was on a panel that worked seven to ten hours a day judging the performance and choreography of ballet, modern, and folk dancers from various parts of Europe and selecting prizewinners to be presented in evening performances. Also on the panel were representatives from Vienna, Prague, Berlin, London, Paris, Greece, Oslo, Warsaw, Stockholm, and Tokyo. Besides her panel work, La Meri was one of two dance artists invited to give solo concerts at the event. The other was Grete Wiesenthal (1885–1970), a well-known Viennese dancer, choreographer, and educator, who had begun in traditional ballet but stretched the limits of that genre during her career (Oberzaucher-Schüller). Since the organizers had asked La Meri to perform work from countries that were not represented at the congress, she did dances from or related to the cultures of Japan, India, Morocco, Mexico, Argentina, North America (native American), Hawaii, and Spain—each "explained" to the audience by a Viennese ethnologist and university professor, Dr. Heine Geldern (1977a, 74–75; Cleve, 1934; La Meri's report under R.M.H. in the *American Dancer*, August 1934).

The concert went very well, however, and was highly praised by Felix Cleve in the *Neue Freie Presse* (June 6, 1934). La Meri writes that after the wonderful triumph in Vienna, "it seemed difficult to return to the bucolic life." Instead, she longed to return to the "siren theater" (1977a, 75–76). Although she continued giving in to Carreras's desire for them to stay settled in their new home, the life of teaching and occasional performances was not fulfilling her dream.

In Castiglioncello, La Meri gave summer courses and organized festivals of dance and music. What was probably the first festival took place in the park of the Castello Birindelli in Castiglioncello on August 23, 1934. A review in *La Nazione* (August 24) says that the event was a benefit for the *Opere Assistenziali* (a term used for various kinds of charitable assistance organizations). The program consisted of two parts: six dances by La Meri and her *corpo di ballo,* and a section of classical music by the *Banda della 350 Legione Avanguardista "Benito Mussolini."* The unnamed reviewer praised the concert and noted the warm reception given to the artists by the audience.

A brochure of 1935 solicited students for classes in preparation for a "Festival Coreografico" that would be offered that summer. An outdoor performance was scheduled for Saturday, August 17, on a cliff in Quercianella (a short boat ride down the coast from Livorno). In an article in *Il Telegrafo* that same day, the prospective audience members were advised that transportation would be provided by a boat leaving Livorno at 9 p.m. for the concert beginning at 9:30. The return boat would leave Quercianella at ten before midnight, indicating that the length of the program was about two hours. La Meri performed eight of her solos; her students, identified as *Signore della Società* (society girls), were in six solo, duet, or group works; and the entire company, including La Meri, performed in the finale, "Hawaiiana." Most of the music was by the usual Western composers, such as Chopin, Vivaldi, Debussy, Ravel, Delibes, Falla—but here also, surprisingly, Gershwin. The Hawaiian suite was performed to the usual recorded traditional music. The program included both old and new works, and some dances that had been performed by La Meri were now set on other dancers.

La Meri and Carreras stayed in Italy through 1935, but then the state of their finances deteriorated to the extent that going back to touring seemed their only choice. While Carreras was undoubtedly disappointed by this, La Meri was delighted, writing: "I welcomed the wolf that came snuffling at our door and forced Carreras to put away his shotgun and dust off his spotlights. The wolf was my ally, pushing my return to deadline rehearsals and the welcome fever of costume creation" (1977a, 76–77). This change in their fortunes brings up the question of the financial situation throughout their time together. Did Carreras have a substantial inheritance from his family in Italy that they had used to live there and buy their house? Had there been great financial gains during their touring that gave them resources for a time? And if either of those were true, why would the financial situation have deteriorated so much at this time?

London (1936)

In January 1936, La Meri, Carreras, and Bertocchi left Italy for performances in London that were organized by L. G. Sharpe, a well-known manager, and his assistant Cameron Stockwell. Her first engagement (beginning February 10) was for a week of eight performances, including evenings and matinees, at the small Arts Theatre Club. By now it had become usual for her to organize a concert into sections (usually three), each featuring a different category of dance. On the opening program, she performed five of the "free interpretations" that were still in her repertoire, five Spanish dances, and five "ethnologic" dances. Probably because she had been off the circuit for a while, La Meri was extremely nervous before beginning her first dance on the first performance. As she writes, "This evening's work was a Rubicon to cross. The butterflies in my stomach metamorphosed into hummingbirds." After she began performing, however, she felt the response of the audience to be very positive (1977a, 77–78). In the *Dancing Times* of London (March 1936, 753), a critic (identified only as the "Sitter Out") expressed some appreciation of her work, writing that "it is obvious that a great deal of intelligent research has been done and care taken with the ethnologic section, and little-known dances of this type are always a pleasure to watch, as well as being of great importance to the dance student and connoisseur." However, this reviewer basically criticized the performance, writing that "the dancer lacks variety in her movements and her choice of dances is not always a happy one; and in spite of some attractive and authentic costumes, she fails to be convincing. She was greatly handicapped by the accompaniment of badly-worn gramophone records." Complaints about the quality of the recordings would continue over the years.

Sharpe was then able to book La Meri for two weeks at the Savoy Theater beginning March 2. In the opening concert of that engagement, the three groups of dances she presented were termed "Spanish," "Ethnologic," and "Oriental." It is interesting that on different programs a dance might be presented under different categories. For example, on the February concert, the "Empress of the Pagodas" was in the group of "Free Interpretations," while on March 2, it was presented as part of the "Oriental" section.

In London, between the engagements at the Arts Theater Club and the Savoy, La Meri also gave some other performances—one "in a hospital for child charity cases." She also created a new work, took lessons in Irish dancing, and "gave a conference on Indian dancing for the Indian Society." The latter engagement raises the same questions as the inclusion of Indian dance in the Accademia curriculum, since La Meri did not yet have any real experience in traditional Indian dance genres and techniques. She must have drawn on the Coomaraswamy writings and what she had learned from Uday Shankar and his company.

After the Savoy engagement, Stockwell informed them that he had arranged an audition for her with the Australian impresario A.D.M. Longden for a tour in Australasia. She was very excited about this because, as she writes, "This opportunity, like the silent swinging open of a huge door, disclosed a long vista of exotic beauty: India, Java, China, Japan, and at the end, Australasia." At the audition, she was "a jelly of nerves," but Longden was obviously impressed (1977a, 79) and she was offered a contract for a tour in Australia and New Zealand that would begin in June.

I. Views from the Life of Russell/La Meri

1. Portrait of Russell as an "angel baby" (ca. 1901). Published in La Meri's brochures in the 1940s.

2. Russell as a child.

Elrod ENAMEL FINISH. 1891. LOUISVILLE, *KY.*

3. Lillian "Lilly" Belle Allan, mother of the two sisters. This photograph and #4 and #5 are from a scrapbook compiled by the young Russell in 1918. It is in the archive of the Kentucky Historical Society and the photos are included here with their permission.

4. Russell Meriwether Hughes, the girls' father.

5. Russell and her sister Lilian.

6. Russell as a teenager with her violin.

7. Photograph by Marcus Blechman (1922–2010) in the *New York Herald Tribune,* with the Walter Terry article, "The Dance: La Meri's Dance" (July 28, 1950). Courtesy of the Marcus Blechman Collection, Museum of the City of New York.

8. La Meri in Cape Cod, *Nauset Weekly Calendar* (July 8, 1977).

II. Early Dances Performed during Russell's Youth

9. Greek inspired dance, perhaps first performed at Travis Park Methodist Church, ca. 1910.

10. Spanish dance, probably ca. 1911.

11. Ballet dance on pointe, sometime before 1920.

III. Early Professional Work of Russell/La Meri in the 1920s

12. Performance of ballet for a movie prologue in San Antonio, ca. 1922.

13. (*above*) Versions of a dance titled "The Doll," "Katinka," or "The Wooden Doll from Russia" were in La Meri's repertoire from 1923 until at least 1943. This picture probably dates from the 1920s.

14. (*left*) Guido Carreras, probably in the early 1930s.

15. "The Shawl Dance," one of various dances inspired by the bullfight movements that La Meri learned in Mexico in 1926. Photograph in the *New York Evening Post* (February 25, 1928). Dances using the Spanish shawl and based on such movements were in her repertoire from 1927 until at least 1936.

16. Movement from "Études Symphoniques" to music by Robert Schumann. This work was performed with Lilian and Billy on tours, 1927 to 1929.

17. La Meri as the Javanese idol in her group work, "In a Temple of Java," choreographed to music by Albert Ketelbey and presented 1927 to 1929.

18. "Empress of the Pagodas," Chinese-themed dance to one section of Maurice Ravel's "Mother Goose Suite." Originally learned from Michio Itō, this was on La Meri's programs from 1927 to 1948—perhaps with changes along the way.

19. In this 1936 photograph from the National Library of Australia, La Meri is posing for a sculpture by Lyndon Dadswell (1908–1986). She is in the costume and pose of the "White Peacock," a work to the music of Charles Tomlinson Griffes that was in her repertoire from ca. 1927 to the mid-1940s.

4

Australasia and Asia, 1936–1937

The contract offered by Longden was originally for a minimum of thirty appearances in fourteen weeks or more.[1] Besides La Meri, the original tour group consisted of Carreras as director; Mario Salerno who played piano and directed small ensembles of local musicians for the concerts; Laura Mollica, a dancer who had been studying and performing with La Meri for a few years in Italy—and Averardo Bertocchi, who was apparently relegated to third-class accommodation on the ship. As it turned out, the tour of Australia and New Zealand lasted for more than four months, and after it ended, La Meri, Carreras, and Bertocchi continued traveling through most of 1937—to Ceylon (Sri Lanka), India, Burma (Myanmar), Malaysia, Java, the Philippines, China, Japan, and Hawaii. La Meri's frequent and multipage letters to Lilian during this time (cited below just as letter[s]) provide a wealth of detailed information about her performances and the dance training she sought and received in the various countries—and also, about the group's travels from one place to another; their daily activities; the difficulties they sometimes encountered; the people they met; the sightseeing and shopping for which they always dedicated time; and their impressions of the landscapes, populations, food, and cultures. Such information, with less detail, was also in the occasional "Installment Letter" that La Meri would send to a group of friends. Each of these summarizes an extended period of time and range of touring.

Australia and New Zealand (June–November 1936)

La Meri, Carreras, and Bertocchi left Genoa on May 5, 1936, and the ship picked up Salerno and Mollica at other Italian ports. Between December 7 and 16, La Meri wrote what was her first "Installment Letter." Written on shipboard as they traveled from Perth, Australia, to Sri Lanka, it covers about

eight months, beginning with the group's May departure from Italy and ending with their departure from Australia. La Meri describes how much they
enjoyed their thirty-eight days traveling from Europe to Australia on the
"S.S.Romolo," and that she "practiced long hours every day." From Italy, the
ship went through the Suez Canal, made brief stops in Cochin (Kochi) on
the west coast of India and Colombo in Ceylon (Sri Lanka), and finally arrived in Melbourne, Australia, on June 10 (1977a, 81–82; Installment Letter).

In her writings—especially in the letters—La Meri frequently expressed
her enchantment with the cities, scenery, and historical landmarks that she
saw and told about her meetings and interactions with people. For example,
in her May 29 letter to Lilian, besides discussing life on the "Romolo," she
writes of their experiences when they were in port in Cochin and Colombo.
Their few hours in Cochin thrilled La Meri since, as she writes, it was "my
introduction to India (of which I have so often dreamed)." While the group
was roaming through the city, they happened to see some kind of meeting
going on in "an open-air pavilion" and were invited to attend by a "handsome
Indian lady." It turned out to be a conference focused on various religions,
including Hinduism, Christianity, and Judaism. Since La Meri and the group
could not understand the language, they didn't stay long but were very impressed with the large audience who was obviously interested in the topic. La
Meri found Cochin "perfectly fascinating," but the experience in Colombo
was totally different. During their short time off the ship there, the music
critic of the city's leading newspaper met them, had them come to its office
for publicity pictures, and then arranged a short tour for them. However, to
La Meri—and surely the others also—the tour had nothing of interest. Instead of being taken to places important in Sri Lankan history and culture,
they were transported around the residences of the English colonists and
finally to an American hotel for cocktails with the newspaper editor.

Mario Salerno and Laura Mollica had fallen in love during the long journey from Italy to Australia and the early days of the tour, and they decided,
rather quickly, to marry (1977a, 84). In her letters to Lilian, La Meri frequently wrote about them, and particularly about Laura—sometimes with
appreciation for the young woman's efforts and more often with annoyance
and scorn for various flaws such as "silliness," "excessive self-confidence," in-
consistency in rehearsing and performing, and lack of respect for the others
in the group. Both La Meri and Carreras were dubious about the marriage,

thinking that it was good for Laura, but not necessarily for Mario and his professional life. In her letter of June 18, La Meri writes:

> I wanted to give a nice girl a "leg up" in her career—& the day before yesterday Laura & Mario announced their intention of *marrying immediately*—in 3 or 4 days (the nuts!). True to type Mario doesn't want her to dance anymore after they leave our company.

Salerno and Mollica waited to receive permission from Laura's mother to marry, and the ceremony took place in Melbourne, probably on July 12. They stayed with the company until early November when the Australian-New Zealand tour was finished.

The first concert in Australia was Saturday, June 20, at the King's Theatre in Melbourne. La Meri performed fifteen dances, and there were at least two piano solos between sections of dances. Besides Salerno, the other musicians were Tom Challen, violinist, and Joan Howley, cellist. As usual, some of the dances were to live music and others to recordings. This first program included four Spanish dances, three dances identified as "oriental," four "free interpretations," and four dances from Latin America. Laura danced with La Meri in "Faunesque," and "El Gato." While there were some variations on different programs, the works were usually organized in the four sections listed above, although sometimes an "ethnologic" or "racial" category replaced the Latin American section. In that case, it would usually include dances from a variety of cultures, including those of Latin America.

In considering most of La Meri's touring, the question arises as to how she had the energy to do so well and survive such a demanding schedule. For each concert, she performed many dances with no more than three minutes for each change of costume—some of which were complex combinations of clothing, jewelry, headdresses, and shoes. Often there were concerts scheduled on subsequent days and sometimes two concerts scheduled on the same day. In addition, before and after each performance, there was work to be done with the costumes—unpacking, ironing, and organizing them in the best way for quick changes; the regular need to repair or clean items; and repacking everything for the next engagement. And every time they crossed a border, the more than fifty trunks had to be opened and the contents spread out for customs inspection. Sometimes for the performances La Meri had help from an assistant or second dancer such as Laura, but not always. Of course, Carreras was overworked as well—on this tour, as overall director and lighting designer. He was overseeing and helping Bertocchi with the complicated stage equipment maintenance and installations, collaborating with Longden in scheduling and promotion, and taking care of any problems that arose. In addition, both he and La Meri had to be present at frequent social events, interviews, and photography sessions that were scheduled to promote the performances. As expressed in her autobiography and her letters to Lilian, La Meri suffered the same degree of exhaustion in Australia as she had during the 1928 Latin American tour—if not more. However, whatever the challenges and difficulties, La Meri loved touring and was very happy that their financial situation had made it necessary for them to go back on the road. And even though they were on a hectic schedule most of the time, she writes frequently in her letters to Lilian about sightseeing, going to movies, and engaging in other recreational activities.

In addition to eleven concerts at the King's Theatre in Melbourne, over the next five months, the group performed in other Australian locations (Geelong, Bundaberg, Maryborough, Brisbane, Sydney, Tasmania) and in New Zealand (Wellington, Christchurch, Dunedin, Invercargill, Oamaru, Palmerston, Hamilton, Auckland, Gisborne). La Meri writes that they gave a total of 108 concerts (1977a, 91).[2] News coverage in each city where they performed was extensive—due no doubt to the efforts of both Carreras and Longden. Articles included discussion of La Meri's life (usually with extreme exaggerations and falsehoods), her personality, her "ideas" and poetry, her repertoire, and her costumes—and sometimes, also, of Carreras, his many languages, and his professional life as impresario, manager, designer, and director. Articles on La Meri's costumes would be included in the women's section of the paper, while reviews of the concerts themselves often mentioned society people who had attended. Some preperformance articles and postperformance reviews compared La Meri with Anna Pavlova, Adeline Genée, La Argentina, or other well-known concert dancers while noting that La Meri's work was unique. One such comparison, by D. L. Waraker in Brisbane is titled "How La Meri Differs from Pavlova—Warmly Human Appeal," and stresses that Pavlova's art—ballet—is less natural than the dance genres performed by La Meri, and because of the characteristics of her art, Pavlova herself appeared more as a spirit than a woman (*Brisbane Telegraph*, October 2, 1936).

Happily, La Meri and her small company enjoyed great success everywhere in Australia and New Zealand. The response throughout the tour was enthusiastic and overwhelmingly positive. The reviewers were amazed and delighted by her art, her technical versatility, her expressive range, and her costumes. For example, a Melbourne review of her opening performance headlined "Dance Concert of La Meri: 'A Magical Journey'" begins with the following statement: "To enter the King's Theatre on Saturday night when La Meri opened her season of dance concerts, was to procure a passport to many picturesque and unfamiliar lands" (*Argus* June 22, 1936). And a review in Wellington, titled "La Meri: An Incomparable Dancer," begins

> Versatility is but one, though not the least of the many gifts bestowed on La Meri. Dancing at the Opera House last night she showed not only understanding by [*sic*] the spirit of many peoples as expressed in their dances, but how to make those dances stir the imaginations of the dullest of onlookers.

The reviewer then goes on to discuss some of the works on the concert in detail (*Evening Post* July 24, 1936). In many reviews there is also favorable mention of Laura and praise for the musicians, each of whom played solos on the program—with Mario Salerno receiving particular notice.

La Meri's season at His Majesty's Theatre in Auckland, New Zealand, was to run from August 22 to 29. By then, she had done more than fifty concerts since their arrival in Australia, and her exhaustion was growing. She writes that, on one of those nights [Friday, August 28], as they were going to the theater, she said to Longden, "If I were the captain of my soul, I wouldn't be doing this performance tonight. I'm dead beat. Lately I've been drawing mental blanks in the middle of my oldest dances." Nevertheless, she went on and got through the first ten dances. Then, at the beginning of the eleventh, as she ran across the stage, she heard a snap and lost control of her right leg. She could not continue, and the concert was completed by the musicians (1977a, 85). In her August 31 letter to Lilian, she relates her frantic schedule on the days before that concert. On Wednesday, August 26, she had had two concerts; on Thursday, three to four hours of rehearsing for the "relatively new program" that was to be given that evening; and Friday morning she "went for a brief shopping tour, and at eleven gave two auditions to budding geniuses." She writes that when she went to the theater Friday evening, she was "so tired [she] could hardly move," and continues that "the night was jinxed," referring to some technical problems. Finally, as she entered the stage for the "Faunesca," she suffered the injury. She was transported backstage, where she says she "threw fits" and, as a result, "[t]hey gave me a shot of whiskey and that knocked out the rest of my self-control, and I had a merry time of making funny cracks and weeping." As was her habit, La Meri expressed to Lilian her upheavals, fits of anger or anguish, complaints, and other personal feelings that she never included in her published writings.

Considering her increasing exhaustion from the amount of performing she was doing—and everything else—it is not surprising that La Meri suffered an injury. To her relief, she was told by the doctor who treated her that it was a torn muscle rather than permanent damage—and she was advised not to dance for three weeks. However, she began performing "an easy program" after about ten days (1977a, 85–86). An article in the *Auckland Star* reported that, because of the injury, her two performances scheduled for August 29 were canceled, but a farewell performance was scheduled for the Auckland Town Hall on Thursday, September 17 (August 29, 1936).

While she was in New Zealand, La Meri had become interested in the culture of the Maori people and, of course, their dance. So instead of staying in Auckland for rest and recuperation from the injury, she and Carreras traveled to the Maori center of Rotorua on September 1.[3] This city is famous for its health spas as well as its culture, so La Meri was able to receive treatment and therapy there as well as making contact with the Maori people. She and Carreras visited Whakarewarewa, one of several Maori villages in and around Rotorua, and there she was welcomed with great hospitality and interest. Despite her injury, she was able to learn the "poi dances and something of the hakas" from a seventy-year-old woman, who, she writes, was "dancing like 20" (1977a, 86). And the Maori princess Rangi invited her and Carreras for meals and arranged an evening of Maori dance for them in which traditional (as opposed to touristic) dances were shown. She, of course, could not dance for them so soon after her injury, but she would do that later, in their next visit.

It is not clear how long they stayed in the Maori area this first time, but they probably had to leave by at least the 6th because La Meri was scheduled to give a concert in Hamilton (about 70 miles away) on September 7. As always, the stage had to be set up with the lighting and sound, and the costumes had to be unpacked and organized for the quick changes. Between September 7 and 14 La Meri gave six concerts in three different cities: Hamilton, Hastings, and Gisborne. They traveled from one to the other on the road, with a passenger car and a truck. On September 15, they returned to Rotorua and Whakarewarewa, and that evening, La Meri performed dances for the Maori. She writes that her program consisted of "milestones on the fabled Maori westward migration—India, Spain, Morocco, North America, Mexico, Peru, and Hawaii" (1977a, 86). One can wonder where she found this "fabled" information, because it is definitely not historical fact. However, the Maoris loved her performance. As she writes:

> Never has there been such an audience. From small children to ninety-year-olds, they were breathlessly attentive. Even a lift of my eyebrow was observed and understood. At the end of each number they fairly squealed with delight. Drunk with their appreciation, I danced better than ever before in my life. (1977a, 86)

In this second visit to the area, they also visited one or more of the other Maori communities and La Meri obtained traditional costumes as well as the training.

After her injury had healed, La Meri continued giving performances and lectures until early November. Her last engagements were in Tasmania on November 7 and 9. In recalling her travels and performing in Australia and New Zealand, she writes that this was

> the most glamorous tour I ever had. More personal adulation than I would have thought possible; kindness, compliments, flowers. I was painted, sculptured and photographed endlessly. A racehorse, a hat style, a popular sundae were named La Meri. I brought away three enormous volumes of press clippings. (1977a, 91)

And despite the intensity of her performing for months and her injury, and despite Carreras's age and desire to settle down, the two of them apparently had no qualms about continuing on the road for another year, to countries and cultures that were entirely new to them—to Ceylon, India, and beyond.

Ceylon (now Sri Lanka) and India (December 1936–March 1937)

After her successes in Australia and New Zealand, La Meri began her Asian travels with three concerts at the New Olympia Theatre in Colombo (December 19, 21, and 23). They had arrived there by ship on Wednesday, December 16, and began preparing immediately for the coming performances as well as attending the usual social and promotional events. Longden was still traveling with them as agent/manager and Bertocchi as technical assistant, but since Laura Mollica and Mario Salerno had departed for Italy, the company was without a musical collaborator and an assisting dancer. From Colombo on, they apparently used only recorded music for the concerts, and for a short time, Mollica was replaced by a seventeen-year-old Australian dancer, Beverley Slaney (stage name, Anne Beverley). In her letter to Lilian (December 15, 1936), La Meri writes that Slaney had taken some lessons with her in Melbourne and, wanting to continue this work, asked to tour with them and perform on the concerts. Her parents offered to pay most of her expenses, so, with some apprehension, La Meri and Carreras agreed to let her join them. In La Meri's opinion, she was a good dancer, very intelligent, and "delightful in every way," but she was also immature, which could require La Meri to "play mama," a role she did not want. An unidentified article of December 12 (probably from the *Times of Ceylon* and written before the first performance in Colombo) identifies Slaney as a "young Melbourne socialite" with experience in ballet and says that she will perform duets with La Meri, including "Valentini's Gavotte," "Faunesque," "Jota Aragonesa," and the "Hulalei Hula." However, later clippings only mention her in "Faunesque." The last references to her are in January programs in Madras and Bangalore. In La Meri's January 31 letter to Lilian, she describes some of the problems with Slaney that led to them sending her home on January 27. So, from then on, until engaging the Indian male dancer who would become known as Ram Gopal (see below), La Meri performed alone.

In her December 21 letter to Lilian, La Meri writes about how sick she was the day of the first performance in Colombo (stricken with her usual monthly ordeal). Despite how she felt, however, the concert went very well. The Colombo performances, like those that followed, were all well received by both reviewers and audiences. In considering her abilities, one critic wrote:

Take the versatility of Ruth Draper, the colour and imagination of the Chauve Souris, add a dash of Argentina and you have some idea of the wonderful varied programme presented by La Meri, the Spanish-American dancer, . . .

The three or four curtains which followed her every appearance showed that Colombo, which has never seen anything quite like this before, definitely wanted more. ("Colour, Imagination and Versatility of La Meri" by J.R.F., *Times of Ceylon*, December 21, 1936)

It is interesting that in comparing La Meri to internationally known performing artists, this Colombo critic refers not only to La Argentina, but also to the actress Ruth Draper (1884–1956), who portrayed a broad array of characters in her dramatic monologues, and to La Chauve-Souris (The Bat), a cabaret show originally from Russia that toured from the 1920s to 1940s and also featured great variety in its presentations. The incorrect, but presumably enticing, identification of La Meri as Spanish-American or Spanish was an image promoted by Carreras throughout their touring.

After the concerts in Colombo, the group traveled to Kandy in central Ceylon for a short stay (perhaps December 23 to 28 or 29). There, in addition to the one scheduled performance, La Meri was able to learn three traditional Kandyan dances.[4] Her teacher, Ratharana, whom she identifies as "Kandy's finest dancer," taught her what she terms "devil dances." These were from the genre of *vannam*, which includes eighteen classical dances depicting animals or objects. She learned the Cobra (*naga*), Elephant (*gajaga*), and Eagle (*ukkussa*) dances and kept them in her repertoire for many years. These were traditionally men's dances, and Ratharana told her that she was only the second woman to whom he had taught them. She assumed that the first must have been the partner of Uday Shankar, the French dancer Simone Barbier, whose stage name was Simkie (1977a, 94). With a generous Christmas check from Lilian and her husband, La Meri was able to purchase an elaborate antique Kandyan costume with headdress and ornaments of silver set with semiprecious stones. She describes in detail their Christmas celebration in Kandy in her December 29 letter to Lilian. And then, after they returned to Colombo, La Meri danced for the New Year's Eve celebration at their hotel. The next afternoon, January 1, 1937, they left for Madras, arriving on January 4 (January 13 letter).

The schedule of travel and performances in India was as heavy as anything they had experienced before. By mid-April La Meri had given between twenty and twenty-five performances in ten cities: Madras (Chennai), Bangalore, Hyderabad, Poona (Pune), Bombay (Mumbai), Nagpur, Calcutta

(Kolkata), Lahore, and Delhi (1977a, 93–107; programs; letters). Transporting their personal luggage, trunks of costumes, stage lighting, and sound equipment, they traveled enormous distances by train between the north and south and east and west of that huge land—an activity that La Meri remembered as "complicated, to say the least." As she writes:

> one had to have a bearer whose duty it was to go to the station hours ahead of train time to take possession of a compartment and hold it, the only known way of obtaining one. He had to carry with him mattresses, sheets, pillows, towels, and toilet tissue.

After packing their luggage and food in the compartment, he would guard everything until the last minute when he would run out to get a huge chunk of ice—presumably to prevent the food from spoiling. Then, after helping the travelers get settled, he would go to his 3rd class wagon for the long journey (1977a, 101).

Not only was the travel demanding, but also preparations for performing and the performance itself. As usual throughout the tour, their stage equipment, sound system, lighting, floor cover, and curtains all had to be set up in theaters with different configurations. The supervision of that and often the work itself were in the hands of Carreras, Bertocchi, and Longden. And La Meri needed four hours to unpack her costumes, iron them, and organize them in the order necessary for the program. Sometimes she had help with this—by the assisting dancer when there was one, or a local staff person—but sometimes not. Also, she was used to having a woman during the concerts to assist with the quick costume changes, but since, for some reason, in India, only men were available for such a task, she had to do it alone (1977a, 93, 99). Despite the rigors of the travel and performing, however, La Meri, now in her late thirties, seemed to thrive on this inspiring introduction to a land and its rich cultures that had long fascinated her. It is interesting that many of the reviewers referred to her as a "young dancer" and praised her energy, which was apparently unflagging. How Carreras, now in his late fifties or mid-sixties, felt about the rigorous travel and the challenges of presenting concerts in ever-changing settings can only be imagined.

La Meri's first concert in India was on Thursday, January 7, at the Museum Theatre in Madras where she performed fourteen dances in three sections: Spanish, interpretive, and "racial." In her autobiography, she writes that the audience at this first performance was all British, including the governor, diplomats, and society people. Although this was advertised as her only appearance in that city, she writes that the next evening, she "danced on the floodlit lawn of a British country club," and on January 9, had another performance at the Museum Theatre, where the audience was all Indian (1977a, 95). In her January 13 letter to Lilian, she says that "several Maharajahs" also attended the first concert, and the reason there were only Indians at the second was because the British elite were attending a "huge party after the races." La Meri enjoyed performing for the Indian audiences and their enthusiastic reaction—and notes that there was "a tremendous lot of anti-British feeling" among them. From her writings and some reviews, however, it seems that, for most concerts, there were mixed Indian and British audiences. Her stay in Madras had a short interruption when she traveled to Bangalore for two concerts on January 13 and 14.

As usual, La Meri received enthusiastic and appreciative reviews for the variety and the beauty of her performances; much attention was paid to her Spanish, interpretive, and other non-Indian dances. But what was crucial to her at this time was how her Indian dances would be accepted—both the two she had arrived with, "Lasyanatana" and "Nacni Nrrta," and the new ones she added to her concerts as she learned them in India. Even in Colombo—not India, but close to it and culturally related—she had felt "trepidation" about performing "Lasyanatana," worried that it would be scorned by a knowledgeable public. There, however, it was a great success (1977a, 94). When she performed in India itself, she was even more nervous, "frightened to death" as she puts it, but the Indian audience for her second concert "reassured [her] by shouting with joy and by demanding an encore after each presentation (ibid., 95). Some of the reviewers, however, criticized the "Indian" numbers. For example, in discussing the January 7 concert, one critic wrote:

> "Lasya Natana," although containing many typical movements, was performed in the wrong *tempo*, according to South Indian ideas, and with too much freedom of movement about the stage. (*Madras Mail*, January 8, 1937)

He was undoubtedly comparing it to Bharatanatyam,[5] which she had not yet studied.

Later, a reviewer of her January 14 concert in Bangalore would write more appreciatively, while noting that La Meri had not yet had direct experience or training in the arts of India. He compared aspects of her non-Indian dances with the characteristics of Bharatanatyam, concluding that there were similarities as well as differences between the dances of "the East and the West." Then he discussed the dances she presented as "Indian":

> The two Indian dance numbers expressing *Sringara rasa*, (the erotic) . . . were tolerably well discoursed, both of them coming under the *Kathak* school of technique of Northern India. In the second, the observer was reminded not only of Menaka [a well-known Indian dancer and teacher], but also Simkie of Uday Shankar's troupe, . . . It was poetry itself. As she herself [La Meri] addressed the audience on the stage, she is not as yet perfect in *mudras, rasas* and *bhavas* of *Bharatha Natya*, though she has exhibited an intelligent understanding of the very complicated technique with a philosophical background, . . . [I]t can be stated with confidence that La Meri, will very soon pick up the details of the Indian Art by practicing the *mudras*, the bedrock of Indian dancing. (*Daily Post*, Bangalore, January 15, 1937)[6]

And that, of course, is exactly what she intended to do.

As early as January 1937, what would grow into World War II was looming. After her first Bangalore concert, in response to a reviewer's question about the world tensions and hostilities that were developing, La Meri commented that

> the present tension which is sweeping the world is due to a lack of understanding of each other among the various peoples of the world. That lack of understanding, . . . could be minimized through the "dance." . . . the soul of any nation was expressed through its dance, and so to study and gain an understanding of the dance of a nation was to study and gain an understanding of the soul of that nation.

The reviewer felt that she had proven this point completely in her concert, that she "lived every part that she played" and "expressed the soul of every nation whose dances she depicted" ("Around the Dance World; With La Meri," *Daily Post*, Bangalore, January 14, 1937). And it is interesting that during World War

II, in response to La Meri performing a Japanese dance in New York City, a reviewer had noted the value of presenting the arts of an enemy nation to illustrate the positive side of a culture that was being seen only negatively.

On January 11, the day after her second concert in Madras, La Meri was visited by G. K. Seshagiri, *régisseur* of the Indian Renaissance Theatre.[7] He invited her to a recital by two young and well-known Bharatanatyam dancers of the *devadasi* tradition, Varalakshmi and Bhanumati. He also introduced her to their teacher, Papanasam Vadivelu Pillai, who belonged to the school of Meenakshi Sundaram Pillai, a noted master of the Pandanallur style of Bharatanatyam (1977a, 95–97; Venkateswaran, 14–15; Jones, 309). La Meri soon joined Varalakshmi and Bhanumati in their four-hour classes with Pillai and then would return to her hotel room and, after lunch and a rest, practice what she had learned for another three hours. The teacher and pupil did not share a verbal language, but through her "young Indian translator," La Meri learned that Pillai was surprised and impressed with her progress. She writes:

> By the third lesson old Pillai remarked that I would learn in a month what it took his girls a year to master and with six months' training he'd make me the best dancer in India. At the end of the eighth lesson he cut the time to three months. (1977a, 96)

Her study with him was interrupted by the Bangalore performances, but when she returned to Madras, she continued her classes with Pillai and also began studying *abhinaya*, the depiction of stories or themes through the dance, with Srimati [Mrs.] Gauri Ammal (1977a, 97; Venkateswaran, 15–16). This may have been the well-known former *devadasi* and Bharatanatyam dancer, Mylapore Gowri Ammal (1892–1971), who significantly influenced the development of Bharatanatyam in the twentieth century (see, for example, O'Shea, 37–39).

On Monday and Wednesday, February 1 and 3, the Renaissance Theatre presented La Meri in a joint concert with Varalakshmi and Bhanumati at the Victoria Public Hall in Madras. She writes that the program was in two parts—the first with different types of western dance that she performed; and the second, all Bharatanatyam by Varalakshmi and Bhanumati, with one solo by La Meri (1977a, 98). However, the printed program gives a different format. According to that, there were four parts to the concert: 1. Three Bharata Natya [*sic*] dances by Varalakshmi and Bhanumati; 2. Four interpretive dances by La Meri ("Caprice Viennoise," "Nocturne," "Adoration of the Virgin," and "Russian Doll"); 3. A Bharatanatyam work combining pure dance and gesture song by Varalakshmi and Bhanumati; and 4. Racial dances by La Meri including two from Spain, one each from North American Indian culture, Argentina, Morocco, and South India. The last was identified as "A short sequence from the pure dance part of South Indian Bharata Natya." For La Meri, these concerts were very special because she was sharing the program with the two professional Bharatanatyam dancers, and she performed a work in that genre herself under the direction of the guru. The audience was so pleased with her rendition of the dance that they wanted encores, and Pillai had her repeat it twice (1977a, 98). In Madras, La Meri also gave a lecture-demonstration for the YMCA Athenaeum on Friday, January 29, discussing Bharatanatyam and how its influence had spread to dance forms in Morocco, Mexico, Spain, and the Maori culture in New Zealand, and she ended with a demonstration of some creative dances ("Spread of the Indian Dance; . . ." *Madras Mail*, January 30, 1937).

On February 4, the day after the second joint performance, La Meri and her team left on the 7:30 morning train for their next destination: Hyderabad. Despite the early hour, they were seen off by Seshagiri, Bhanumati, Varalakshmi, and, what La Meri describes as "half of Madras . . . dancers, poets, musicians, critics" (1977a, 99; February 7 letter to Lilian). After the twenty-four-hour trip, they arrived and began preparing for the two Hyderabad concerts on February 6 and 7. La Meri had no help with the unpacking or packing there, nor with her changes of costume; and, at the theater, she was told that she had to be very careful to steer clear of a resident cobra! (1977a, 99–100). After these concerts, they remained in Hyderabad for almost a week and spent some time sightseeing, shopping, meeting with people— and going to a Laurel and Hardy movie. Most important, however, La Meri spent many hours working on her dances—on what she says were "about 15" to "be learned, re-hashed [?], or made." In the evening of February 14, they left for the overnight trip to Poona where they stayed a couple of days, had two performances (one at a "Club"), and did some sightseeing. On February 17, they traveled to Bombay, where they would stay until February 27 (February 14 and March 9 letters to Lilian). According to an announcement in the *Evening News* (February 12), there were four performances scheduled there at the Capitol Theatre, February 20 to 23.

The art critic for the *Bombay Sentinel* wrote that La Meri's concert on February 20 was "one of the rare treats of dancing which Bombay has witnessed in recent years," and he praised her for demonstrating "brains" as well as dancing ability:

> There is an Indian saying that dancing is not mere pretty footwork but all brains. The truth of that statement is obvious in many of La Meri's interpretations. . . . More than mere entertainment, La Meri's dances must make students of art think. . . . [The] underlying unity in the dances of the world, despite the artificial barriers erected by "stylists" should not be missed.

And he suggests that Indian dancers could learn from this American artist ("La Meri Gives Rare Treat at Capitol," February 22, 1937).

After Bombay, the group traveled to Nagpur, where there was one concert (March 1) and then to Calcutta by overnight train (March 2–3) where there were six performances between March 6 and 12. They left Calcutta the day after the last performance, and arrived in Delhi on Sunday, March 14—another overnight journey. After a concert on March 16, they traveled to Lahore for one concert on March 18, but it was such a success that the management engaged them for two more (March 19 and 20). As usual, the day after the last performance, they packed up and got on the road again—this time for a return to Delhi for three more performances. In her letters to Lilian, La Meri includes, as usual, detailed information about their extensive sightseeing and shopping; her almost daily practicing; the creation of new dances; sewing, mending, washing, and ironing costumes and street clothes; packing and unpacking; having interviews and photography sessions. One can only wonder how she maintained her energy and enthusiasm during all of this. The chores related to the stage equipment were equally demanding for Carreras and his team—but they did not have to perform on top of all that work. (1977a, 102–4; letters of March 9 and March 22).

La Meri writes that when she was performing in Bangalore in January, a "handsome young boy" named Bassano Ramgopal (1912–2003) came to her hotel to audition for her company (1977a, 97). Born in Bangalore, he began dancing as a child, eventually becoming trained in the four major Indian dance genres—Bharatanatyam, Kathakali, Kathak, and Manipuri (Kothari 1998, 199). Impressed with both his knowledge about Indian dance and his performance, La Meri and Carreras arranged with his family that he could become a part of their small company. He joined them in Bombay on February 25, went with them to Nagpur (February 28 to March 2) and then on to Calcutta and beyond. La Meri writes about their long hours of working together to develop dances for him to perform. For example, after their all-night train ride and morning arrival in Nagpur, they worked seven hours setting two pieces to add to the concert programs: an Indian duet, "Krishna and Radha," and "Jarabe Tapatío," the Mexican dance that La Meri had often done with Lilian as partner (1977a, 100–101; March 9 letter to Lilian). His first appearance on stage with La Meri was at her Globe Theatre concert in Calcutta on March 10 when he performed his own solo, "Siva," and "Krishna and Radha" with La Meri (*Star of India*, Calcutta, March 9, 1937). He also danced with her in Delhi and in performances scheduled in other countries after India. Later, under the name, Ram Gopal, he became an internationally recognized concert dance artist on his own. He performed in Europe and the United States as well as in India, opened his own school in Bangalore, and wrote about Indian dance (Kothari 1998, 199).

Sometime during their travels in India, they also added to the small company Reginald Rajoo ("Jim" or "Jimmy"), who played the Indian drum called *tabla*, helped Carreras and Bertocchi with the stage and sound work, ran errands, and generally supported the production side of the touring (1977a, 112–13). One can continually wonder at the ability of the three men to get everything set up for each performance. While they usually had some assistance from the technical staff of the theaters, that was sometimes more hindrance than help (see ibid., 104).

In addition to Bharatanatyam, La Meri wanted to study Kathak, the major dance genre from northern India; so between her performances in Lahore and Delhi, she went to Lucknow to train with the aging master Ram Dutt Misra. After a few days of four-hour lessons and three-hour rehearsals, she felt that she was ready to begin performing her Kathak dance, probably with his encouragement, so she added it to her concerts in Delhi (1977a, 104–5). As noted above, one of the reviewers of her January 14 performance in Bangalore had stated that the two dances she had brought to India were both "under the *Kathak* school of technique of Northern India" (*Daily Post*, Bangalore, January 15, 1937), but while her early "Indian" dances might have included some of the Kathak vocabulary, this study with Ram Dutt Misra provided her with a more accurate and deeper sense of the genre and its technique.

Years later, La Meri recalled her experiences in India and summed up their effect on her and her continuing life in dance:

> I think now of those months in India with a strange detachment. It seems almost that they happened to someone else. It was a time of grinding work and petty harassment. But it was also a time of great enrichment—an enrichment so profound that it has taken me nearly twenty years to savor it fully. Perhaps unwittingly I found in the golden, dusty landscape, in the great serenity of the temples, in the dark, deep eyes of simple people a clearer sense of values and a philosophy for living. I know that it was in India I reached a point at which my work became predominantly important to me, a point at which I began to feel that I was important to my work. I began to find new strengths within myself, fresh faith in my own capabilities. (1977a, 105)

On to Other Asian Countries and the Pacific (April–October 1937)

From early April through late September, La Meri, Carreras, Ramgopal, Rajoo, and Bertocchi were touring from Southeast Asia to Japan for scheduled concerts, with La Meri continuing to learn new dances for her repertoire. While Longden had arranged the contracts, he was apparently not with them until they reached Japan. In April, the group was in Rangoon, Burma (now Myanmar); in Malaysia (Penang, Ipoh, and Kuala Lumpur); and in Singapore. In May, they spent about five weeks in Java, Indonesia, in early June went to the Philippines, and in July to Hong Kong. The final destination turned out to be Japan from mid-August to late September. More performances and touring had been scheduled for Japan and China, but the Japanese invasion of China prevented any further travel in the area (letters to Lilian from April through September; 1977a, 109–27; clippings).

The group was in Rangoon only six days (April 9–15), but during that time, there were two concerts—on April 10 and 14,[8] the usual sightseeing, shopping, attendance at a movie, and social meetings. Most important was La Meri's study of Burmese dance with Po Sein (1882–1954), identified in Wikipedia as "an influential 20th-century traditional actor, singer, and dancer, who has been credited with innovating and modernizing Burmese performance arts in dance, song, costumes, and stagecraft." In her April 17 letter to Lilian, La Meri writes in detail about her study with U Po Sein (the U is a Burmese honorific) and says that what he taught her was influenced by seeing her performance on April 10. Apparently, he taught her what he considered a Burmese version of one of her concert dances—and he insisted that she perform it in her second concert. She did that in a traditional Burmese costume and the audience loved it (ibid.; 1977a, 110–12; "Farewell Matinee," *Rangoon Gazette* April 15, 1937). In her autobiography (109), her April 17 letter to Lilian, and the "Third Installment Letter" that she sent to the group, La Meri expresses how much they loved Rangoon.

After eight days in Malaysia, with concerts in Penang, Ipoh, and Kuala Lumpur, they traveled to Singapore for one performance on April 27 at the city's largest theater, the Capitol. The concert received extensive press coverage and promotion and was highly praised by the reviewers. An unidentified promotional article, dating sometime before April 21 when tickets would become available for the performance, focuses on the sound accompaniment in La Meri's concerts. The author praises the well-recorded traditional music, played on the high-quality amplifiers that were carried as part of the stage equipment. He notes the various advantages of using the recorded music: that the traditional accompaniment for many of her dances was "played on weird and exotic instruments" with sounds that could not be replicated by a classical orchestra; that "records have been specially made for her, with her own timings, pauses, and breaks, so that she is always assured of a perfect accompaniment for her art"; and that even for the dances done to Western music, it is good to have pieces played by the most appropriate ensembles or orchestras. And he suggests that the technological advance of recording music "marks an interesting step forward in the life of the theatre." Unfortunately, as the recordings aged, they would get scratchy, which detracted from the performance—something that would elicit criticism in reviews.

La Meri's concerts also attracted attention for the stage lighting that had been developed by Carreras. Another article promoting the Singapore concert focuses on that, noting that her recitals have

the full lighting and staging effects exactly as produced in London, Paris, Vienna, and other great cities of the world where she has appeared. This is made possible by the fact that La Meri is always accompanied on tour by her producer, Guido Carreras, and by Averardo Bertocchi, the Italian lighting and sound expert . . . Many of the lighting effects have never before been seen in the East, and the lighting is changed completely for each dance, . . .

Then the author gives some examples of the lighting variations for the different dances (*Morning Tribune*, Singapore, April 7, 1937).

The next venture for the group was more than a month in Java—engaging in all the usual activities. After six days on a ship from Singapore, they arrived on May 2 in Batavia (now Jakarta) and spent two days getting through customs. They were in Java until June 5 with performances, lecture-demonstrations on Indian dance, shopping, and sightseeing in the cities of Batavia, Bandoeng (Bandung), Jogjakarta (Yogyakarta), Solo or Solokarta (Surakarta), Soerabaya (Surabaya), Malang, and Semarang. Of course, La Meri continued with the regular practicing of her existing repertoire and the search for teachers of the local dance genres. For their travel in Java, they had a car for the passengers and a truck for the luggage, costumes, and stage equipment—both driven by local drivers. La Meri discusses the difficulties with their car's chauffeur, whose English was "sketchy" and who treated them as if they were unknowledgeable tourists who had to follow his decisions regarding itinerary and stops. She writes that his name was "Moan"—which she found very "appropriate"—and says that there were hilariously funny episodes when Carreras was struggling to explain or insist on something through a combination of pantomime and talk (1977a, 113–16; letters of May 9, 16, 21, and June 3; Third Installment Letter). But, despite the problems with Moan, there was much to enjoy in Java. Regarding the scenery, La Meri writes:

> Java is a beautiful land to drive thru [*sic*]. The roads are perfect, and nature lush and laughing, . . . it is nearly too richly lovely, and after a week of it one begins to feel that one has had too much whipped cream. (Third Installment Letter)

She also speaks of Java's beauty in her autobiography (114) and in her May 9 letter to Lilian. But, of course, the most important aspect of Java for her was to study its dance.

La Meri was particularly interested in the cities of Jogjakarta and Solokarta because they were the centers of the classical dance forms of Java, which had developed under royal families, were traditionally performed by members of those families, and were still being supported by the "princes" of each city. La Meri writes in some detail about her experiences with these two dance communities, noting that they were "bitter rivals" who considered each other's practices "unorthodox." Contacts were established in each city, and La Meri and the group were invited to observe classes and rehearsals. On Sunday evening, May 16, they went to the "house of the Prince" in Jogjakarta where they were given a demonstration of the teaching at different levels—from beginners to third-year students, and then saw the professionals rehearsing some parts of a dance-drama (probably *wayang wong*). On Tuesday, May 18, they arrived in Solokarta and went to observe that prince's dance classes, which were open to all. In the class they watched, there were more than 100 participants, ranging from "the royale professionals" to "anybody of the folk who cared to enroll." The class was mostly men with only six or eight women and "several dwarfs"—and Bassano joined in (1977a, 115; Third Installment Letter; May 16 and 21 letters).

Besides observing these demonstrations, and attending Javanese performances in Djojakarta, Solokarta, Surabaya, and Semarang, La Meri and Bassano were able to obtain dance instruction in Solokarta and Batavia, and by the time they left Java on June 5, La Meri writes that she had three additions to her repertoire: the "Srimpi of Djojca [Djojakarta]; the Slendang, a Bedojo dance of the popular theater; and Sriewkandi and Rsi Bisma, an epic battle in the Solo [Solokarta] style" (Third Installment Letter). The *srimpi* or *serimpi* was one of the traditional court dances, but her identifications of the other two are unclear. By *bedojo* she may be referring to the court dance *bedaya*, which might have had popular theater versions. The last item does not appear again in her writings or in her list of dances, but both the *srimpi* and various versions of *bedojo* were in her repertoire until the late 1940s.

On Saturday, June 5, the group left Java to return to Singapore for three more performances (June 8, 11, 12); then they traveled to Manila, arriving on Thursday, June 17. While their experiences in most of the locations on this tour were wonderfully positive, their time in the Philippines was an ordeal. This country was under United States control at the time, and only La Meri was a United States citizen; therefore, entrance was initially denied the two Italians—Carreras and Bertocchi—and the two Indians, Ramgopal and

Rajoo. La Meri writes that "three hours and forty dollars of palm oil" after the ship's arrival, they were finally allowed to disembark, but more money had to be paid to prevent Ramgopal and Rajoo from being sent to a detention center. And there were still their "sixty-odd trunks and crates" of costumes and production equipment that "the authorities would not release . . . without a two-thousand dollar bond!" On top of all that, there had been no announcements or publicity for their performances. During the next three days, the problems began to be resolved with visits to the British and Italian consulates, contact with the local manager of their Manila concerts, and Carreras's intense efforts to get publicity created and dispersed. As a result of the problems, and the bribes they had had to pay, their financial situation, which had been good after the Asian touring, was in dire straits. It was essential that they earn a substantial amount of money from the concerts given in Manila to be able to continue their touring. However, they ended up giving only two out of the planned four performances. Despite all the problems, La Meri managed to learn three Philippine folk dances and buy costumes (1977a, 117–18; Third Installment Letter; June 18 and July 2 letters).

On June 30, the group boarded a ship for Hong Kong, where they had concerts scheduled for July 5, 8, and 9. Everything went well while they were there, but La Meri writes that soon after they left, "bombs dropped on the city" (1977a, 119; July 10 letter). While Hong Kong was still under British control, the Japanese had already begun to attack it as part of the Second Sino-Japanese War, which began July 7, 1937, and continued until the end of World War II in 1945 ("Second Sino-Japanese War" Wikipedia). On the boat trip from Hong Kong, they spent one day sightseeing in Shanghai before arriving in Yokohama on July 15 (1977a, 119; July 10 letter).

La Meri and Carreras planned to spend three months in Japan, so they decided to rent a house in Tokyo for their group of six (Longden had joined them again). After much searching, they found the residence of a British family temporarily away on vacation. Since the house and its furnishings were Western in style rather than Japanese, it was ideal for them—and they had a cook and a maid to take care of the household work. After moving in, they emptied the dining-room of its furniture to use that space as a studio and converted the living room into an office for Carreras, Longden, and Longden's secretary. Averardo had the garage for his work with the stage materials, and Rajoo helped all of them in various ways. La Meri had her usual rigorous schedule of practicing and learning dances, teaching Bassano, performing, shopping—and unpacking and taking care of her costumes, which she says "had taken an awful beating." During their stay in Tokyo, she was able to have each item in this large collection cleaned, mended, and, in some cases, even remade (1977a, 119–22; Fourth Installment Letter; letters of July 10 and 23).

La Meri writes about the theater productions they attended in Tokyo—all beautiful, but typically about six hours in length, which they found exhaustingly long. She describes a performance at the huge Takarazuka Theater, which included two parts: excerpts from Japanese dramas and dance works and then a "western revue . . . titled 'Manhattan Madness.'" And they went to performances of Kabuki, the classical dance drama form; and Noh theater, the classical music drama form. She also writes about seeing a festival performance in the garden of one of the temples—a "combination of Dengaku and Nogaku" [two forms associated with rural cultures]. This was performed continuously throughout the day and open to all viewers (Fourth Installment Letter; 1977a, 120).

To find instruction in Japanese dance, Carreras went to the Kokusai Bunka Shinkokai (KBS—The Society for International Cultural Relations), which was committed to promoting Japanese culture outside Asia through films, publications, and other means. La Meri writes that they "recommended as teacher the wife of an authoritative writer on Japanese dance and herself a dancer and teacher of repute." On Saturday, July 24, after they dined together, "Mme. Kodera" demonstrated some classical and folk dances—probably for La Meri to make choices as to what she would like to learn. They scheduled three private lessons a week in the studio the group had arranged in their house, and Mr. Kodera was always there to translate. La Meri describes in detail her learning experiences with the Koderas and the kind of notes she made. In her autobiography she says she had a total of fifteen lessons during which she learned six classical dances. Of course, the Koderas were amazed at how quickly La Meri could master the foreign techniques and rhythms. Outside of the lessons, Mr. Kodera accompanied La Meri to assist her in shopping for costumes and other performance necessities. Unfortunately, La Meri's demanding activities were interrupted in the beginning of August when she developed a severe cramp, a "charley-horse." The doctor put a splint on that leg, and for five days, she could only do what she termed "chair-practice"—limited to the arm movements of the dances. She could still work with Bassano, however, and on her letters, the lecture discussed below, and other projects (1977a, 120–25; Fourth Installment Letter; letters from July 29 to September 4).

The same organization (KBS) that had recommended the Koderas to La Meri invited her to give a lecture-recital on September 10 in the auditorium of the historically significant Meiji Seimei Kan building in Tokyo. Her presentation was titled "Tracing Early Indian Influences on the Japanese Dance" and featured her lecture, spoken in English with Japanese translation after each paragraph. She and Ramgopal demonstrated some of the Indian dance techniques and dances that she was discussing. On this program, she also debuted the first Japanese dance she had learned. In addition to all the other preparation, the day before the lecture-recital, La Meri and the others spent six hours arranging a display that was part of the event. It included 14 mannequins in different costumes, instruments, props, and other related items on "tables, racks and cabinets filling 2 large rooms"—each item with an identifying card (1977a, 125; Fourth Installment Letter; September 10 letter). Among La Meri's archival materials is an invitation in English for this event, which was sent out by Count Ayské Kabayama, Chairman of the Board of Trustees of the KBS—so apparently they expected English-speaking as well as Japanese attendees. In addition to this engagement, La Meri gave three performances in Tokyo at the large auditorium of another historical landmark, the Hibiya Public Hall—on September 16, 20, and 22. They received very enthusiastic reviews in two English-language papers: the *Japan Advertiser* (September 17 and 21) and the *Tokyo Nichi Nichi* (September 24). Longden had originally scheduled five concerts in Tokyo, but the increasingly dire situation in Japan and the beginning of "practice blackouts" at night cut the season short. On September 24 La Meri, Carreras, and Bertocchi sailed on the ship *Chichibu Maru*, which was bound for Hawaii, sadly leaving Rajoo behind for his return to India (Fourth Installment Letter).

In her autobiography, La Meri writes that while on the ship approaching Japan in mid-July, she had had no idea that she would "fall in love" with that land. But she did. She found that "everything was delightful. Everyone was so kind and polite. Everything was so sweet and clean. There was beauty of line and color everywhere" (1977a, 119). And her various experiences in Japan were especially satisfying to her and valuable for her career.

When making their own travel arrangements, La Meri and Carreras were planning to send Ramgopal back to India along with Rajoo. However, he decided to stay in Japan (1977a, 126–27). Some letters written at the time by La Meri and Carreras shed light on problems that had developed in their working with him. In an undated one addressed to "My dear Bassano," La Meri details negative aspects of his behavior as their "guest" and a student member of the company, chiding him for spending nights away from them without notice or explanation and his lack of gratitude and respect. Another, dated July 8, 1937, was La Meri's response to a "public letter" that had been published in the July 8 *Morning Post* and was apparently critical of the way Ramgopal was being treated or presented in their company. In this, La Meri stresses that Ramgopal was a beginner—not an established artist—and that they were doing him a great favor to include him in their concerts. On July 9, Carreras wrote a response to what he identifies as an article on "Indian Dancing" in the *South China Morning Post* of July 8 (probably related to the "public letter" that elicited La Meri's response). He addressed it to "My dear Mr. Indian," and in it, complains of the author's lack of knowledge about Indian dance, his criticism of how Carreras was running "the show," and his consideration of Ramgopal and La Meri as equal artists. He emphasizes that "Mr. Ramgopal is a beginner who is still under severe tuition." From his side, in his 1957 autobiography, *Rhythm in the Heavens*, Gopal writes that, during his touring with them, he was unappreciated and mistreated by La Meri and Carreras and that, at the end, they abandoned him in Japan (40–45). However, his feelings about La Meri seemed to have changed by the next year. In 1958, he invited her and one of her former students (who had also studied in India) to perform with him in Trinidad as guest artists, and the two apparently stayed in contact after that, as there is a very warm letter from him in July 1981 that he signs "Much love;" and, in 1988, he wrote to Bill Adams about his grief over her death.

After about a week at sea, the three travelers—La Meri, Carreras, and Bertocchi arrived in Honolulu on Friday, October 1. Somehow, two performances were soon arranged with the assistance of a local manager, Mrs. Mable Thomas—a full concert on Monday, October 4, at the McKinley High School Auditorium and a shorter program Thursday, October 7, at the Honolulu Academy of Arts, where La Meri danced in the patio (clippings; 1977a, 130). Her arrival and the performances elicited enthusiastic coverage in the newspapers including both announcements and reviews of the concerts. For example, Edna B. Lawson, dramatic critic for the *Honolulu Advertiser,* wrote:

> Mme. La Meri is not one woman. Last evening in her solo dance recital at McKinley auditorium, she was fourteen—and each one a distinct and different entity. The magnificent program . . . is something to be remembered.
>
> La Meri is an exponent of the dance which is governed by intelligence. She showed genius in each of her numbers. They were scholarly interpretations. She created perfect rhythms. Her body control is flawless and the movement of her hands may be compared to delicate flowers swaying in a light breeze.

This critic goes on to praise every aspect of the performance, including her quick "two-minute" costume changing and the lighting, and ends by saying, "It was an exhibition of the art of dance in its highest form (October 5, 1937).

The Hawaiian press also wrote about La Meri's interest in the Hawaiian hula and seemed proud that such an internationally revered artist wanted to learn more about an important element of their culture. Prior to this visit to Honolulu, La Meri's only "hula instructor" had been her sister Lilian, who had been in Hawaii in 1924 while her husband was stationed there. During that time, Lilian studied with Ana Hila, whom La Meri describes as the "last representative of the old classic style of technique." While in Hawaii only a few days, La Meri managed to take lessons at the Betty Lei Hula Studios and was given a certificate of completion of a hula course dated October 8. She also attended a performance of Winona Love, a noted Hawaiian dancer (1977a, 130–31; Fourth Installment Letter).

After nearly 18 months of being on the road (and on the seas), La Meri, Carreras, and Bertocchi sailed out of Hawaii on October 9 and, on October 14, arrived in Los Angeles. Thus began the next segment of their lives in the United States and Latin America.

5

Here and There in a World of Turmoil, October 1937 to October 1939

During these two years, La Meri's performing was often as tightly scheduled as it had been in the preceding eighteen months. And the travel ranged
over a similarly large—but different—part of the world. After their arrival
in Los Angeles on October 14, they were in the United States until February
18, 1938, when they left for Mexico, the beginning of La Meri's second Latin
American tour. In August, they returned to Italy and stayed there until
January 1939, when they spent a short time in London. From February to
April, they were back in the United States, and then La Meri and Carreras
embarked on her third Latin American tour. That ended abruptly in October because of World War II. Of course, that disaster made it unfeasible
to return to Italy, so they settled in New York—the best choice at the time.[1]

The United States, October 1937 to February 1938

When the ship arrived in Los Angeles on October 14, 1937, La Meri, Carreras, and Bertocchi were met by Lilian and Longden. It was a great joy for
the two sisters to be together again after having been apart for so long. Their
relationship was now very different from what it had been on the Caribbean
tour in 1927. In the many letters La Meri had written to Lilian from Australia
and Asia, she frequently expressed her love and appreciation for this person
whom she considered her closest friend in life. For example, months before
their reunion in Los Angeles, she had written from Tokyo:

> I do hope to get to the States soon. It's been an indecent long time since
> I saw you all . . . I believe one of the very finest things life has given us

in a long line of blessings, is our deep friendship for one another. . . . I know you are a legend and an inspiration to everyone who knows me. And heaven forbid that you should ever find out that no one could be as grand as you think I am. (July 29, 1937)

Lilian was with La Meri and the others during their time in Los Angeles and their return to New York in November, where they were given lodging in the Newcomers' Manhattan apartment.

Longden spent a few days with the group in Los Angeles and then took off for Mexico. He had been trying through correspondence to get the Mexico City concerts that had been scheduled for March updated to an earlier time—to help with the group's financial situation. But, since he had had no success up to that point, he decided to travel to Mexico and try to accomplish the change in person. For about a month, La Meri, Carreras, Lilian, and Bertocchi stayed in Los Angeles—a city La Meri did not like—waiting in vain for news from him about the hoped-for earlier engagements. They finally "gave up in despair" and traveled to New York, with stops in San Antonio and Louisville. In San Antonio, they wired Longden and found out that he had been totally unsuccessful in dealing with the Mexicans at the border, and, in fact, his lack of deference to officials had even landed him in jail. They wired money to bail him out, and he visited them briefly in New York before leaving for Europe (1977a, 131–33; Fourth Installment Letter). The tour dates that Longden had originally scheduled for Mexico and other parts of Latin America from February through July were still in place, however.

As soon as they arrived in New York, the group resumed their professional work. Carreras rented a large studio near the Newcomers' apartment where, besides having enough open space for La Meri to practice her dances, the trunks could be stored and their gramophone and typewriter set up. Each day they would go there—La Meri to dance, Carreras to write letters, and Bertocchi to work on the stage equipment. Early in December, Carreras completed a contract with a Mr. Coppicus[2] of Columbia Concerts, which would provide bookings both locally and beyond. Before the first New York engagement on December 12—and probably with future touring in mind—Coppicus requested that La Meri show him all or most of her dances, and it took her about six hours to do that. She undoubtedly did each dance in its appropriate costume, which would explain the length of time needed.

For the December 12 matinee at the Guild Theater, Coppicus had La Meri perform dances from the international repertoire, making this her first totally "ethnic" concert (1977a, 133). The program included works from India, Ceylon, Java, Japan, Spain, Cuba, Argentina, Hawaii, and the Philippines as well as one Native American dance—and the audience loved it. La Meri writes that, after she had danced two and a half hours, they still wanted more. It was such a success that Coppicus booked her for two more New York concerts after Christmas, before she would be leaving for the Latin American tour that Longden had organized (1977a, 133; Fourth Installment Letter). The reviews of this first concert were almost totally positive, although the noted dance critic John Martin questioned the claim on the program that all the dances were "authentic." While he acknowledged that the dances might all be "meticulous reproductions" of the traditional movement and choreography, some of them were originally done only by men, and if performed by a woman could not be considered "authentic" reproductions ("Varied Program by La Meri," *New York Times*, December 13, 1937).

After this concert, there was Christmas to prepare for and celebrate. This was the first year since 1931 that La Meri and Carreras were able to share the holiday with Lilian and David. Besides enjoying their Christmas dinner amid the lavish decorations they had installed, there was a total of 180 gifts to open (Fourth Installment Letter). La Meri writes that in the evening, they went to see the movie *The Wizard of Oz* and "skipped all the way home singing 'The Wonderful Wizard of Oz' at the top of their lungs" (1977a, 133). One can only wonder if Carreras joined them in the skipping and singing at the top of his lungs. Regarding this time of her life, La Meri wrote in her autobiography: "The days sped by with work and happiness" (ibid.); and in her Fourth Installment Letter, that this time was filled with "[f]un and work which make an excellent combination."

On Sunday, January 30, at 3 and 8:45 p.m., La Meri gave two different concerts at the Little Theater in New York City. The afternoon included three of her "interpretive" works, as well as dances from Java, Morocco, India, Japan, Panama, Cuba, Hawaii, and the Philippines, while the evening program of ten dances was totally "ethnic."[3] One can marvel (as always) at the energy she had to perform so many dances in one solo concert, and here—as happened sometimes on tour—there were both matinee and evening performances. She writes that, after the two, she was tired, "but a *good* tired" (1977a, 133).

There is no indication in these New York performances of assistance from any musician or other dancer—or what, if anything, filled the time when she was changing costumes between dances.

La Meri, Lilian, and Carreras traveled to San Antonio where they had three engagements before beginning the Latin American tour arranged by Longden. They arrived on Thursday, February 10, and, on the 12th, La Meri gave a private matinee performance for the nuns of San Antonio in the auditorium of Our Lady of the Lake College—where she had been a student for a while. Then she had two concerts at the San Pedro Playhouse (February 16 and 17), with almost totally different programs. Not surprisingly, the society editors of the local press were excited by the return of this former San Antonio "society girl" and current world-renowned artist. It had been about ten years since she had performed in what she identifies as "the scene of [her] first feeble terpsichorean efforts" (1977a, 134)—of course, this return brought back many memories. Although the audiences at the Playhouse included people she had grown up with and their children, the performance felt to her like any others. However, the reception after one of the concerts was something very different. Instead of being surrounded by strangers, she felt "swept up in a crowd of old friends, calling out half-forgotten nicknames, remembering hoary local jokes" (ibid.; Fourth Installment Letter). This reconnection with old friends and teachers was quite an experience for La Meri, and one reunion was particularly significant. She met with Olivia Baldessarelli, whom she identifies as "a girl we had long ago 'adopted' as a member of the Hughes family" and a valued friend. Surprisingly, Olivia volunteered to join them on the coming tour as "social secretary and backstage helper" (1977a, 133, 135). As it turned out, she ended up staying with them until their return to the United States the following year.

As she writes in her autobiography, La Meri was excited about returning to Mexico, the country where she had begun performing internationally. As she remembers from many years later,

I was going to the land where I made my first foreign appearance twelve years earlier. I remembered the flowers of Xochimilco, the charros [cowboys] in the park on Sunday mornings, the courtesy and appreciation, the culture and dignity of Mexico. . . . I was so happy to be

going back to dance in a country where the rewards of my first appearance, . . . had been so much better than I deserved. Now I would be able
to prove that I had grown as a creative artist. (1977a, 135)

And, she definitely did that.

Latin America, February to August 1938

On February 18, the team—La Meri, Carreras, Bertocchi, Lilian, and Olivia—began the drive from San Antonio to Laredo on the Mexican border.
La Meri writes of the harrowing experiences they had in the next two days
getting their sixty-seven trunks of costumes and stage equipment through
the United States and Mexican customs and, after they finally made it across
the border, the difficulties of traveling from city to city by car or by train
with all that gear. Of course, every time on this and other tours that they had
to enter a different country and go through a customs check, it was a long
ordeal. The group arrived in Monterrey at 8 a.m. on Wednesday, February
23, had a concert that evening, and the next morning were off to the next
destination. After Monterrey, there were performances in Saltillo, Torreón,
and San Luis Potosí before their month in Mexico City (1977a, 135–39; Fifth
Installment Letter). There is no evidence that Longden was with them, although, as noted above, he had organized the bookings, arrangements, and
publicity for the entire tour. On several programs, he is listed as overseeing
the "La Meri World Tour Publicity and Management" or as its "director."

For the most part, despite the problems at the border, La Meri enjoyed
very much being back in Mexico. She writes about the beauty of the forty-
six-mile drive from Monterrey to Saltillo, which she found to be a "delightful town." After one concert there, they drove about 160 miles farther
inland to Torreón where their next performance was scheduled. That was
one of the few places she did not like at all, considering it "a thoroughly
ugly, vulgar town." After their concert there, they had planned to go to
San Luis Potosí by train but discovered that there was neither train service
nor a highway that connected the two cities, so they drove back to Saltillo
to catch a train there. They had a few free days in Saltillo, and La Meri
writes that, besides practicing (as always), she worked on a lecture she was
preparing on the Hindu dance, walked around the city with Lilian, and

attended "several local celebrations and parties—while Guy went shooting." On another day, both she and Carreras went shooting. Along with their performance equipment and personal baggage, they had also packed "three shot-guns and a rifle" so they could both engage in this recreational activity that they enjoyed. La Meri also writes of other shooting sessions in Mexico and elsewhere on the tour (1977a, 137–38; Fifth Installment Letter).

On March 7, after their performances in San Luis Potosí, they traveled by train to Mexico City. On March 14, La Meri and Carreras presented the lecture-demonstration on dance in India that she had been preparing, and after that, there were eight performances (from March 16 to April 3) at the Palacio de Bellas Artes, the city's (and country's) major concert venue. Six concerts had originally been scheduled, but then two more were added (1977a, 139; programs and announcements). As could be expected, her performances received very positive reviews, one writer noting that: "Esta gran artista fue recibida por nuestro público con el calor cordial que merece su proeza de ofrecernos un panorama seductor de la danza universal." [This great artist was received by our public with the cordial warmth that is merited by her endeavor of offering us a seductive panorama of the universal dance.] (El Nacional, Mexico City, March 19, 1938). And there are many more reviews that praised her work. Apparently, the interest in her art was great enough to attract audiences to this large hall—and for so many concerts. Its capacity is 1,800, but there is no information as to how full it was for each of La Meri's performances. Since the group spent a whole month in Mexico City, they had time to attend bullfights, festivals, and other events—and to climb pyramids! La Meri writes that on one of those, they became so dizzy, they had difficulty getting down. She also met with people she had known early in her career—such as Federico Flores, the baritone with whom she performed in movie prologues. And a very special party was given in her honor by someone La Meri doesn't name but identifies as "an old friend" of Carreras who was "director of a private conservatory of music" and "president of the Bach Society." At the party, he gave a "laudatory speech" and the 100 or so pupils and society members attending honored her with music, flowers, and shouts of "Viva La Meri" (1977a, 139–40; Fifth Installment Letter). Sometime toward the end of their stay in Mexico City, Lilian returned home—an emotional separation for the two sisters, who loved to be together.[4]

After Mexico City, the group spent six days in Guadalajara with two concerts. A major newspaper there published a long and enthusiastic article by Armando de María y Campos, a noted theater and arts writer and critic, that discusses her studies of dance around the world, some of her dances, and her publications. ("La Aparición de La Meri . . ." *Suplemento Dominical de "Las Noticias,"* April 17, 1938). It is interesting that this same article was also published in *El Mercurio* in Santiago de Chile, May 15, 1938, and in *El Universal* in Caracas, Venezuela, May 21, 1939 (full citation is in the bibliography under María y Campos, Armando de).

After Guadalajara, the group took a twelve-hour, exceedingly uncomfortable train trip to the Mexican port city of Manzanillo to sail for Lima, Peru. Getting through the Mexican customs in order to leave the country was difficult and took the whole day, but as they were waiting with the "trunks and boxes" for the officials to get through the process, everyone had something to do to pass the time. La Meri writes: "Carreras, sitting on a suitcase with the typewriter on a trunk, catching up with overdue correspondence and routine matters; I on another trunk waving my hands vaguely as I mentally choreographed a new dance; Averardo, addressing postcards against a wall; Olivia, notebook on knee, forever verifying her list of my costumes and accessories. This was always the time for doing our 'homework'" (1977a, 140). The ship they were finally able to board was the Japanese *Heiyo Maru*. La Meri writes, "Like the Japanese themselves, the ship was phenomenally clean" and "was something to bring peace to the soul" (ibid., 140–41). Being on this ship was a great pleasure for the group in contrast to the time they had spent on land before boarding. In her Fifth Installment Letter, La Meri asks the reader, "How can I make you feel what it is to go aboard a Japanese boat after Manzanilla!" She also tells of some of the many pleasures during the journey—such as her participation in a festivity on the ship—putting on one of her Japanese costumes and dancing two Japanese dances for the passengers and crew, which was highly appreciated.

During the next three months, the company traveled and presented concerts and what she terms "conferences" (lecture-demonstrations) in Peru, Chile, and Argentina. One can marvel, again (as always), that La Meri had the vitality and the energy to occasionally perform twice in one day, often on consecutive days, and sometimes with only one day and travel between concerts. The regimen was also a strain on Carreras, Bertocchi, and Olivia. As in Mexico, it is impressive that there was apparently sufficient audience interest to justify scheduling multiple concerts in large urban theaters and concert halls. There were seven performances in Lima from May 7 to 15; more than ten in Chile from May 28 through July 5 (mainly in Santiago, but also two each in Valparaiso and Viña del Mar); and probably five in Argentina between July 20 and 28 (three in Buenos Aires and two in Rosario).

La Meri writes that the concert in Lima on her birthday (May 13) was a very special occasion because it was sponsored by the Japanese ambassador to Peru for members of the large Japanese colony there, many of whom "had been born in Peru and had never seen Japanese dancing." At the ambassador's request, she performed her six Japanese dances as well as dances from Java, India, and Ceylon, and three "interpretive" pieces (1977a, 143–44; "De Arte: La Meri Bailará Esta Noche," *El Comercio*, May 13, 1938). When the group returned to their hotel after the concert, there was a surprise birthday party for La Meri that was attended by local artists, musicians, and journalists. Most notable was the presence of the well-known art and music critic, Carlos Raygada (1898–1953), who had perhaps organized the event. Later in the month, in Santiago de Chile, he published "La Meri, poetisa, danzarina, escritora," a very appreciative and in-depth article about her life and work (*El Diario Ilustrado*, May 29, 1938).

From May 17 to 24, the group traveled by ship from Lima to Valparaíso, Chile; and, as usual, when they arrived, getting through customs was a trial and took much time. On Wednesday, May 25, they traveled the sixty-three miles to Santiago, where there were several engagements scheduled. La Meri's first program (May 28) was a conference on the dance of India for La Escuela de Bellas Artes (The School of Fine Arts). Then, from May 30 to June 6, she had five performances at the Teatro Real (a major film and performance venue in the city from 1930 to the early 1990s). They left Santiago for a couple of weeks with engagements in Valparaíso and Viña del Mar and returned for two more lecture-demonstrations at the Escuela (June 25 and July 7). There were also performances on June 26 and July 3 at the Teatro Municipal (the national opera house of Santiago, which dates from the mid-nineteenth century).

The three conferences in Santiago were on the following topics: "Derivatives of the Hindu Dance in the Orient," "Derivatives of the Hindu dance in the Occident," and "Spanish Dancing." She writes that each one "had to be translated into Spanish, corrected, and re-written [which] was a big, nerve-wracking job in the limited time that we had. But we managed to get it done—we generally do." She doesn't say who did the translating. The third conference was in response to a "special request," and it attracted such a large audience that "many of the students were sitting in windows and hanging onto fresco scaffolding in the back of the Bellas Artes hall." While La Meri was in the middle of one of her demonstration dances, "a strong earthquake rocked the building" which caused some of the students to lose their hold and fall, but while La Meri felt "frightened to death," the audience members seemed to have no reaction—apparently they were used to such experiences (1977a, 144–45; Fifth Installment Letter). The conferences and performances both received very positive reviews. For example, after a detailed discussion of the Spanish dance conference, the reviewer writes that the three conferences together "han constituido un completo curso sobre la historia y la estética de la danza" (have constituted a complete course on the history and aesthetics of the dance) and that this contribution to their knowledge and culture demonstrates "una generosidad de espíritu que oblige la gratitude de los chilenos" (a generosity of spirit that calls for gratitude from the Chilean population) ("Bellas Artes: La conferencia sobre 'Danza española'" by C.H.S., *El Mercurio*, July 7, 1938). So, obviously, all the hard work putting this together in Spanish was worth the effort.

Returning to Chile after so many years was also a great experience for La Meri. She felt that she was received as a "valued friend," still remembered from her first tour in winter 1927–28. She was "flowered with gifts, entertained at parties," and recalls her joy at "[h]ow we danced the cueca, handkerchiefs snapping and flying in our hands, our feet tingling with banquet champagne!" (1977a, 144).[5] She wanted to learn more about the *cueca* in its "pure, unadulterated country" form, but since there was not time to search in rural areas, she tried some possible city sources. In one place, she was shown "stylized concert variations of the dance"—not what she was looking for. Then she writes that a friend took them (La Meri, Olivia, and Carreras) and "two society girls" to a brothel [!], where it seems that the traditional *cuecas* were regularly danced. However, the "professional girls" did not want to perform in front of four "respectable ladies," so the "Madam" insisted that the maid and a male worker demonstrate the dance.

La Meri writes that what they saw was only "a sort of cueca" (Fifth Install-ment Letter).

The last country on this tour was Argentina. On July 7, the group left Santiago and traveled south by train to Los Andes and across the border. There, because a "mountain had crashed down on the railway line," they were "bundled into a fleet of Ford autos" to get to Mendoza, where they could then continue by train to Buenos Aires. One can imagine the dif-ficulty of having to get all their trunks off the train, into the cars, and then back on the next train. The drive was more than 100 miles, and La Meri describes it as "the bumpiest and most hair-raising trip" she had ever expe-rienced—high speed travel on a "narrow gravel road" with tight curves and steep inclines. But they enjoyed the view of the Andes and the contact with the country and its inhabitants that they would not have had otherwise (1977a, 145; Fifth Installment Letter). As always, La Meri was interested in experiencing the country areas, the cities, and the cultures of both.

The group arrived in Buenos Aires on July 9, the national holiday when Argentina celebrates its independence from Spain. Because the customs offices were closed, they could not continue to Montevideo, Uruguay, as planned, and they ended up not going there at all. Instead, they stayed in Buenos Aires until July 26, and some unexpected—and welcomed—engage-ments were scheduled. In her Fifth Installment Letter, La Meri writes that Carreras had founded the "Wagnerian Society" there many years ago. That cannot be true since the "Associación Wagneriana de Buenos Aires" was founded in 1912, but he probably had contact with it in 1929 when they were there during their first Latin American tour. Carreras contacted some of his friends in the Society and La Meri was invited by the organization to present her conference on Indian dance at the Teatro Odeón on July 20—under their auspices. She writes that it was so successful that the Odeón management en-gaged her for three concerts. I have found newspaper documentation for two (July 21 and 24), but perhaps there was also a third. La Meri was surprised and pleased that each performance was attended by dancers and staff from the city's major opera house, the Teatro Colón.

La Meri's work in Buenos Aires was very successful. In her autobiogra-phy, La Meri had written that Buenos Aires was "a difficult city to conquer," and that on her earlier tour, she "had made no very deep impression on this city." She wondered if the reaction would be equally cool this time. Happily, the opposite was true, with some reviewers favorably comparing the work of the mature artist with that of the young woman they had seen some ten years before. She quotes one critic who may have wondered about his own previous reaction as saying: "having seen both Argentina and La Meri in their formative years, Buenos Aires had failed to discern the genius of either" (1977a, 145–46), and he was not the only critic who referred to her early visit in praising her current work. After Buenos Aires, the group traveled to Rosario, more than 100 miles to the northwest, for concerts on July 27 and 28 at that city's Teatro Colón, also a grand opera house (1977a, 145–46; Fifth Installment Letter).

After their return to Buenos Aires on July 29, the group had almost two weeks to enjoy their last days in Argentina and prepare to leave for Italy on August 10. In her Fifth Installment Letter, La Meri writes in detail about how busy they were. She had promised "auditions" and lessons to some of the dance students she had met there, and many friends and fans invited them to events. Most important, of course, was to get all their clothes, costumes, and performance equipment ready for customs and for the ship. La Meri and Carreras also found time for their favorite recreational activity. She writes: "best of all, we spent three days in a little town called Chascomús for shooting. It would certainly have been a shame to have encircled the world with a trunkful of shooting things, . . . and then miss using them in Argentina, the paradise of hunters." They took a train to Chascomús, seventy-six miles south of Buenos Aires, and spent the night in a hotel. The next morning, they visited their first site (a ranch), but it turned out to be flooded from heavy rains and without any game present—and Carreras had to carry La Meri over some areas of knee-deep water. They then went to another ranch where they "shot all afternoon," and they visited other ranches as well. In two of the ranches, the owners requested that, in addition to shooting "game," they shoot the birds that would fly in and eat the feed of their chickens and horses. La Meri didn't want to do that and writes, "though I can shoot a game bird like any man, I get all romantic about the little gray and green parrots." It is interesting that she felt "romantic" and protective of some birds but boasts about murdering others. Did she and Carreras have any feelings about their destruction of living beings? It seems not.

Most of the events scheduled on this tour were concerts, but, as noted above, she was also engaged in some places for the lecture-demonstrations on the dance of India, on Indian influences on dance in other parts of the world, and on the dance of Spain. In her book, *Total Education in Ethnic Dance*, La Meri writes that "all the facets of my career seem to have been preparing me for the role I have found myself playing during the past fifty-odd years. It seems I have been cast in the character of explainer" (1977b, vii). As she had done and would continue to do, La Meri was not content with only performing international dance arts but was also eager to "explain" them. In different countries, she was assisted in this by the multilingual Carreras, who often delivered the lecture segment of the presentation in the local language. During her performing career as well as her later years of teaching, La Meri typically brought together practice and theory—the learning of techniques and choreography coupled with a study of their histories, contexts, purposes, philosophies, and aesthetic principles. One can look back at her voracious reading as a teenager on the "Orient" after seeing the performance of Denishawn. Her curiosity and probing never abated—nor her commitment to sharing the knowledge she gained.

After their three vacation days in Chascomús, La Meri and Carreras returned to Buenos Aires, and on August 10, they, Bertocchi, and Olivia departed by ship for Italy. La Meri writes that many friends came to the dock to see them off, and after stops along the coast in Montevideo, Santos, and Rio de Janeiro, they crossed the ocean and arrived in Genoa. It was on this ship that La Meri wrote her Fifth Installment Letter. In her autobiography she says the trip took six days, and then they traveled by train and car from Genoa to Villa Alegrias, the home in Castiglioncello that they had not seen for more than two years.[6] La Meri wondered if her beloved dog, "Booch," would remember her. Well, she did. She met them on the driveway with "ears flapping, rear end in hysterical spasms of welcome," and "[h]er serious little white face, framed by the long black ears, was alight with joyful recognition." And by then, Booch had a son named "Wop" (1977a, 146–47).

Europe, United States, and Third Latin American Tour (August 1938 to October 1939)

La Meri was extremely happy to have returned to Italy, and Olivia was fascinated by what she was experiencing there for the first time. The three settled in for a couple of months of what was to some extent a vacation—swimming, taking long walks, riding bicycles to different towns, and shooting clay pigeons—not live ones! But they also spent time on work—La Meri's daily practice, of course, and refurbishing costumes, and other preparations for future performing (1977a, 146–47). It is not clear if Bertocchi stayed with them in Tuscany or went to visit his own family or friends.

La Meri had a few engagements in Italy in November and December. The first ones were in Florence, at the *Teatro Sperimentale dei GUF (Grupi Universitari Fascisti)* (Experimental Theater of the Fascist University Groups).[7] There, she gave her two lecture-demonstrations—with Carreras reading the text—on the dance of India and its influence abroad (November 12 and 16) and a concert (November 19) that included both international repertoire and some of her own creative works. It is interesting that this politically committed theater was open to nonpolitical presentations. In Rome, there were three lecture-demonstrations at the Teatro delle Arti (November 23 and 29, December 2) and a concert at the Teatro Quirino (December 10). This short tour ended with a concert in Naples on December 13 (clippings). La Meri writes that after one of the lecture-demonstrations in Rome, "a charming grande dame came backstage," praised the performance, and asked, "where are the six little ladies who danced for you? I want to tell them how much I enjoyed them too." She had no idea that the dances were all done by La Meri, and it was difficult to convince her of that (1977a, 147).

The group spent Christmas at Villa Alegrias, and La Meri writes that their celebration was "in the old-fashioned American tradition" and was a "lovely, lovely" holiday. They enjoyed very much being in this beautiful place but couldn't stay long because of engagements that were scheduled in London, the United States, and Latin America. The European war was already looming, and La Meri and Carreras were well aware of the dangerous situation, but they could not have imagined that, after departing this time from Italy, they would never again be able to return to their home in Castiglioncello, and La Meri would never again see her "beloved Booch" (1977a, 147). The schedule they followed for the next several months was as daunting as anything in their previous tours; and, in addition, there was the developing conflict to worry about. Despite that dire situation, however, they traveled, and La Meri performed right up until the actual outbreak of World War II.

As usual, this tour included "explaining" along with performing. The first engagement in London was the lecture-demonstration on Indian dance on

January 16. This was cosponsored by the India Society and the Anglo/Bata-vian Society, and its text published in the 1939 edition of the India Society's journal, *Indian Arts and Letters* (see bibliography). Then, beginning January 18, La Meri had a ten-day concert season at London's Duke of York Theatre, with evening performances each day and Saturday matinees. All went well, and La Meri felt that she "should have been very happy" about her return to London. However, she writes that

> a cloud lay heavy across the world, so heavy that it penetrated even my art-insulated consciousness. All mankind was marching stubbornly toward a tragic destiny, and we felt an odd psychic need to hurry and live normally while normal living was yet possible. As though to some temperamental giant orchestra, I danced frenetically against the omi-nous accompaniment. (1977a, 148)

Of course, the whole world was feeling that heavy cloud which soon ex-ploded into war.

In February, La Meri, Carreras, Olivia, and probably also Bertocchi, sailed for New York. La Meri writes of that journey: "we crossed an angry North Atlantic. Seas broke unceasingly over the decks; . . . Tempo was quickening and it was as though this sea change were affecting all things in our changing world" (1977a, 148). Life did not calm down after their arrival in New York, as a heavily scheduled two-month tour in the United States was to begin almost immediately—what was announced as La Meri's "first American tour." Since Olivia was returning to San Antonio, Carreras's niece, Juana,[8] replaced her as secretary and backstage helper. Later, she would be performing both with La Meri's companies and in her own concerts (see chapter 6).

The American tour, from mid-February to mid-April, had been arranged by Columbia Concerts and included cities in Pennsylvania, Michigan, In-diana, Kentucky, Iowa, Tennessee, Arkansas, Idaho, and Illinois (clippings and programs). La Meri writes that the tour consisted of "endless one-night stands" with the group traveling "in a chauffeured Cadillac, which pulled a trailer carrying the luggage." And she notes that, at some point, she "con-tracted a virus and too often danced with a temperature of 104" (1977a, 148). Fortunately for La Meri, her beloved sister Lilian had joined the tour. Bertoc-chi was undoubtedly also with them, so that made a group of five. Despite the ordeals of this venture and La Meri's illness, it seems that the programs went well—as usual. Reviews throughout the tour were generally very positive, although there are some that criticized the quality of the recorded music, the waits between dances for the costume changes, and the choice of some of the dances that were shown. One would assume that Lilian would have danced with La Meri on all the programs, but she is seldom mentioned in the reviews, except in relation to the Philippine dance "Tinikling," in which she and Bertocchi operated the bamboo sticks around which the dancers move (in this case, only one—La Meri). Lilian might have also danced the "Jarabe Tapatío" with her sister, but there is no evidence of this. While Lilian's presence during these months was a great pleasure for her sister, it was not a benefit to this book—because there are none of the wonderfully detailed letters that La Meri would have written if they were not together.

A particularly notable engagement on this tour was the concert on February 27 in Louisville, Kentucky, the city of La Meri's birth, which elicited enthusiastic coverage in the press. One article, "La Meri Dances in Louisville for First Time in Her Career," begins by referring to the lack of appreciation this artist had received as a child from a local dance teacher: "La Meri, who twirled her world-famed dancing toes Monday night in Memorial Auditorium, shed her first professional tears many, many years ago in Louisville." The writer had interviewed her and discusses aspects of her life, her studies, and her thoughts and feelings. The article concludes with information about her family and states that two surviving members attended the performance. These were Ben T. Allen, the uncle with whom she had maintained contact over the years, and a cousin (*Louisville Courier Journal,* February 28, 1939). The United States tour ended with a concert on April 22 at the Brooklyn Academy of Music, an important venue for dance and music events.

To follow the United States bookings, Carreras had prepared for what would be their third—and last—Latin American tour. Sometime, probably in late April or early May, the small company, including Juana and Bertocchi, embarked for Caracas, Venezuela. There is no information about Lilian accompanying them—nothing in the clippings or in La Meri's autobiography. However, in the broad collection of La Meri's letters to Lilian, there are none sent from this tour—which could mean either that Lilian was there, or that somehow letters from this time were lost. In any case, if she was with them, Lilian would have returned to New York sometime before the tour ended as there are two letters she wrote to La Meri from there in August and September.

During the almost four months of the tour, La Meri had engagements in Caracas (May 23 to June 10), in Rio de Janeiro and other Brazilian cities (July 1 to August 10), in Montevideo (August 15 to 26), and in Buenos Aires (September 1 to 28). And, as usual, the lecture-demonstrations with Carreras were scheduled as well as performances. Also, as usual, there were the positive sides—wonderful receptions and reviews—and the negative sides, such as dealing with tight scheduling, long jaunts of travel, and getting through customs. La Meri writes in her autobiography that in one of the Rio de Janeiro concerts, she wrenched her ankle, had it put in a cast, and could not perform for two weeks (1977a, 149). After Brazil and Uruguay, the group's last engagements were in Argentina. La Meri writes that they "had given only a few performances in Buenos Aires when all-out war was declared in Europe" (ibid.). The last event of this tour, their lecture-demonstration on Indian dance and its international influence, was given in that city on September 28. Realizing that with the war, continuing the tour was impractical and returning to Italy impossible, they sailed to New York City on the SS *Argentina*—and on October 14, La Meri and Carreras—always ready to be on stage—presented their Indian dance lecture-demonstration on board.

In the United States, La Meri's career—and her life—would be reinvented.

6

A Reinvented Life in the United States
as a Teacher, Innovator, and Woman, 1939–1956

On October 16, 1939, La Meri, Carreras, Juana—and probably also Bertocchi—arrived in New York City on the SS *Argentina*. Since there were several "celebrities" on the ship who had left Latin America because of the war, the arrival was written up in the next day's *New York Times* with information on violinist Mischa Elman, pianist Alexander Brailowsky, La Meri, and others. The article also mentions the Indian dance program that La Meri gave during the voyage.

New York City would now be La Meri's base through the 1950s. During that time, she performed, taught, and choreographed in Manhattan and occasionally elsewhere. She also toured in the United States and, later, Latin America, but nothing compared to her travels before World War II. As in the early 1930s when she and Carreras had settled in Italy, this new era of her life would be in stark contrast to the excitement and rigors of being constantly on the road, performing, learning new material, and adjusting to different cultures and environments. In New York she continued her professional activities with her usual energy and commitment, but she had to adapt them to new contexts and conditions. While the aspects of La Meri's life as performing artist, choreographer, educator, writer—and woman—were intimately related, it is useful to consider them separately. After information about how La Meri and Carreras got started in New York and embarked on their new life and work there, this chapter focuses on La Meri's schools and teaching in the 1940s and 1950s and then on her personal life. Chapter 7 is devoted to her work in performance and choreography during the same years, and her writings are discussed in chapter 9.

Getting Started (October 1939 to May 1940)

Carreras, always the skillful promotor, saw to it that La Meri's return to the United States would not go unnoticed and that she would have engagements after they arrived. During the Latin American tour, he began working with a New York booking agent, Mark Byron of Embree Concert Service, but apparently some of their correspondence got lost. On August 29, 1939, Lilian wrote to La Meri that Byron had visited her the night before with concern that he had not yet heard from Carreras about photographs, information needed for publicity, and the terms of the contract. Contact was reestablished, and in an October 8 news release, Byron announced that, while La Meri's United States engagements had originally been scheduled to start in 1940, since the war had cut short her Latin American tour, performances would begin at the end of October. That might have occurred, but there is no evidence of 1939 performances in the archives. La Meri's national visibility was growing, however. Promoting her availability for bookings after the beginning of the year was a full-page advertisement with two photographs in the October issue of *Dance* and one with eight pictures in the October 25 *Musical America*. These two ads and a promotional brochure distributed by Byron emphasized La Meri's triumphs in Latin America and other parts of the world and the broad range of her international repertoire. In its December issue, *Dance* featured her picture on the cover—and also published a long letter to the editor from Carreras criticizing the presentation of Javanese and Balinese dances by a group from Indonesia.[1]

When the group arrived in New York City with meager financial resources, David, who had a teaching position at New York University, and Lilian displayed their usual generosity by providing La Meri and Carreras with free lodging in their home. A hotel room was rented for Juana and a small studio for rehearsals and the storing of the costumes and other equipment. In the studio, La Meri was able to practice her dances each day, the kind of disciplined regimen that she had followed for years. There is no information as to where Bertocchi was staying. This residential and working arrangement lasted until around the middle of May 1940, when La Meri, Carreras, Juana, and Bertocchi moved into the building where the School of Natya was opened (see below) (1977a, 150–51). Sometime during 1940 or 1941, David was transferred, and from at least June 1941 to June

1942, he and Lilian were in Fort Belvoir, Virginia (as shown on the letters La Meri wrote to her sister).

Carreras was able to schedule a few performances and lecture-demonstrations for his wife in New York and elsewhere, but the nation was still suffering from the aftermath of the Great Depression that had hit in the 1930s, and involvement in World War II was approaching. La Meri's 1973 chronology states that she gave eleven concerts in eleven cities in January and February 1940 (under the management of Byron), and there is archival material on some of those (see chapter 7).

One of La Meri's early 1940 appearances would significantly affect her professional life. The Museum of Costume Art was sponsoring a series of programs on different cultures, and its president, Irene Lewisohn,[2] invited La Meri to give a lecture-demonstration as part of the series. She was happy to accept—and as she wrote, to be able to "speak in English to English-speaking people" (1977a, 150). This presentation, "Demonstration of Costume and Dancing of India," was at the New York Junior League, 221 East 71st Street on March 6, and an announcement had appeared in the March 4 edition of *Newsweek* with a full-length picture of La Meri in an East Indian dance and eight other pictures of her "expressive feet" in shoes and poses from different cultures. The program was lauded by the noted dance critic Walter Terry (1913–1982). He began his review by expressing distaste for such events in general, but then went on to praise this one:

> The term "lecture-demonstration" connotes such dull scholarliness that most of us evade it unless we are out for self-improvement. . . . Last Wednesday evening, however, New York had a lecture-demonstration which was not only extremely scholarly and factual but also dramatically exciting. ("To a Greater Dance," *New York Herald Tribune,* March 10, 1940)

He discussed what La Meri presented in relation to trends in American dance and suggested that "the American dancer might learn something of thoroughness from his Indian colleague." It is interesting to compare this with the suggestion made by an Indian reviewer of La Meri's February 1937, concert in Bombay, that it would be beneficial to Indian dancers to learn from her (see chapter 4). Another critic, noting La Meri's introduction to the costumes, principles, and techniques of Indian dance and her performance of both traditional and modern Indian dances, concluded that anyone attending the lecture would have gained "new insight into the art of Uday Shankar and a quickened interest in Indian dancing (S., "La Meri Illustrates Dance Forms of India," *Musical America*, March 25, 1940, 35).

In addition to eliciting good press coverage, this lecture-demonstration brought La Meri into contact with two dance figures who would become very important in her re-created life—the renowned Ruth St. Denis, whose performance had strongly influenced her as a teenager in San Antonio, and the as yet unknown Hadassah, a young dancer who would work with La Meri and then gain respect and admiration on her own as a concert dance artist.

La Meri writes that at the end of the Costume Museum event, "a beautiful tall woman . . . burst into my dressing room." This was the iconic Ruth St. Denis, who was clearly excited by the knowledge and artistry she had just witnessed. She immediately insisted that La Meri must open a school and that together they should "found a center for the study of eastern arts—dancing, painting, sculpture, philosophy!" (1977a, 150). La Meri was not so sure. She had done some teaching in Italy, but that wasn't her main interest at all. As she expressed it,

> I truly did not want to teach. I did not want to open a school. But I was to find out that Miss Ruth had not become a living legend for nothing. She was a torrent of embodied enthusiasm, as easy to avoid as a hurricane. Perhaps she was right, perhaps America *was* actually hungering for knowledge and therefore might be persuaded to pay a living wage to receive it. Thinking practically, I well knew that, so few were engagements now, we were very close to living off my sister and her husband, . . . so by mid-May . . . we had opened The School of Natya. (1977a, 151)

The school's first location was 66 5th Avenue (between 12th and 13th Streets), where Martha Graham had had a studio since the early 1930s (O'Donnell, 59). That building also provided small residence spaces for St. Denis, La Meri, Carreras, Juana, and Bertocchi.

The other contact that resulted from La Meri's March 6 presentation was with Hadassah (Spira Epstein, 1909–1992), who had already been studying Indian dance with the well-known writer on Southeast Asian dance, Claire

Holt (1901–1970). On March 11, Hadassah wrote a passionate letter asking La Meri to be her "guru," because she was convinced that La Meri's

> lovely hands have touched the heart of Bharata and her feet have trod the roads of Eternity—for they re-echo the divine rhythms of Siva's foot-beats in the Halls of Chidambaram. . . . I'm sure you won't refuse me because I feel in the depths of my heart that you who have been an Apsara in the court of Nataraj and probably have the instincts of a priestess, will surely understand what it means when the soul of a disciple is aflame with the desire for Wisdom and Knowledge of Natyasastra.

This request was supported by a March 13 letter from Holt, who said that she had taught Hadassah as much as she could and hoped that La Meri would be able to help her further.

Hadassah studied with La Meri at the School of Natya and performed with her group, the "Natya Dancers" (see below) from at least July to December 1940. After that she established herself as a major performing artist and choreographer, specializing in dances on Jewish themes as well as dances from Southeast Asia (Danitz). She and La Meri kept in contact, and after reading La Meri's 1977 autobiography, Hadassah wrote saying that she would like to know more about her parents than had been included there. La Meri sent her thirty-two typed pages about her family and a letter, dated November 20, 1979, that ended: "So I make you this offering with gratitude, with love and with a profound admiration for you and your great artistic works."

The School of Natya (May 1940 to October 1942)

The "School of Natya" officially opened on Sunday, May 19, 1940, with the first "reunion" (see below). The opening of the school was reported and highly praised in an article by the noted Indian-American journalist and author, Basanta Koomar Roy (ca.1883–1949). He later lectured at the school and chaired its advisory board. It is interesting that Roy speaks of the institution as if it was totally La Meri's and not a collaborative project with St. Denis. He writes of having attended La Meri's concert on March 31, 1940, at the Saint James Theater in New York (see chapter 7) and being very impressed. And then, after discussing her experience and accomplishments, he ends the article, saying that the school is "A splendid achievement for the message of India's art of the dance. Let India bow to America's La Meri in gratitude; even as America bows to India's Uday Shankar in reverence" ("La Meri Opens Her School of Natya").

While La Meri had not been eager to teach, she had a great deal to contribute in this area. She had studied many kinds of dance with native teachers, each of whom had his or her traditional and/or individually devised pedagogical method. She had learned how to practice on her own to develop her proficiency in the varied techniques, taught some in Italy, written on dance, and presented lecture-demonstrations. With all this experience, she had a breadth of knowledge and a range of skills that would serve her well in preparing curricula and teaching American students dance languages from around the world. La Meri's classes at the School of Natya included the Indian genres of Bharatanatyam, Kathak, Kathakali, and what she termed "Renaissance"; and the Spanish genres of flamenco, regional, and classical dance. The latter probably referred to the balletic *escuela bolero* (bolero school). It is surprising that Kathakali was included in her teaching as well as her performances as there is no record of her having studied that form. In her autobiography, La Meri writes that her first pupil at the school was the dancer and choreographer Jack Cole (1911–1974), who became known for his fusions of Western and non-Western dance forms. He had worked initially with Denishawn, and he came to the School of Natya for private lessons (probably in Bharatanatyam) with La Meri (1977a, 151; Loney, 184).

In her biography of St. Denis, Suzanne Shelton writes that the school "was a shared venture in name only. While La Meri offered classes in a variety of techniques, St. Denis rarely taught—but when she did, La Meri allowed her the day's 'take' from the student fees." But, while the two artists did not really share students, they did share ideas and movement practices—St. Denis to learn "authentic" movements from La Meri and La Meri to discover "some of the secrets of St. Denis' genius" (Shelton 1981, 251–52). St. Denis was more involved and active in the "reunions" of the school. As a regular feature, every two weeks or so, one was held on a theme related to Asian, Spanish, or other dance traditions—usually in the form of a lecture-demonstration and presented by La Meri, St. Denis, or invited guests. These were a means of spreading knowledge about world dance—one of La Meri's continuing goals—and also a source of needed income. Between May 19, 1940, and August 12, 1941, twenty-nine reunions were given. As they were trained, students would participate in the demonstrations and sometimes give entire student recitals. By early 1941, the student dancers were presented as the "Natya Experimental Group" or the "Natya Dancers."

At the first reunion on May 19, St. Denis spoke briefly on "Dancing in India," and La Meri and Carreras gave the same lecture-demonstration that they had presented on March 6 for the Museum of Costume Art. This format was repeated on June 11 with "Oriental Derivatives of the Indian Dance" and on June 25 with "Occidental Derivatives of the Indian Dance," both of which had previously been presented by La Meri and Carreras on tour. Other re-unions focused on subjects such as costumes and ornaments in relation to the dance; genres and techniques of a particular geographical location, such as Spain, the Middle East, China, or Japan; types of movement expression, such as gesture language; or aspects of a culture or religion in relation to the dance. And there were guest presentations such as Basanta Koomar Roy's "The Poetry of Rabindranath Tagore" (August 6, 1940), in which La Meri interpreted the poems in Hindu gesture language.

On July 14, 1941, some of La Meri's dancers gave a performance at the theater of the Master Institute of United Arts (MIUA),[3] and the Institute's administration invited her to transfer all her activities to their establish-ment—to teach in their studios, give performances in their theater, and have a room and bath for her personal use—all without rental costs. So the School of Natya became affiliated with MIUA, and October 1 was its official opening date (October 4 letter to Lilian). An undated brochure announces, "La Meri's School of Natya (founded by Ruth St. Denis and La Meri) in af-filiation with the Master Institute of United Arts," thus identifying it now as La Meri's school, but recognizing St. Denis's role in its beginning.

The School of Natya remained in its original location, with everyone liv-ing in the same cramped quarters, until sometime in the summer or fall of 1941. Suzanne Shelton relates that St. Denis "decided she needed more space and moved uptown to a studio and apartment formerly occupied by Isadora Duncan" (252). Located at 110 East 59th Street, between Park and Lexington, this structure had reportedly been built for Duncan by Paris Singer, her lover and the father of one of her children (Fay, 63). St. Denis was not alone in her dissatisfaction with the 5th Avenue location. La Meri writes that by the late summer of 1941, Carreras had decided that the way they were living was "ridiculously impossible," and it seemed obvious that with the free facilities at the MIUA, they would earn enough from classes and presentations to cover rent as well as other expenses. In early August, La Meri and Carreras began looking for an apartment in Manhattan, but since Carreras did not like New York City at all, they changed their search to New Jersey. There they found an affordable house with three floors and a basement, a two-car garage, and a "huge beautiful lawn" in Montclair, a relatively short commuting distance from the city. Carreras, Juana, and Bertocchi began to move in on September 1, but La Meri did not plan to be there all the time until October 1 when she would totally move out of the 5th Avenue building (1977a, 153; letters of August 9, 16, and 24). These changes of location marked a break in the initial collaboration of La Meri and St. Denis, however close it may or may not have been. There is no indication of any kind of conflict between them, however, and they maintained their friendship until St. Denis's death in 1968. They continued to appear together in various events in New York, and La Meri visited St. Denis after she had moved to California.

The classes of the School of Natya at the MIUA began on October 3, 1941; and the opening was publicly celebrated on October 8, when La Meri gave a recital of Indian dances (probably with her Natya Dancers). From then on, La Meri would travel three times a week from Montclair to the school and teach all day and evening (1977a, 153; letter of October 4, 1941; clippings). In the school brochure, the classes in "Hindu" and Spanish dance were divided into one group for "artists" and another as "popular" classes (for beginners). Also announced was a class for the artist level students in theory and pedagogy. It is interesting that La Meri was already concerned with providing more than just training in dance techniques. And, in addition to the regular courses in Spanish and Indian dance, special courses in the dance of other cultures would be offered for a minimum of five students. There would also be an "Experimental Group" chosen from students enrolled in at least three classes a week, and their fees might be reduced. Scheduled from fall 1941 through spring 1942 were six performances by La Meri and her group in the MIUA theater and six lectures (comparable to the former "reunions") with slides, music recordings, and short dance demonstrations in its lecture hall.

In the beginning, this seemed like a wonderful opportunity for La Meri and her work as artist and teacher, but unfortunately, it turned out to be unviable financially. The audiences who had flocked to the programs on lower

5th Avenue were apparently not willing to travel all the way uptown to the Institute at Riverside Drive and 103rd Street, and with low attendance, the performances and lectures did not provide the needed income. La Meri began looking for a studio closer to midtown and found one (at 5 West 46th Street near 5th Avenue) with enough space for both classes and reunions (1977a, 154–55). While she still used the name "School of Natya" at times, she now began to identify the institution as the Ethnologic Dance Center.

Ethnologic Dance Center (EDC) (October 1942 to September 1956)

On October 15, 1942, the EDC's new location formally opened with a reunion featuring Felix Cleve, the Viennese dance critic who had praised La Meri so highly when she performed in Europe. Included in his speech, "A Quarter-Century of Artistic Dance," is information about his life as a dance critic in Vienna, three important dance artists he had seen or met there (Grete Wiesenthal, Anna Pavlova, and Uday Shankar), and the seeming opposition between ballet and modern dance. All of this led into a detailed account and analysis of La Meri's January 19, 1930, matinee performance at the Reinhardt Theatre in Vienna, which he had attended and reviewed—and finally to his conclusions. Of the artist during her years of touring, he writes:

> By her ethnologic dancing, La Meri had been preaching to all mankind, all the time while traveling around the earth-ball, the olden never-fading gospel of human brotherhood. Hers was a global thinking, long before this slogan of today was coined.

And, of the school:

> This Ethnologic Dance Center is La Meri's great contribution to the peace effort of mankind. She is convinced that "should the diverse folk of the earth," to say it in her own words, "be taught to know each other, they would automatically learn how to respect and love each other." And as she considers the dance to be that means of expression which communicates most directly and intimately the very nature of a people, she [believes knowledge of the dance of different cultures] to be particularly apt to bring forth and promote a mutual understanding and brotherly love among the dwellers of this earth.

> La Meri hopes and faithfully believes . . . that this Center will become a nucleus of an ever growing community of dance missionaries of this cheerful creed.

Cleve thus believed that La Meri's contributions were as important to the world at large as to the world of dance and the performing arts.

The EDC remained at West 46th Street until July 5, 1943; and the reunions were now attended by substantial audiences—thus providing essential income. Those invited to be "honored guests" and make presentations included well-known figures such as the Spanish dancers Federico Rey (Freddy Wittop, 1911–2001) and La Argentinita (Encarnación López Júlvez, 1898–1945), the noted writer on Asian cultures, Pearl S. Buck (1892–1973), the historian and philosopher of Indian arts, Ananda K. Coomaraswamy (1877–1947), the Chinese writer and translator, Dr. Lin Yutang (1895–1976) and, of course, Ruth St. Denis and Ted Shawn.

In 1942, St. Denis decided she wanted to move permanently to California, which she did either at the end of that year or early in 1943 (Shelton, 254). Before leaving New York, she offered La Meri all her costumes; and, most significant for the future of the EDC was that La Meri and Carreras were able to take over her lease at the 59th Street facility. As La Meri writes, this studio and apartment "occupied a whole floor and had two very large rooms, two baths, and several smaller rooms" (1977a, 157). In her 1987 interview with Patricia Taylor, La Meri said they had the entire second floor and two rooms on the ground floor—all for $200 a month. They decided to construct a dance theater in one of the large rooms and accomplished that with borrowed money and the hard work of Carreras and Bertocchi (1977a, 157). They moved into the new space in June 1943, and the opening reception on Thursday, July 8, featured several of the notable figures who had given presentations for reunions at 46th Street: La Argentinita, Pearl S. Buck, Felix Cleve, and Lin Yutang.

The new center gained notice and appreciation from many in the dance community. In a short review of the July 27 reunion, Rosalyn Krokover (1913–1973), dance editor for the *Musical Courier*, provides a detailed description of the facility:

> While the studio is rich in dance traditions, having been the home and workshop of . . . Isadora Duncan and Ruth St. Denis, the skill and

untiring efforts of Guido Carreras has turned the suite into one of the most completely equipped studios in this country. A spacious reception room leads to an auditorium which comfortably seats over two hundred people. It has a raised stage with a platform of about eighteen square feet luxuriously framed in black velvet curtains. A complete stage lighting system has also been installed.

Krokover also notes the "professional dressing and make-up room" for the dancers ("The Dance," August 1943, 12). In a later review of the same event, Margaret Lloyd (1887–1960), critic for the *Christian Science Monitor*, gives a history of La Meri's schools since she returned to New York and praises this new site ("Theater for Ethnologic Dance—I," August 28, 1943). And the editor of *Dance Magazine* showed his appreciation by publishing a short article about the facility with photographs (Rudolf Orthwine, "A New Type of Intimate Dance Theatre," November 1943, 17).[4]

The first full season of EDC presentations in this new location opened September 14, 1943, with a reunion that included six dances of India and five of Spain, performed by La Meri and her Natya dancers. There was an overflow audience; so, for those who had not arrived early, it was "standing room only." From that event until the end of 1943, there were nine more reunions, three guest lectures, and two concerts, one by La Meri and the Natyas and the other by noted Spanish dance artist Carola Goya (1906–1994). In 1944, the EDC offered four more reunions between January 11 and February 22. After that, the term "reunion" was dropped, and all the presentations were identified as either concerts or lectures.

Each year, the EDC teaching program ran from September to late April or early May. Brochures were printed, but they lack dates until the one of 1950–51. A brochure distributed in 1943 or later announces a curriculum of sixteen hour-long classes that included instruction in Spanish and "Hindu" dance on Mondays, Wednesdays, and Fridays (day classes for "artist" training and evening ones for beginning and intermediate students), modern dance on Tuesdays, Thursdays, and Saturdays, and single classes in unspecified genres for children (Saturday mornings) and teenagers (Wednesday afternoons). There is no information as to who taught which classes, but surely La Meri did all or most of the Spanish and Indian instruction. The other classes must have been covered by one or more of the Natya dancers—and Lilian after her return to New York.[5] It is not clear what is meant by "modern dance" in this brochure—one of the current modern dance techniques, modern creative work with traditional ethnic forms, or something else. The term does not appear in later brochures until 1950–51 when classes by modern choreographer and dancer Myra Kinch (1904–1981) were included in the curriculum.

Usually, the EDC also had a summer session—a financial necessity to keep up with expenses. According to an announcement for July and August 1944, there would be intensive training in dances of India, Spain, Latin America, Java, China, Morocco, Hawaii, New Zealand (Maori), and the Philippines—a seemingly impossible breadth of genres in two months or less. This program was in collaboration with courses at the Vilzak-Shollar (or Schollar) School, an institution in New York City from 1940–46 that was run by two former Russian ballet stars, Anatole Vilzak (1896–1998) and Ludmilla Schollar (1888–1978). La Meri writes that this summer EDC course attracted "a number of out-of-town teachers," and that she, Lilian, and some of the Natyas were teaching eight hours each day (1977a, 161). Other summer programs did not include such a range of techniques but focused more on Spanish and Indian dance.

In June 1949, La Meri was a guest artist at Ruth St. Denis's studio in Hollywood where she gave two lecture-demonstrations and taught a three-evening course on dance in India. While meeting with St. Denis, La Meri told her of the continually dire and discouraging financial situation at the EDC, which, of course, made it difficult both to continue the school and to keep up with living expenses. St. Denis encouraged her to perhaps find a new way to give of her "knowledge and inspiration" that would provide more income. Coincidentally, it was after this discussion with St. Denis that La Meri had an engagement to teach one month at Iowa State University (ISU). In her autobiography, she writes that "the offer from the university was so fortuitous that it seemed like a nod of approval from a benign destiny" (1977a, 180). She goes on to explain: "It was my first experience in the field of higher education, for I held no degree and my two somewhat slapdash years of college study were in the far-distant past. I plunged in, haunted the library between my classes and quizzed fellow teachers on a range of pedagogical approaches in this field that was so new to me" (ibid., 181).

La Meri seems to credit both St. Denis and the ISU experience with inspiring the expanded EDC curriculum, which was first offered in fall 1949. She writes:

In my dance center background lectures had already become regular fare for my students, but on my return to New York I added to the already overloaded schedule, making such study compulsory for those dancers who elected to go for the three- or four-year course. In forty-five hours of classes a week they took not only dance techniques but the study of ethnic dance—history and culture as well as choreography, music fundamentals, pedagogy, and costume design.

They were required to keep notebooks, to do outside research. They were given a short course in public speaking and twice a year took stiff oral and written examinations. (ibid.)

A student in the three-year curriculum could focus on developing as an artist or teacher, in one or more of the following fields: "ethnologic," Indian, or Spanish dance. Required for all were classes in production (lighting, costuming, makeup, and publicity) and in writing and public speaking—the latter on the assumption that anyone presenting dances of different cultures would be called on to speak or write about them. On completion of the three years, the student would be given a certificate.

The program that La Meri developed was complex in that she was trying to draw students who wanted to train for careers as artists and/or teachers, and she felt strongly that the successful and effective artist or teacher would need knowledge and experience in all the areas mentioned above. There are undated brochures from the first years of the expanded curriculum that give some information about the EDC and its programs, but more informative is that announcing the 1954–55 season. It includes photographs of La Meri, Peter di Falco (see below), Lilian, Matteo (Matteo Marcellus Vitucci, ca. 1919–2011), and others who taught, studied, and performed at the EDC and gives the full curriculum for the three-year course for teachers. The requirements included technique, choreography, fundamentals of music, writing, and speaking. Recommended were courses on topics such as Spanish or East Indian culture, Spanish or East Indian percussives,[6] aspects of production, costuming and makeup, pedagogy, and ballet—the latter to prepare students for the Spanish classical dance, the *escuela bolera*.[7] This woman, who had said (and surely believed) that she had no interest at all in teaching, had become a pioneer in the development of education for the dance artist or teacher who was interested in one or more genres from the international world of dance.

The EDC on 59th Street lasted for only a few more years. The initial—optimistic—hope was that it would be financially self-sustaining with student fees and receipts from the reunions and concerts, which attracted sizeable audiences. It soon became clear, however, that it was not taking in enough for the rent and for La Meri's constant preparation of new works with costume and other production costs. The problems were intensified in fall 1949 when the city fire department required extensive and expensive wiring alterations for the theater to have its license renewed (*Dance Magazine* 23: 8, August 1949, 31). The next month, however, there was a news item that La Meri would not be suspending presentations at the EDC theater but would temporarily change to a "subscription and contributions events basis" (*Dance Magazine* 23: 9, September 1949, 41). In fact, a limited program of lectures, lecture-demonstrations, and an occasional recital continued until at least May 1952, but whether these were done formally on stage or as studio presentations is unclear.

With continuing financial difficulty, La Meri was only able to keep the EDC operating until the end of the 1956 summer course (June 18 to August 25). She spent the next few years still living in New York City; performing in various venues; and giving courses, workshops, or master classes at institutions such as Teachers College, University of Texas, Texas Women's College, Oklahoma College for Women, Boston Dance Circle, and New York University (1977a, 187; *Chronology 1973*).

Between 1942 and 1967, La Meri also taught and performed at Jacob's Pillow (see chapter 7). As I mentioned in the preface, I first met and had classes with her, Peter di Falco, and Lilian at the Pillow in summer 1953, and I continued studying with them at the EDC from the fall of that year through the summer of 1956. Since I had to work full-time in New York to support myself, I was not able to enroll in any of the three-year certificate programs. Nevertheless, La Meri's premise that to master a dance language, one needed to study and gain an understanding of the culture and history of the form influenced me greatly. I would spend any spare hours I could find reading in the library, and, as I stated, I credit her with starting me on the path that would lead me to the profession of "dance historian." From my contact with fellow students while I was at the EDC and with others who had been there earlier, I know that she influenced many to read and learn about their art in depth.

La Meri's Personal Life from 1939 to the Late 1950s

In 1944, La Meri suffered two losses. Sometime in the spring of that year, her relationship with Carreras ended, and in August, her brother-in-law, David Newcomer, who had been stationed in France, was killed in action. His death was a deep blow for La Meri. As she writes, she "had loved him like a brother" (1977a, 158), and from the earliest years of his marriage to Lilian, he had treated her like a sister, providing financial and other kinds of support. So this was very sad for La Meri, although, of course, not as devastating as it was for Lilian. It was good that the two sisters were so close. On the personal level, they could share feelings about their losses as well as enjoy each other's company in the ways they always had. In the professional realm, their collaboration in teaching and performance provided Lilian with a continuing focus and purpose in her life that probably made the mourning process somewhat easier than it would have been otherwise. And it was very good for La Meri to have her sister's helpful support, advice, and sharing of responsibilities since, with the loss of Carreras, she was now in charge of everything involved in running the school, preparing productions, and organizing performances.

Guido Carreras

There is much information available about the relationship between La Meri and Carreras from their meeting in the mid-1920s through their thirteen years together as a married couple (1931–44). An obvious source is La Meri's autobiography, which focuses on their professional activities but includes only short references to aspects of their personal life together. More knowledge and insights into the latter may be gained from the large archive of 31 letters she wrote to Carreras from 1926 to 1933 and some of the 121 written to Lilian when they were living in separate locations. These provide evidence of La Meri's strong feelings for Carreras in the early years of their relationship, and, in letters to Lilian, information about the problems that developed. More information can also be found in diaries and other documents in the Jacob's Pillow archive and the Indira Gandhi National Centre for Arts in New Delhi, India. Another important source is some of La Meri's poetry. In a 1938 letter she sent to her brother-in-law, David, along with a copy of the newly published *Songs and Voyages*, La Meri gives short explanations of each of the poems in that book, including to whom they were directed. Seven of the eighteen in the "Love Song" section were for "Guy," Carreras's nickname, but others also seem to be about their relationship.

All the documents show that the relationship between La Meri and Carreras was for some time and to some extent a passionate union. However, with the difference in age, and Carreras's role from the beginning as manager, director, producer, and promoter of La Meri's work, it seems that he was as much (or more like) a father or supervisor rather than an equal partner. And, often, in her correspondence with Lilian, La Meri would refer to him as "The Boss." The relationship was always characterized by inequality—Carreras being in charge and La Meri expected to follow. This, of course, was the usual situation in male-female relationships then—and is still prevalent in many places today.

As discussed in chapter 2, the love relationship between La Meri and Carreras began before May 9, 1926, as shown by her letter of that date. Its continuing development is obvious from the letters she wrote on the ship as she, Lilian, and Billy were traveling from Puerto Rico to Mobile, Alabama, in October 1927. How long the passion lasted is not clear, but certainly for some time after their marriage in 1931—as shown in the twenty letters she wrote to him while in the United States with Lilian from August to October 1932 (see chapter 3). La Meri opened each letter with a greeting, such as: "Dearest," "My Blessed Husband," "My Own Dear Lover," and often ended with words about her feelings, such as: "Once I loved you with the rush of a waterfall, . . . Now I love you like the great deep river: steady, swift, but voiceless. I can no more find the words to express my love! Your Wife" (probably written September 7, 1932). It is interesting that in the saved copies of those letters some of the loving passages were scribbled over with pencil—probably after the painful break-up.

While living in Italy from 1931 to 1935, the relationship between La Meri and Carreras might have simmered down somewhat as each followed separate interests. However, poems in the 1938 *Songs and Voyages* indicate that her feelings for him were still strong up to then. During the 1936 to 1939 touring and their first four years in New York, Carreras and La Meri continued their professional collaboration, and his dedication to promoting her and facilitating her projects never wavered. But, while their life as a married couple also continued, problems between them had apparently been brewing for a long time. Whether the decision to part was mutual or from one side or the other is not clear. In her autobiography, La Meri only writes that "Carreras and I separated with a good deal of drama and nervous tension" (1977a, 158). There is no detailed information as to why they broke up, and apparently no legal action was taken until 1950 when La Meri filed for an annulment in the court of the County of Kings in Brooklyn, New York. The court tried without success to contact Carreras in Italy, and the annulment was granted October 26, 1950, on the basis that his previous marriage had never been ended with a legal divorce.

Regarding the problems that led to the breakup of La Meri and Carreras, Venkateswaran quotes from documents in the Indira Gandhi Center in which La Meri writes about the tensions and anger between them, and her conflict over feeling dependent and needing to be "obedient," on one side, and her desire for independence, on the other (30–31). It is interesting that La Meri's concern about independence and her need to feel that she was in control of her own life, decisions, and activities would also come up at future times—when she refused to marry Charles Miller, for example (see below) and, much later, when deteriorating vision took away her freedom to drive a car—something she had been doing since her teenage years (see chapter 8).

While in her autobiography, La Meri gives no details about her positive or negative feelings toward Carreras or the ending of their marriage, she does write about the challenge of taking on the administrative work that he had done so well—and her problem finding a replacement for him in the role of the Ghost in *El Amor Brujo*, which he had apparently "mimed" in its initial partial production (see chapter 7). This is the only mention in La Meri's autobiography, or any other source, of Carreras performing. Regarding the administration and management responsibilities, she jokingly writes of her own ineptness in keeping track of finances, and that after a year, she hired a certified public accountant, Sam Prussak, who she says "kept me sorted out ever since" (1977a, 159–60). In addition to his abilities in financial matters, Carreras had always been an exceedingly skillful agent and manager, promoting her art, making contacts and contracts, scheduling performances, and arranging the technical needs and publicity. Now all of that would be on her shoulders. In another passage quoted in Venkateswaran, La Meri writes that, sometime after she and Carreras parted, she heard that he had gone back to live in Italy and that she "never saw him again and he died there in 1957" (31).

La Meri describes the continuing overload of her life after this break-up—with the school, new productions, touring, and the establishment of the Exotic Ballet Company—and writes that "work and worry had taken up all my mind and energy." But as she became used to being alone, she says that she "began seeking momentary release from the bitter-sweet joy of creation" and returned to her previous "offstage life," which she had abandoned after "meeting Carreras in 1925." She continues: "Frenetically I took up smoking and cocktails and assiduous nightclubbing. Every night after the curtain went down in my theater, I rushed out on the town, gleefully squired by men of any and all ages, and all financial brackets. For a little while it was a delicious never-never land and I was as happy as a subdeb" (1977a, 164). Her "never-never land" probably also included intimacy with some of the men with whom she caroused.

Charles James Miller

After World War II, some veterans came to study at the Ethnologic Dance Center—first under scholarships La Meri offered to attract male dancers for her company, and then, under the auspices of the G.I. Bill.[8] As it turned out, La Meri became seriously involved with two of these students. The first was Charles James Miller (1915–2004), variously referred to in correspondence and programs as Charles or Chuck Miller, or Carlos (sometimes by other nicknames, as well). According to a short biography in the summary of his archival collection, while serving in the United States Army during World War II, Miller both interpreted "in French and Spanish for the Arabs" and was "director and choreographer for Army Red Cross shows in Algeria" (see "Charles James Miller Papers 0333," *Online Archives of California*, 2). I have found no other information about his previous dance or theater background. Miller first appears on an Ethnologic Dance Center program, January 2–3, 1945, as a member of the new "men's group" that La Meri had formed. Since he was performing on that date, he must have begun his studies with her somewhat earlier. There is mention in his archive that he was still in the army in late August 1944, so he might have started working with La Meri in the fall of that year.

Throughout 1945 and in part of 1946, Miller appeared in some of La Meri's major works, such as *Swan Lake, Scheherazade,* and *Iberia* and in individual dances from the Caribbean, Latin America, the Middle East, the Philippines, India, Ceylon, and other cultures. His name is on La Meri's programs at Jacob's Pillow during the summer of 1946, at the University of Connecticut in October, and at the EDC in November, but Peter di Falco (discussed below) remembered Miller being "banished from the studio" before the Jacob's Pillow programs in June 1946 (correspondence, June 28, 2009), so it is not clear how long Miller was active in the company.

At some point, the relationship between La Meri and Miller developed from teacher-student and choreographer-dancer to that of lovers. From letters in Miller's archive that La Meri wrote to him in February and March 1946, while she was away from New York City, it seems to have been a passionate connection, for perhaps a year or less. The letters were sent from Tennessee, Alabama, Texas, Kentucky, and Florida, while La Meri was on tour, performing in solo concerts and with Shawn and others in a program to promote Jacob's Pillow. She writes about missing him, how much he means to her, her disappointment when she hasn't received a letter from him, and how eager she is to return to New York and be with him. It is interesting that the content of these letters and the emotions expressed are very similar to those in the letters she wrote to Carreras in 1932. But then, in an undated letter written on School of Natya stationery (so probably from New York), she seems to be defending herself against accusations or complaints Miller must have made. She writes: "I am quite good enough to be loved, whatever you or your mother may think to the contrary; and no one has ever been in any way degraded by any association with me." Apparently, Miller had wanted La Meri to give up her professional life, marry him, and live as a "traditional" wife, subservient to her husband. She goes on to say that she was always clear about not being willing to marry him but, still, had not just been playing with his love. And she felt hurt "at being assigned the role of the designing female" (Miller Collection, box 9, folder 8). In another undated letter, she writes that she realized that being with Miller had "all the disadvantages of being married and none of the advantages" and ends with "I cannot help it if I do not love you" (box 9, folder 11).

After the end of their sexual relationship, however, La Meri and Miller continued to be friends. In another undated letter, which is obviously a response to what he wrote to her after she rejected him as a lover (or husband), she writes that she is glad that they can be friends and that she had experienced great happiness during the year she was with him (box 9, folder 9). And in undated letters probably from 1946, she introduced Miller to figures in the dance world in Los Angeles, such as Jack Cole and Ruth St. Denis, expressing the hope that they would be able to help him get started there. In the rest of box 9 and much of box 10 of the Miller archive, there are more than 130 documents of their correspondence from the early 1960s to 1987. These include letters that Miller received from La Meri and carbon copies of letters he wrote to her. This collection attests to the continuing friendship these two former lovers maintained, but La Meri never mentions Miller in her autobiography.

After Miller left New York, he moved to Los Angeles and completed three degrees at USC: Bachelor of Arts, 1951; Master of Arts, 1952; and PhD in Communicative Arts, 1957. While working on his dissertation, "Descriptive Study of the Contribution of Edward Gordon Craig to Modern Theatre," he was in contact with Craig, himself, who was still alive until 1966, and with Craig's son, Edward Carrick; that correspondence is also in the USC collection (box 1, folders 1–58). After finishing his doctorate, Miller taught courses in Asian and Asian-American studies and language training at various colleges and universities. In addition to his academic research and teaching, he traveled internationally (visiting Edward Gordon Craig, who was by then in his nineties, in France), performed dances from different cultures in various venues, and taught special courses in ethnic dance forms for summer and other courses— and at some point he married. Since he was actively carrying on the work he had begun with La Meri in the 1940s, in his correspondence with her, he often asked for her advice regarding sources for information, music, and the content of dance courses he was preparing. They also shared information about their families and former students and dancers who had worked with La Meri in New York when Miller was there. Since Miller apparently saved everything from his experiences with La Meri, his archive is a rich source for information, pictures, and publications related to her life and work.

Peter di Falco

Another of the veterans who came to the EDC to study after the war was Peter di Falco (1924–2017), who would become a major figure in both the personal and professional life of La Meri for more than ten years.[9] Di Falco was born in Johnstown, Pennsylvania, of Sicilian parents. He developed an early interest in dance and began in his teens to take classes in tap, ballet, Polynesian dance, and perhaps other forms at the Eleanor Oliver Dance Studio in Johnstown in exchange for work such as doing cleaning tasks and assisting in some of the classes. He must have shown strong potential in his dancing because Oliver encouraged him to continue in the field and helped him to do that after the war. In February 1943, di Falco had either enlisted or was inducted into the army, and because he was fluent in Italian (something his father had insisted on), he was stationed in Italy, where he served as a translator and interpreter. He was demobilized December 15, 1945.

Sometime after the war began, probably in 1943, Oliver moved to New York City to study with La Meri. She is listed in performances at the EDC from August 1945 to mid-1949, and she also did some teaching there beginning in the summer of 1948. She recommended the EDC to di Falco as a place to continue his dance training and performance and asked La Meri to save one of her scholarships for him—which she did. Early in 1946, di Falco came to New York City and began his work at the EDC. He was performing almost immediately and was soon listed as a member of the company. By the late 1940s, he had become La Meri's partner; and they performed together professionally until the mid-1950s—in and around New York City, at Jacob's Pillow, and on tour. As a student he completed three of the EDC certificate programs: the Iberian Dance Course (May 1950), the Indic Dance Teachers Course (May 1952), and the Ethnologic Dance Artists Course "with highest honors" (1956); and he was listed as faculty in the 1950–51 EDC brochure. His performing and choreography will be discussed in the next chapter.

Di Falco recalls that his personal relationship with La Meri began in the fall of 1946, sometime after they had returned from Jacob's Pillow. While it went through some tense times as she was deciding whether to be with him or with another veteran whom she had gotten to know that summer, they ended up coming together in a relationship that lasted about ten years. From 1946 to 1956, La Meri's age was 48 to 58 years and di Falco's 22 to 32. That might have been somewhat of a problem in her mind, but not in his. He said, "We had fun. We sang. We would do silly things . . . I felt that I was with a girl my own age" (interview March 26, 2003). La Meri obviously still had a great ability to enjoy life as well as to work hard in performance, choreography, teaching, and writing.

In September 1948, La Meri decided to stop living in the EDC studio—which had been her home at least since the break-up with Carreras in 1944—and moved to an apartment in Queens. After she and di Falco came to an agreement about sharing all expenses and joint income, he moved there with her, and they lived together for the next eight years. They were performing in New York and on tours through 1954, but then, because La Meri had developed a severe allergic reaction, she had to stop dyeing her hair. She writes: "I was stricken—inexplicably—with a case of the itch! Doctors cried 'allergy!' but it eluded all manner of pills and shots. My poor body, overworked for twenty-five years, broke out all over. I could not sleep at night and would burst into tears at the slightest provocation—or no provocation at all. For nearly two years I fought this undignified and hysterical disease before, most grudgingly, I gave up and admitted that, in all probability, it was hair dye that was the villain of the piece" (1977a, 184–85). In spring 1955, she stopped using the dye and exposed what was, by that time, totally white hair. She decided that she should no longer perform with di Falco since the change in her hair would make their age difference so apparent.

In 1956, La Meri and di Falco left Queens and moved to separate apartments in Manhattan. They continued their personal and professional contact, however, as reported by di Falco (email of September 20, 2009) and by La Meri in her long unpublished hand-written *Chronology Notebook*, which notes their meetings and collaborations until at least July 1960. In December of that year, La Meri moved permanently to Cape Cod, and from that point on, there was no contact between them—which is strange, considering the very close and long-lasting personal and professional relationship they had had. Remembering his relationship with La Meri, di Falco wrote: "I probably knew La Meri as a woman better than anyone else including her husband Guido. She never could talk to him as she used to [to] me. Imagine 8 years together night and day, every day. We were entwined both humanly, intimately and artistic[ally]. . . . I do not believe either of us were truly in love with [each] other. The symbiotic relation perhaps was for some other reason. It is interesting that in 8 years, we never had a harsh word said to each other or expressed any anger" (ibid.). This relationship must have given La Meri a great deal of joy and peace in her life, but one can wonder why she maintained a friendship with Miller after they broke up but not with di Falco. Was that her choice, or his, or a mutual decision?

• • •

In the La Meri archive at Jacob's Pillow, there are two handwritten undated letters addressed only to "Dearest" and, while it is probable that they were meant for Carreras, it is impossible to know if they might have been intended for another man with whom La Meri had had an intimate relationship (such as Miller or di Falco). And whether they were ever sent or given to this "Dearest" is also impossible to know. They are very interesting because they provide deep insight into La Meri's inner demons, which somehow she seemed to be able to set aside or quiet down while she was performing, teaching, choreographing, and writing. In her autobiography and in the draft section that was not published, she mentions her lack of confidence and worries as a child and young person, and apparently such feelings continued into her adult life as well—at times becoming more and more intense. In these two letters she speaks of fear. For example, in one section she writes: "I reckon I'm a coward. I'm afraid to say what I think, & half afraid to think. In speaking I'm afraid I'm wrong: afraid I'll be misunderstood. Thinking, I'm afraid I don't rightly judge myself; afraid lest I shatter something intangible, delicate . . . You see I harbor a bugbear of fear that I try to keep buried, but that jumps up in spite of me, now & then. I'm afraid of myself, mortally afraid of my judgement, afraid of the future; or of that more distant future we call life; afraid of my love for you, & afraid of you." There are also other indications of her fear in the *Chronology Notebook*. Interspersed among notes of performances, travel, meetings with people, and so on are short statements about problems with health, anger, exhaustion, money worries—and fear. For example, in February 1956, she writes, "I am terribly afraid. I feel like I am at the bottom of a well screaming for help—no one hears me!"

In looking at the hundreds of photographs of La Meri both in performances and everyday life, in reading her published writings, in seeing how the critics around the world praised her and appreciated her art—it is hard to imagine that she suffered at all from any lack of confidence or debilitating fear, but such feelings were apparently there—and very intense at times— probably most intense during her time with Carreras. She is to be admired and honored for working through such anxiety and tension to accomplish all that she did in her life.

20. A Spanish flamenco dance in a *bata de cola* (dress with a train). This photograph was in the program for La Meri's performance March 25, 1938, at the Palacio de Bellas Artes, Mexico City.

21. A dance of the Spanish *escuela bolera* (bolero school), the dance genre that dates from the eighteenth century and combines ballet with regional Spanish dance forms. The dance in this photograph is probably "Bolero Antico of 1830," with music by F. Boghen, which was in La Meri's repertoire from ca. 1930 to the mid-1940s.

22. La Meri's sister, Lilian. In the 1948 edition of La Meri's *Spanish Dancing*, the dance is identified as "Sevillanas *circa* 1900" and the photographer as Philcox.

23. La Meri with Peter di Falco in their "Sevillanas." This is a traditional couple dance from Seville in southern Spain. La Meri probably first learned it during her study with Otero in 1929, and it was in her repertoire until the 1950s and in her teaching until her retirement. This photograph from the late 1940s is by Dwight Godwin.

24. La Meri teaching Spanish dance at Jacob's Pillow in 1953, with Mariano Parra front left.

25. "Chethat-al-Selah," translated on La Meri's programs as "Harem Dance of Salutation." One of La Meri's dances on Middle Eastern themes performed in the 1940s and perhaps 1950s. Photograph by Marcus Blechman. Courtesy of the Marcus Blechman Collection, Museum of the City of New York.

26. "Carabali," a Cuban-themed dance to music by Ernesto Lecuona, that was on La Meri's programs from the early 1930s to the 1950s. This photograph is dated 1944 and attributed to Mario Rosel.

27. "Jarabe Tapatío," or "Mexican Hat Dance," which La Meri learned during her first visit to Mexico in 1926 and kept in her repertoire until at least the end of the 1940s.

28. As a *gaucho* (cowboy) in "El Gato," a traditional Argentine dance with music by Andrés Chazarreta that La Meri performed from 1929 to the early 1950s. Photograph probably by Mario Rosel in 1944.

29. La Meri with di Falco in a version of the popular Andean dance "Huayno" which they performed from the late 1940s to the early 1950s. Their brochure of ca. 1950 credits Mario Rosel as the photographer.

30. Native American dance, probably of one of the Umatilla tribes in Oregon.

31. (*above*) "Tillana," a dance of the Bharatana- tyam genre that La Meri studied in India in 1937. She first performed this in Madras that year and it remained in her repertoire until the early 1950s.

32. (*left*) "Serimpi" (or Srimpi), a slow and elegant court dance from Central Java performed by women to *gamelan* music. After learning this in Java in 1937, La Meri performed it through the 1940s.

33. This is the dance that La Meri learned in Burma (Myanmar) in 1937 and first performed there. Sometimes titled the "Burmese Pwe," it remained in her repertoire until ca. 1950.

34. "Kikuzukushi" (traditional Japanese "chrysanthemum dance"), performed by La Meri 1937 to 1947.

35. Another addition to La Meri's repertoire was this comic Japanese folk dance identified as "Kappore," which she performed at least through 1939, in Latin America and perhaps elsewhere.

36. Marcus Blechman photograph of La Meri in 1945 with the masks of a "swollen woman" and "laughing man." These were the characters in the comic dance, "Nasu to Kabocha," which was choreographed for her in Japan in 1937 and remained in her repertoire until the early 1950s. Courtesy of the Marcus Blechman Collection, Museum of the City of New York.

37. A scene from one of La Meri's performances with Rebecca Harris who played the "lady's maid" on their concerts and touring from ca. 1946 to 1949. Harris would assist with the costume change on stage as La Meri gave the audience information about each dance.

7

Performance and Choreography in New York and Beyond (1940–1956) and Jacob's Pillow (1940s–1970s)

After settling in the United States, La Meri's own performing continued unabated until the mid-1950s. She presented her groups of dancers in various kinds of programs, her choreography developed in new and innovative ways, and she became a major figure in the Jacob's Pillow summer festivals and classes. In this section I will first discuss aspects of her performing and the development and activities of the groups; then her major innovative choreographic works; and finally, her involvement with Jacob's Pillow.

La Meri, the Natyas, and the Exotic Ballet

As noted in chapter 6, after their return to the United States, La Meri was engaged for performances in various locations. There are articles about a recital in Lansing, Michigan, on November 21, 1939, and many others on programs in New York and other states in the first two months of 1940 and later. A review of her January 12 concert in Middletown, New York, is particularly useful for anyone researching La Meri's works. It contains short but detailed descriptions of pieces that were in her repertoire for years, but for which there are no film records. Some of what is included probably came from the printed program for the concert—for example, that "The White Peacock" is "a musical visualization of the king of birds wandering among the flowers in a garden, proudly parading the richness of his plumage"; and "The Doll" is a "simulation of a mechanical toy, with its jerky movements and apparent jointlessness." In addition, however, for several of the dances, the unnamed critic summarizes the work beginning to end, which gives the reader a sense of its choreographic structure ("Versatile Art of La Meri Captivates Audience Here," *Middletown Times Herald,* January 13, 1940).

Very significant for La Meri to become known in New York City was her March 31 matinee at the St. James Theater. Performing with her were Lilian and Juana (cited on this program as Giovanna, the Italian version of her name). Introductions to each dance were given by Lilian, and this became a regular feature of La Meri's concerts. Since most audience members were unfamiliar with what they were viewing, explanations were a useful and appreciated addition—and they filled the time La Meri needed for costume changes. The printed programs also often contained some information about each piece. Such efforts to expand the public's knowledge of the genres were probably adopted in response to the occasional complaints from reviewers in London and the United States about the strangeness of La Meri's repertoire. And they were in line with La Meri's ongoing commitment as an "explainer."

The St. James program included dances from India, Java, Burma, Japan, the Middle East, Spain, Hawaii, and the Philippines—the usual broad range, and it elicited thoughtful and mainly positive responses. One of the most appreciative reviews was by John Martin (1893–1985), a well-known dance historian and critic who wrote for the *New York Times*. Martin appreciated the variety, costumes, and music of the concert and particularly noted the value of the explanations and how they added to the audience's understanding and enjoyment of these dances from "alien cultures" ("La Meri Appears in Racial Dances," April 1, 1940). La Meri also received praise for this concert and for the School of Natya from Basanta Koomar Roy (see chapter 6), who wrote, "Her work is more than an abiding message of the art of the dance; it is also a transcendent lesson in human brotherhood which is the real and the only sure foundation of permanent peace on earth." He noted the appreciation La Meri had received from organizations such as The India Society of London, the Institute of Oriental Research in Rome, and ministries of education in various countries that had sponsored her lecture-demonstrations and performances ("La Meri Opens Her School of Natya in New York").

There were some questions raised, however—perhaps because this sort of performance seemed so strange to those only familiar with the current ballet and modern dance arts. For example, Joseph Arnold Kaye, who regularly covered events for the magazine *Dance,* praised La Meri as "unique," the program as "fascinating," and the explanations as enlightening and "entertaining," but he also wrote: "Purely as a dancer, La Meri suffers somewhat from her absorption in the ethnographic details. One feels that she has subordinated herself to the dances, instead of combining natural artistry with the technical requirements of her medium." He also criticized a dance that La Meri had choreographed as an introduction to the Philippine "Tinikling," as "amateurishly done" ("Dance in Review," *Dance* 7/5, April 1940: 32–33).

Walter Terry, who had praised La Meri's lecture-demonstration, also expressed a mixed reaction, writing,

> La Meri is not, in my opinion, a great artist, for she lacks that indefinable essence that touches the beholder with great beauty, that seems to reach his very heart and that seems to actually influence his creed of living. But La Meri is a splendid craftsman of the dances and a true scholar. She is mistress of a variety of techniques and her mimetic powers enable her to capture the spirit of the place she is representing. ("La Meri Offers 'Dancing Tour of the World,'" *New York Herald Tribune*, April 1, 1940)

Over the next twenty years, as La Meri's work developed—and, probably, as he became familiar with the various genres she presented—Terry became a more appreciative reviewer and would invite her and members of her company to participate in events that he organized.

Radio also contributed to La Meri becoming known in New York. She was invited by Douglas A. MacKinnon, founder of the classical music station WXQR, to share her knowledge of world dance on his program, "There's Nothing New in Music," on March 26. After he interviewed her and she demonstrated "the rhythms of India and Spain with ankle bells, drums, castanets," he recommended the listeners attend her March 31 concert. He then invited La Meri back on May 28 to present on the "melodic forms of the dance-songs of India and of Spain" and opened the program with an announcement about the School of Natya, the classes offered there, and the lectures (reunions), which he also highly recommended (typed texts in Jacob's Pillow archive). On May 28, La Meri was performing with other dancers and musicians at the studio of Juan de Beaucaire Montalvo,[1] so either she had rushed from one event to the other, or the radio show had been prerecorded.

La Meri and St. Denis collaborated in various performance projects in addition to establishing the School of Natya and organizing its reunions. One of their most interesting endeavors was a joint concert on August 7,

1940, at the Dance Theatre of the Y.M. and Y.W.H.A. (Young Men's and Young Women's Hebrew Association) in which they contrasted "authenticity" and "theatricality." Each one performed dances from what was termed their "Oriental" repertoire. Except for one "creative" work ("Lasyanatana"), La Meri's were all stagings of actual dances from India and Java that she had learned while in those countries. And, except for one "authentic" work (the Javanese "Srimpi"), St. Denis, "in her own words 'did what she darn pleased,'" as quoted by Rosalyn Krokover, while presenting "her own romantic interpretations of the eastern countries." In Krokover's opinion: "The contrasts were startling. We owe a deep debt of gratitude to Miss St. Denis for having aroused our curiosity over a period of years in this distant, fascinating world, and to La Meri for her untiring efforts in satisfying our curiosity ("St. Denis and La Meri in Joint Program," *Musical Courier*, August 15, 1940, 9).

In his review for *The New Leader*, noted author and critic Joseph T. Shipley (1893–1988) wrote about this concert in relation to the world at war:

A fuller life, a richer civilization, is measured by its culture, its arts. And if we who live through troubled years are to preserve any measure of the civilization we want for our children, we too must find it—despite the pressure of all our burdens—in the pursuit of the arts. . . . It is for art, not money, not food: freedom to grow in wisdom and in art—that the forces against Fascism ultimately stand.

He notes that "[t]hese thoughts came to me while watching, last week, a significant new step in the interpretation of the Orient to America" and writes with great appreciation about the work of St. Denis and La Meri and their concert ("There Is Still Dancing," August 24, 1940, 6). There were also appreciative reviews in other publications, such as *American Dancer* and *Dance Observer*.

Remembering this event from many years later, La Meri writes that St. Denis "was absolutely wonderful to work with. Though I felt she loved me and wanted me to succeed, there was, nevertheless, a sense of competition between us that made each of us work to give the very best performance possible" (1977a, 152). Even though she was sixty-one—twenty years older than La Meri—St. Denis had not lost her ability to perform well or her competitive spirit.

While La Meri had done most of her performing as a solo artist, or, at times, with one or two "assisting" dancers, in New York (as previously in Italy) she began to include her best students in the concerts. In the beginning, they would only perform dances they learned from her, but later, some began to develop and present their own choreographies. The Natya Experimental Group or Natya Dancers (sometimes referred to as La Meri's Company) debuted in 1940, and by the middle of that decade had grown to more than ten members. Then, in October 1947, La Meri introduced what she called the Exotic Ballet, a group of twelve to fourteen that included several of the Natyas, other former students, and her recently recruited male dancers.[2]

Two dancers who worked regularly with La Meri in New York were her sister Lilian and Carreras's niece Juana. In the 1940s, both Lilian (as she progressed from the age of forty-eight to fifty-eight) and La Meri (going from forty-one to fifty-one) appeared in numerous performances (more than fifty or sixty each in 1947, for example) as well as keeping up their heavy teaching schedules (and La Meri her choreography). Lilian continued performing until at least 1952. Juana was not listed as a member of the Natyas or the Exotic Ballet, but from July 1940 through around May 1949, she danced in many of La Meri's productions as well as her own—after which she embarked on a six-month tour in Europe (see Schwarz). Juana lived with La Meri and Carreras in the early 1940s, and in her letters to Lilian, La Meri frequently wrote of conflicts with "Jo"—both as housemate and student.

Other important Natya and Exotic Ballet dancers (with the years for which there is evidence of their participation) were Edna Dieman (1943 or '44 to 1950), Marilyn Duberstein (1946–52), Richard Cressy (1944–48), Renato Magni (1944–49), Lillian Rollo (1944–48), Rebecca Harris (1945–52), and Peter di Falco (1946–54). A fifteen-page brochure for the 1947–48 season includes La Meri's biography, brief biographies of the twelve company members, descriptions of eleven of La Meri's choreographed works, including the "ethnic ballets" discussed below—and photographs of all. One can wonder how La Meri's dancers were able to cover their living and course expenses while studying, rehearsing, and performing with her. Those who taught at the EDC would have gained some income from that, but not enough to live on.

After the war years, La Meri toured several times—with her solo performance "Dances and Costumes around the World," with an ensemble of dancers that included di Falco, and with programs that she and di Falco shared as "artistic partners" (*Chronology 1973*). Because there were constant financial problems in maintaining the EDC and funding La Meri's new productions, touring seemed the only feasible way to gain sufficient funds. As she writes: "Every cent I made on the road—and it was not much, for I was too desperate to hold out for high fees—-went into the seemingly insatiable maw of the Ethnologic Dance Center. And I shudder to think how often Lilian threw what money she could muster into the same cause." She adds that "it was not the school but the road work and the theater that were paying the bills" (1977a, 162).

For her solo performances, La Meri was assisted on stage by Rebecca Harris as her "lady's maid."[3] In addition to engagements in the United States, from late April to late July 1948, La Meri and Harris toured in Mexico, Panama, Ecuador, and Peru with three versions of the solo program (1977a, 168–72). In her autobiography, La Meri describes the stage setting for these performances:

> It consisted of a little dressing room with table and costume rack placed upstage center behind the cyclorama. At the end of each dance the cyclorama opened, and I went into this dressing room to change, chatting with the audience as I donned the next costume. Becky, dressed as a maid, helped me change, and with carefully routine movements she screened me with the larger portions of my costumes. (1977a, 168)

In her "chatting," La Meri would tell the audience about the next dance and its costumes. She writes that while this "commentary became a confusing mélange of English, Spanish and Italian, it proved very successful" (*Chronology 1973*, 11).

It was apparently not easy to obtain bookings for the ensemble groups. A 1944–45 tour brochure announced that La Meri and seven Natya dancers would be available for performances of "Dances of Many Lands," but there is nothing in the archives about any engagements outside New York in that season. The following year, under the management of Vera Bull Hull (1885–1953), there was some touring of La Meri and five dancers with a few performances in late 1945 and early 1946. A March 1946 article in *Dance News* announced that La Meri had signed with the National Concert and Artists Corporation (NCAC) for a twenty-four-week cross-country tour beginning in October 1946 but noted that she would only be able to accept a few of the possible engagements because of prior commitments ("La Meri Signs with NCAC," VIII/3, 1, 7).

There was more ensemble touring in 1948 and 1949, mostly scheduled in central and northern states during the winter months—when travel could be difficult due to the weather. From January to March 1948, there were performances in Michigan, Iowa, Missouri, Illinois, and Minnesota with no problems on the road; but the next year was a totally different story. For the 1949 tour group, which included di Falco, Eleanor Oliver, and Marilyn Duberstein, everything was fine in January and early February as they traveled in La Meri's station wagon to cities in Illinois and Missouri. However, as they tried to get through Colorado and on to Utah, they experienced what La Meri has called "a never-to-be-forgotten trip." There were severe snow storms on the west side of the Rocky Mountains, travel advisories giving strong warnings not to drive on the roads they had to take—and all over those highways, crashed and stalled cars and trucks. However, despite her extreme anxiety about both the travel conditions and the reliability of her car in that weather, the indefatigable La Meri couldn't imagine giving up and stopping. They pushed on and with great difficulty made it through the worst of the winter weather—and finally to Salt Lake City for their February 16 performance. La Meri was the only experienced driver in the group, so she had to cope with the challenges. Di Falco had been learning to drive from her but was not yet ready to take the wheel on this kind of journey (1977a, 175–79; 1987 interview with Pat Taylor).

As noted in the previous chapter, di Falco had come to New York City early in January 1946 to begin his work with La Meri. Almost immediately he began to acquire a growing repertoire of dances. His first role was as one of the Five Rivers in La Meri's *Krishna and Radha* at the EDC (January 14–17), and in the February 19–20 program at the EDC, he performed in *Swan Lake* and *Voodoo Moon*. On March 7, while La Meri was touring with Shawn in Texas and Florida, di Falco and other members of the company presented a program of Pacific area dances at the American Museum of Natural History (AMNH). In the summer of 1946, in addition to taking the courses at Jacob's Pillow, he performed there with La Meri's group, and, as discussed in chapter 6, his personal relationship with her began sometime after that.

The career of di Falco as a dance artist continued to develop. He was listed as a Natya dancer in the September 1946 program brochure, and as a member of the Exotic Ballet, when it debuted under that name in October 1947, and after that, he performed in the ensemble tours to various parts of the United States. By the late 1940s, di Falco had become La Meri's artistic partner—as well as her student and lover. In her autobiography, where she makes no mention of the close relationship they had, she writes that she had "decided to groom di Falco as a partner" (175). Beginning with early April 1947 performances in Florida and continuing through 1954, they performed as collaborating artists in New York, at Jacob's Pillow, and on tours. The agent Clark H. Getts promoted their work with illustrated brochures such as "La Meri & di Falco Offering the Most Varied Program on the American Stage." A typical concert would include both solos by each and works that they performed together.

Di Falco began to choreograph solos and duets for himself and his students as well as humorous works derived from literature. These included Voltaire's 1750 story, "Bababec and the Fakirs," and Thomas Mann's 1940 novella, *The Transposed Heads*, which he developed using Indian dance techniques. An unidentified article in volume 20 of La Meri's scrapbooks in NYPL speaks very highly of his performance and choreography. Referring to the concert of La Meri and her company at the Needle Trades High School on December 1, 1952 (part of the Students Dance Recital series), the reviewer wrote: "Di Falco is an unashamedly graceful, masculine dancer, has formidable stage presence and his one satiric Indian group work, Bababec, and his three Latin-American dances show choreographic flair. It is greatly to be hoped that he will find many friendly stages open to his flowering skill." He continued choreographing and performing "ethnic" and related dances for the rest of the decade. As noted in chapter 6, he and La Meri stopped performing together when she could no longer dye her hair, and the age difference between them became too prominent. Their last performance was on May 24, 1955, in Worcester, Massachusetts. After that, di Falco helped La Meri with the production design of her "Little Show" (see below). He also created the Di Falco Dance Theatre which debuted on March 9, 1956, in a benefit for the Gold Star Wives of America at the High School of Performing Arts in New York City. There followed other performances in New York and on tour until sometime in 1959, when he decided to stop touring, to settle in New York, and to begin a new career in ballroom dance.

La Meri's "Little Show," which she performed from July 1955 to sometime in 1956, was a totally new venture. With what seems to have been her

unflagging energy, even in her late fifties, she had put together a purpose-
fully light entertainment with her own career as the theme in order to raise
money for her "serious" endeavors—and she worked several months to
develop it. She writes:

> For laughs—that commodity so prized by American audiences—I
> would relate my experiences during my studies in foreign lands, dra-
> matizing myself as a stupid one who could not comprehend anything.
> I would wear glamorous evening dresses, using only castanets for props
> and scarves for the dances themselves. . . . I pictured myself as the Vic-
> tor Borge of the dance. (1977a, 186)

This new direction was motivated by the dire financial situation of the EDC
and the lack of funds for her choreographic projects. Since both seemed
doomed without some source of income, she "contemplated the rocky road
of commercial 'showbiz'" (ibid.).

The first presentations of the "Little Show" were probably those of July
28 and 29 at the Berkshire Playhouse in Stockbridge, Massachusetts. While
there was some positive reaction to this and other performances, La Meri's
reputation as "an erudite and serious artist" seemed to prevent approval
among many. In his review for the *Berkshire Evening Eagle*, critic Richard V.
Happel (1903–1988) praised it highly as "a polished and sophisticated tour
de force of showmanship"; and included interesting details about its contents
("La Meri Little Show Bridges Two Arts," July 29, 1955). However, most of the
later reviews were critical. For example, after the December 5, 1955, performance at the Brooklyn Academy of Music, Doris Hering praised the first half
of the program, but said of the second part:

> Where before she had been lightly ironic in talking about herself,
> yet straight forward in her little dances, La Meri suddenly began to
> mock the dancing that had occupied her whole professional life. . . .
> The deprecation of the dance forms robbed the program of its point.
> It was as though La Meri were publicly questioning her own artistic
> faith. ("La Meri's 'Little Show,'" *Dance Magazine* XXX/2, February
> 1956, 11)

In another review of the same performance, the critic describes it as an autobiographical travelogue via [La Meri's] study of the ethnic dance forms. She began here in the USA and traveled southward through South and Central America and then across the seas to Spain. The second half of the program toured the Near and Far East, returning home to the American Indian. Snatches of dance accompanied each stop on the tour. However, there was little evidence of the one-time serious artist. It was all in fun and all for fun . . . [a] travesty of her own art. (L.G. "La Meri's 'Little Show,'" *Dance Observer* 23/3, March 1956, 43)

La Meri was disappointed by the negative reactions. She writes "Too many influential persons were disturbed by my laughing at myself," and while she could have obtained bookings in supper clubs rather than theaters, she was not comfortable with that and abandoned the project. Her "Little Show," as she writes, "failed to save the center financially." She then writes that, while she was very depressed, she "just hung in there for two years doing whatever presented itself"—until she decided to move to Cape Cod (1977a, 186–87). Her last years in New York and life in Cape Cod will be discussed in chapter 8.

A New Direction: The "Ethnic Ballets"

In the 1940s and early 1950s, in addition to her exhausting schedule of teaching, preparing programs for the EDC and other venues, developing the skills and artistry of her ensemble dancers, choreographing single dances for herself and for members of the ensemble, rehearsing, and other activities, La Meri set off in a new direction. She began choreographing what she termed ethnic or ethnologic ballets. These were longer works, usually with a story line and characters, that incorporated the technique of one of the international dance languages she had learned. Such works became regular features in her reunions and concerts in New York City, and at Jacob's Pillow and other locations. In the beginning, the male as well as the female characters were danced by women, as there were no men in La Meri's company until 1944.

Indian Themes

The first "ethnic ballet," *Krishna Gopala*, was premiered September 3, 1940, and continued to be performed until at least November 1947. Based on pas-

sages from the *Gita Govinda* of the Indian poet Jaidev (Jayadeva, twelfth century CE), it depicted the Hindu god Krishna enjoying the company of Gopis
(milkmaids) including Radha, who became his eternal love. The music was
by Vishnu Dass Shirali, composer and music director, who had collaborated
with Uday Shankar in the 1930s. Its debut in a School of Natya student recital
featured Hadassah in the role of Krishna. In its second performance, November 2, on the Washington Irving High School Students' Dance Recital Series,
La Meri danced the title role; St. Denis spoke as the "Voice of the Ages"; and
eight Natya Dancers portrayed Radha and the other characters. In a long and
appreciative review, a critic pointed out that, with this work, La Meri "draws
attention to an aspect of the Indian dance which has been largely overlooked;
that there is as much room . . . for original creation within the framework
of long tradition as there is in ballet" (F.X.G. Unidentified publication in La
Meri's archive in the NYPL).

By the end of August 1941, La Meri had completed two more works on
Indian themes: *Gauba's Journey to Paradise*—in the repertoire from August
12 until at least February 1948, and *Devi Murti*—from August 26 until at least
December 30, 1947. *Gauba's Journey,* set to recorded music of Vishnu Dass
Shirali and Wana Singh, was a comic piece based on a folktale published in
the early twentieth century by an Indian author named Baba Trinco. It tells
of an unhappy gardener with a talkative wife who tries to escape to paradise
hanging on the tail of a "celestial elephant." Despite his annoyance with his
wife, Gauba invites her to come along, and she invites the entire village and
begins her continual talking. In reaction, Gauba lets go of the elephant's tail,
and they all fall back to earth. Always one for a new challenge, La Meri
danced the role of the elephant, and in three of her August 1941 letters to
Lilian, she writes about how hard Carreras was working to construct and
decorate the elephant head for her costume. In his review of a 1947 performance of this work, Walter Terry praised "the slim and lovely La Meri" as
"surprisingly, a wonderfully lumbersome elephant ("The Dance," *New York
Herald Tribune,* December 29, 1947). In contrast to her comic role in *Gauba's
Journey*, La Meri's character in *Devi Murti* was that of the Hindu "Supreme
Goddess" in five serious and dramatic manifestations: Maha-Deva (the Abstract), Parvati (the Wife), Ambika (the Teacher), Dourga (the Embattled),
and Kali (the Destroyer). The Natyas served as the goddess's handmaidens
and performed interludes while La Meri changed costumes.

The three works on Indian themes were presented together on November 13, 1941, in a concert at the Barbizon-Plaza Theater (sponsored by the India League of America), and at the Guild Theater on December 21. Both performances received serious press coverage. In his enthusiastic review of the Guild Theater concert, Terry discusses all three ballets in detail, and expresses particular appreciation for the fact that before each work, La Meri briefly related its story and explained the meanings of the *mudras* (hand gestures) that were used in the telling of it. He considered *Devi Murti* "the most rewarding work, from an Occidental viewpoint," but praised the other two as well. Of La Meri, he wrote that she "is not only a fine dancer, but also a vivid theater personality, handsome and skilled in the ways of dramatic projection." He was apparently becoming more appreciative of her strengths—and more open to the strangeness of her non-Western repertoire. Of the Natya dancers, he wrote: "The American girls of the company have absorbed both the technique and the style of the Indian dance to an amazing degree ("La Meri Shows Lore of India in Dance Program," *New York Herald Tribune*, December 21, 1941).

In the magazine *The American Dancer*, H.D. (undoubtedly Helen Dzermolinska) also highly praised *Devi Murti*, writing that

> all of the aspects of the Supreme Goddess are exalted (and thrillingly theatrical), and probably of them all, the last, the aspect of Kali, the goddess of destruction, disemboweling her victims and drinking their blood is genuinely pulse-stopping. La Meri uses such devices as fangs and claws to suggest the savage goddess, but her art alone is device enough to frighten the onlooker into stone.

She notes that this work was followed by *Gauba's Journey*, with La Meri as the "droll" Celestial Elephant, a role "worlds removed" from the divinities in *Devi Murti*. This reviewer also expressed great appreciation for La Meri's introduction to each work and the strengths of the company members ("LA MERI, An Evening of Hindu Natya at the Barbizon-Plaza, November 13," *American Dancer* XV/2 (December 1941): 19, 28).

In contrast to such enthusiastic appreciation, John Martin (in his review of the December 21 concert), found the works "well-conceived," but felt that "the performance itself never passed beyond the stage of a school exhibition." He states that this was the students' "first public appearance" (apparently not considering either the EDC or the Barbizon Plaza performances as "public") and wonders

> if it is possible to put a group of young girls into such a highly developed and totally alien medium as the Hindu dance and keep them from being patently amateurish. The school entertainment atmosphere was not diminished by the fact that all male roles were played by girls, and in one number the prettiest of them appeared with mustache and chin whiskers painted on. . . . Judged according to school standards, however, it was a creditable showing, excellently rehearsed and lavishly costumed.

He finishes by noting that "[t]he audience was of good size and applauded heartily ("La Meri Presents 3 Dances of India," *New York Times*, December 22, 1941).

Hawaiian, Other Indian, and Spanish Themes

The next ethnic ballet that La Meri choreographed was on a Hawaiian theme. *Ea Mai Hawaiinuiakea* (Legend of the Birth of the Islands) was first presented at the Master Institute of United Artists Theatre on March 11, 1942, and stayed in the repertoire until at least the end of 1947. Based on an ancient Hawaiian chant, it was performed to recorded traditional Hawaiian music and chants and included explanations in English between the dances of various characters. La Meri was "Hawaii" and the six Natyas played Pele (the volcano goddess), The Trees, The Flowers, The Waters, and The Skies. In his review of its presentation at the Barbizon-Plaza Theatre on February 2, 1943, noted dance writer, critic, and editor Anatole Chujoy (1894–1969) praised the professional quality of the company members, particularly noting their "substantial dance technique" and "fine quality of projection" ("Dance in Review: La Meri" *Dance News*, March 1943).

During the next several years, La Meri created and presented more such works. They include *Rama Breaks the Bow*, a Javanese dance-drama premiered in 1943; *Krishna and Radha*, a work on the Hindu legend co-choreographed with Ted Shawn, and with La Meri and Shawn dancing the title roles (1945–1946); *Surpanakha in Love*, a South Indian dance drama (1944); and a scene from Delibes's 1883 Indian-themed opera *Lakmé*, which included dances using Kathak and other Indian techniques, first shown in 1946. She also developed works on Spanish themes such as *Iberia* (Debussy), which portrayed a young Gypsy woman in the time of Goya married to an elderly duke and *El Amor Brujo* (usually translated as "Love the Magician").

La Meri was first introduced to the music and theme of *El Amor Brujo* in the early 1930s when she and Carreras met with the composer Manuel de Falla and discussed his vision for how the story and characters should be staged (see chapter 3). From 1933 through the early 1940s, she worked on choreography related to the theme, and at times presented sections in performances. Her creation of the entire work debuted at the EDC reunion of April 11, 1944, and a new complete version was created for the 1953 season at Jacob's Pillow. In his very positive review, Walter Terry noted that La Meri treated the work

> as a narrative rather than as a series of dances. Foreboding lulls alternate with tempests of passion and of terror . . . And as, from time to time, heightened dance action springs forth from pantomimic preludes, so also does formal choreographic pattern emerge, sometimes slowly or again with shocking speed, from the restless strolling or taut inaction of the figures in the drama.

About the characters, he wrote that La Meri, in

> the principal part of the haunted and terrified Candelas . . . performed superbly, communicating emotional intensities of almost unbearable compulsion as well as the formal outlines, aristocratic and tempestuous, of Spanish dance. Ted Shawn . . . appeared as the Spectre and gave a stunning enactment, subtle yet dramatically powerful, and so expertly did he generate the air of fateful magic necessary to his part that his presence was felt, mirrored in the fear-stricken faces of the others, even after he had left the stage.

Terry also praised the performances of Carola Goya as Lucia, di Falco as Carmelo, and Lilian as the Witch ("Jacob's Pillow Festival," *New York Herald Tribune*, August 13, 1953). A silent film was made of this production and is in the La Meri Archive at the New York Public Library Dance Collection.[4]

Swan Lake

In addition to creating dance theater works on themes from the cultural contexts of the different ethnic dance genres, La Meri also began exploring another direction—the use of the Indian dance language—particularly that of Bharatanatyam—with Western music and themes. Probably the most innovative and lauded of these was her production in 1944 of *Swan Lake* using the Tchaikovsky score and telling the traditional story in Hindu gesture language. On February 19, there was a preview for the press at the EDC and three days later a sold-out performance for the public. Either the entire work or excerpts from it continued to be presented until at least 1985.

At some point during or after her creation of this work La Meri wrote a fifteen-page essay, "Tchaikowsky's 'Swan Lake' in the idiom of the Indian Dance" (copies are in NYPL and SAPL). In it, she relates that she and one of her Natyas had attended a performance of *Swan Lake* by a major (unnamed) ballet company. La Meri had seen this work before, but this time, she and her student began noticing and discussing the "inadequacy of the pantomime." Soon after, during a chance meeting with dance specialist Anatole Chujoy, La Meri mentioned her reaction to the performance, and during their discussion, he talked about the traditions and characteristics of ballet pantomime. She writes in the essay that these experiences led her to the idea of staging a version of the work using Hindu dance gesture and movement (1–2). Her purposes for embarking on the project were "to show the great clarity of Hindu gestures when applied to a well-known story"; and to show the range and completeness of the Hindu technique—that it is not limited to depicting only the stories and characters of Hindu traditions (2–3). Not wanting to do the entire four-act ballet, she developed a two-part structure: a pantomimed prologue followed by the main section, which was similar to the second act of the traditional ballet.

The first production was reviewed and discussed in several publications, including *Dance News, Modern Music,* the *Christian Science Monitor,* the *New York Times* and the *Herald Tribune.* For the most part, those responses as well as reviews of later productions highly praised both the idea of the Hindu *Swan Lake* and its realization—although a few critics were not so enthusiastic. As could be expected, Chujoy was highly supportive, writing that "La Meri has achieved a remarkable choreographic feat in translating

Swan Lake into the Hindu Dance Idiom." He notes that, while the "die-hard balletomane" seeing this version might feel "nostalgia and shock," such reactions will "wear off as soon as one gets used to the idea of this not being a ballet performance." In fact, in his opinion, "[t]he story of Swan Lake . . . comes forth in La Meri's version with much greater coherence and clarity than in any other production." He goes on to praise every aspect of its conception and realization as well as the performances of La Meri and the rest of the cast ("Dance in Review: Swan Lake in Hindu Idiom," *Dance News*, March 1944).

Writing in the New York German language paper, *Staats-Zeitung und Herold*, Felix Cleve, long an enthusiastic supporter of La Meri's work, described her *Swan Lake* as "one of the boldest experiments in the history of the dance art," which succeeded totally. He discusses the "nature of the experiment" and its significance in relation to practices in both ballet and opera and to La Meri's work from her January 1930 performance in Vienna through her subsequent travels and research. He concludes: "The performance emerged as from a perfect mold. Never was La Meri more herself as in this case; never had her always talented and enthusiastic co-workers given their finest best with more enthusiasm than on this memorable occasion" (Cleve, 1944. Original and translation in NYPL Archive, vol. VII). As usual, Cleve expressed his complete respect and admiration for La Meri's work as an artist and innovator.

Chujoy was not the only critic to find La Meri's *Swan Lake* superior to the traditional balletic version. Joan Brodie, in her *Dance Observer* review of the December 30, 1947, performance at Times Hall in New York City, felt that "[t]he stylized language of the Hindu dance gave the work a touching folk character which the ballet idiom cannot do, because it is too flashy and too much concerned with technical brilliance" ("La Meri," XV/2, February 1948: 21). And in response to the same performance, Walter Terry wrote:

> In some instances it seems to me to be superior to the Occidental original, particularly in the purely pantomimic passages where the eloquence of the Hindu gesture language far surpasses the communicability of ballet's circumscribed and half-forgotten mime. In its pure dance passages as well as in its wonderfully patterned story-telling, La Meri's "Swan Lake" is an enchanting work, a manifestation of dance poetry at its loveliest. ("The Dance," *New York Herald Tribune*, December 31, 1947)

Terry had also written an informative and appreciative review of a July 19, 1946, program at Jacob's Pillow, when both La Meri's two-part *Swan Lake* and excerpts from the Petipa-derived ballet were performed one after the other to provide an opportunity to compare the two versions. He notes that determining which version is better would be "a matter of taste," and that "[i]n matters of all-around virtuosity, Petipa wins, but when it comes to transforming a legend into theater, La Meri's Hindu 'Swan Lake' must receive first honors" ("The Dance," *New York Herald Tribune*, July 20, 1946).

Scheherazade

Another narrative work in the Western repertoire that La Meri reconceived in the Indian dance language was *Scheherazade*. This premiered March 6–7, 1945, at the EDC with the title role announced as played by La Meri or Lilian and other roles by members of the Natya group. Excerpts or the entire work continued to be performed until at least 1951. The music by Nikolai Rimsky-Korsakov dates from 1888, and ballet works had been created to that music since 1910, when Michel Fokine's *Scheherazade* was first presented by Diaghilev's Ballets Russes in Paris. For her version, La Meri chose the same four stories from the well-known *One Thousand and One Nights* that Rimsky-Korsakov had used for his composition and choreographed them in the Hindu gesture language and dance vocabulary.

This work also received enthusiastic critical responses. For example, in April 1945, Ruthelle Wade, executive editor of *Dance,* wrote:

> La Meri's *Scheherazade,* . . . shows up to an even greater advantage its superiority over the opera and ballet company productions of the same subject. . . . The Hindu idiom seems most suited for interpreting the violent emotions and dazzling imagination encountered in the oft-told adventures of Sinbad the Sailor, of Arabian princes and princesses . . . and of festival time in Bagdad. The choreography is a coherent, altogether satisfactory expression of Rimsky-Korsakov's music. . . . The performance of La Meri and her Natya dancers in this new *Scheherazade* is both refreshing and intelligent. (R.H., "Current Reviews," *Dance* XIX/4, 40)

In the May issue of *Dance,* a short article tells about the April 8 television presentation of this work, which was directed by Raymond Nelson for the

Charles B. Storm series of "Televisuals." Nelson had come to rehearsals at the EDC to watch *Scheherazade* and become familiar with its sections, entrances and exits, and overall structure. It was filmed from different angles by three cameras, and since the movement was spatially more contained than that of some other dance genres, Nelson considered the work "perfect for television" (quoted in "Televising a New Scheherazade," *Dance* XIX/5, 28–29).

Bach-Bharata Suite

La Meri's next innovation was the *Bach-Bharata Suite*, which officially premiered at the EDC on May 21, 1946 (after a preview performance on May 20). The whole work or parts continued to be presented until at least 1952, and La Meri performed the solo section during her 1948 Latin American concert tour. In contrast to the other "ethnic ballets," which had story lines and characters, this was a nonnarrative work. It incorporates the Bharatanatyam *nrtta* (or *nritta*)—pure or abstract dance vocabulary—in contrast to the *nrtya* (or *nritya*)—dance interpreting a story or song—which she had used in her previous works.

In a four-page statement about the suite (copies of which are in SAPL and NYPL), she states three reasons for doing this work. The first was to demonstrate "that Bharata-Natya is a *style of movement* [her emphasis] and far from being a purely racial and ethnologic vehicle, can be used as a technique to interpret the abstract dance-art of any nationality of artist." Secondly, she wanted "to remind Westerners that the hand gesture is only a very characteristic fraction of the complete dance-science of Bharata-Natya," and she enumerates the many other aspects of its movement. Finally, she wished to "set forth the universality of the artist-creator" by bringing together "two widely separated sources—Bach (1685–1750) and Bharata (who in the third Century drew into manuscript notes the technique which had been building since the 3rd Millenium B.C)." She ends the statement with an outline of the five sections of her *Bach-Bharata Suite*.[5] For each part, she names the Bach piece used and explains what she has done with it. For example, she writes that, in her solo to "Air on the G String," "the dancer's upper body follows the melodic line while the lower body follows the accompaniment." For the finale, to the Allegro of "Concerto in D Minor," she says that "the dancers move in a freer floor design, utilizing some of the more dynamic techniques of Bharata-Natya. . . . The soloist (La Meri) interprets the solo piano while the four other dancers . . . move for the orchestra. It will be easily seen that choreographic design repeats with repetition of musical design." In reading her notes, one is reminded of Ruth St. Denis's "music visualizations." However, St. Denis never used a set dance vocabulary for her works but found whatever movement she felt was appropriate to "visualize" the elements of the score she had chosen.

Like La Meri's other ethnic ballets, this work also received strong praise from the critics. In his review of its July 26, 1946, performance at Jacob's Pillow, Walter Terry termed it "a magnificent pure dance work" and continued: "The great music of Bach and the ancient Hindu dance find that they have in common elegance, economy, structure and emotional compulsion. . . . The result of this strange union of the classic East with the classic West is a work of storyless and timeless beauty" ("The Dance," *New York Herald Tribune*, July 27, 1946).

In her review of the same performance, Margaret Lloyd writes that the audience had "received it with wild enthusiasm," and notes that La Meri is "the first seriously to visualize Bach's music in Hindu dance terms" and that her earlier experiments in using Hindu dance with Western music and themes "perhaps may be regarded as preludes to this latest and loftiest work." After discussing the objections or prejudices that might oppose such a mixing of different cultural heritages, Lloyd concludes that the work "emerged in performance as a new artistic entity making its own intangible communication of the human spirit through the common instrument of the human body, turning incongruity into harmonious contiguity, and overcoming the sense of racial separateness with a sense of the oneness of mankind" (*Christian Science Monitor*, August 3, 1946). This statement brings to mind Lloyd's earlier question during World War II—about the potential for La Meri's work to have broad influence beyond the world of dance. In a short item on the EDC reunions, she had asked: "Who can say but that the work she is doing, interpreting through their dance forms the thought processes of the Oriental peoples, will not play its part in paving the way of understanding which must come in that union which will make the world whole" (*Christian Science Monitor*, January 1, 1943). La Meri herself had expressed the belief that world knowledge and experience of dance could contribute to world harmony and peace, and others had also come forward with similar beliefs—or hopes.

Drishyakava (The Seasons)

La Meri continued her exploration of combining Indian dance techniques with Western music in *Drishyakava (The Seasons)*, which was set to selections from Antonio Vivaldi's 1725 work, *The Four Seasons (Le quattro stagioni)*. Over twenty-five years, this was presented only four times: at Jacob's Pillow, August 11–15, 1953; in New York at the Juilliard School of Music, April 9 and 12, 1960; on Cape Cod, July 26–27, 1973, as part of La Meri's annual Summer Festival of Ethnic Dance; and a restaging by Matteo for his EthnoAmerican Dance Theatre performances in New York, February 16–19, 1978 (programs). The work was, of course, divided into four sections, each representing one of the seasons. "Spring" made reference to birds, streams, storms, children, and a dreaming shepherdess; "Summer" to heat, winds, a cuckoo, a dove, and folk dancers; "Autumn" to a "Drunkard's dream after the grape harvest" and then hunters, rabbits, and a stag; and "Winter" to "early rains," "icy winds," and slipping on icy surfaces (Neal 1989, 151–52; program for EDC production).

In his review of the 1953 performance at Jacob's Pillow, Walter Terry writes that, in this work as before, "La Meri has been wonderfully successful in uniting Eastern dance forms with Western musical forms," and he praises her "application of the classical gesture of the Hindu dance to the images inherent in the music." He notes that "La Meri, in the principal part, danced exquisitely and there were expert supporting performances by Di Falco, Matteo, Maria Fenton, and Jerane Michel ("Dance: Jacob's Pillow Festival," *New York Herald Tribune*, August 13, 1953).

The noted ballet choreographer Antony Tudor (1908–1987) taught at Jacob's Pillow along with La Meri and others, and in 1953 he had seen the premier of *The Seasons*. He was so impressed with it that he invited La Meri to stage it in New York for his students at the Juilliard School of Music. Richard V. Happel, reporter for the *Berkshire Eagle*, writes that Tudor had highly praised the work to him, and notes that this was an unusual reaction since "Mr. Tudor has never been one to drop words of praise with easy abandon." Happel goes on to report Tudor's invitation to La Meri, who agreed to restage the work but felt "trepidation" about "using students from the Juilliard dance department, who were untrained in ethnic work such as this suite demanded." However, her worries were apparently unfounded. As Happel writes, the first Juilliard performance on April 9, "with full orchestra of Juil-

liard students . . . quite bowled over the large audience," and its second per-
formance, on April 12, was totally sold-out ("Notes and Footnotes," *Berkshire Eagle*, April 12, 1960). It is interesting that in these Juilliard concerts, two of the student dancers in *The Seasons* (who were also cast in other works on the program) would eventually become internationally important leaders and innovators in the field of dance: Phillipa "Pina" Bausch (1940–2009), German choreographer and developer of the genre known as *tanztheater*; and Carl Wolz (1932–2002), a leading dance scholar and educator and the founder in 1988 of the World Dance Alliance, which is still in existence and has continuing international influence and importance.

Jacob's Pillow Dance Festival

La Meri taught and performed at Jacob's Pillow from its beginning into the 1970s. Her work there and relationship with Ted Shawn were important elements in her professional life. The roots of this institution go back to 1931, when Shawn purchased what was then a farm in the Berkshire Mountains in Massachusetts.[6] Beginning in 1933, he began to develop something that was hitherto unknown—an all-men's group of concert dancers. The members lived, rehearsed, and performed in that location—and toured nationally and internationally until 1940. During those years, more acreage was acquired, and the group constructed studios, performance spaces, cabins, a kitchen, and a dining hall—and with these facilities, summer courses for male dancers could be held both to further the profession of male concert dance and to help with expenses. In 1940, Shawn was trying to sell the property but was only able to lease it for summer festivals that year and in 1941 (Shawn, 3–6).

In the summer of 1940, the site was leased to dance educator Mary Washington Ball for what she titled the "Berkshire Hills Dance Festival," an event that featured performances of a variety of dance genres (Cunningham, 571; Shawn, 5). La Meri was one of the invited guest artists, and in addition to a matinee concert with dances from Spain, Asia, the Pacific, and Latin America (July 20), she gave three lecture-demonstrations: "Dancing in India," "Ethnologic Dance Costumes" and "Dancing in Spain." Walter Terry wrote that her concert was "a program rich in the dance treasures of the world" and that the "enthusiastic audience bestowed generous applause upon this dancing pilot and her rhythmic world tour" ("La Meri Offers Berkshire Hills Dance Recital," *New York Herald Tribune,* July 21, 1940). Being chosen to lecture and perform at this festival attests to the stature and reputation as a dance artist that La Meri was already developing in the United States. And this engagement marked the beginning of her many years as performing artist and teacher at what became "Jacob's Pillow." The next summer Shawn leased the property for a school and festival directed by the ballet artists Alicia Markova and Anton Dolin, which featured many prominent Ballet Theatre dancers. Shawn also participated as teacher and performing artist (Shawn, 5).

In 1941–42, a group of Berkshire residents formed a nonprofit corporation that bought the property, built a theater designed for dance performances, founded the Jacob's Pillow Dance Festival, Inc., and hired Shawn as its director (Shawn, 6, 14; Cunningham, 571). He continued in that position until his death in 1972, with a couple of years off. Each summer, the festival lasted several weeks and included both performances by dance artists and courses at the school—which Shawn termed "The University of the Dance." The variety of dance genres that were presented and taught through the years reflected Shawn's belief that dance should be appreciated in its many different aspects. Thus, the performances and curriculum at the Pillow included ballet, modern concert dance, and "ethnic" dance (Cunningham), and La Meri, of course, was a major contributor in the third area. In the 1952 and 1953 souvenir programs, she is identified as director of the Ethnic Dance Department and a member of the board of directors—roles that she might have also held in other years.

Once the Jacob's Pillow Dance Festival was established, La Meri frequently taught, staged works, and/or performed as soloist, with a partner, or with her group. In some years she was there for the whole season and in others for a few days or a week. During the 1942 opening season, she and her group presented works from India and Hawaii on the July 30 to August 1 program, and she taught Spanish dance classes from July 27 to 31. Such brief teaching and performance engagements were typical during the next three years, and in some of her other years at the Pillow, but 1946 was totally different. La Meri was engaged for the entire summer season (which ran from early July to late August), and her group of dancers (somewhere between fifteen and twenty) was the resident company and performed throughout the season along with other guest artists. In the press reviews and articles on the 1946

Pillow performances, the dancers are just referred to La Meri's "group." During this time, the EDC classes were continuing, so, for eight weeks, La Meri and Lilian were rushing back and forth between New York and the Pillow to cover the courses in both places (1977a, 164).

During this 1946 season, La Meri taught "ethnologic dance" (probably mainly or totally Spanish and Indian dance) and teachers' courses. The group's performances featured the ethnic ballets and were scheduled as follows: *Devi Murti* (July 5–6), Latin American dances (July 12–13), *Swan Lake* (July 19–20 and August 16–17), a scene from *Lakme* (July 23 and August 1), *Bach-Bharata Suite* (July 26–27), Indian gesture songs performed by La Meri (August 2–3), *Krishna and Radha* with La Meri and Shawn in the title roles (August 9–10), and *Iberia* (August 23–24). For each presentation, there had to be at least one rehearsal to prepare the dancers for their performance in a new theater space and the technical staff for their work.

It is hard to imagine how La Meri could have managed all the teaching, rehearsals, and performances that year, but she had planned to do even more. She writes that she "took typewriter and reference books to the Pillow with every intention of writing a book on Spanish dancing that had been commissioned by A.S. Barnes and Company." That turned out to be impossible. As she explains: "Alas for my good intentions, for the Pillow proved even more madly active than usual that summer. There were thirty-odd ex G.I.'s enrolled as students . . . When the last class of the day was over, my car stood ready to take a group of these pleasure-hungry ex-soldiers to the surrounding towns for movies, for drinks, for dancing." (1977a, 165). As noted previously, di Falco was one of the veterans at the Pillow that summer who had received G.I. Bill funding to study with Ted Shawn for two weeks prior to the regular session and then in the regular session itself. He also performed in nearly all of La Meri's concerts. That summer was not only extremely busy for La Meri. Shawn remembered it as "a complete nightmare" for himself. He had scheduled opera and opera ballet performances as well as the other dance events, there was major and extremely loud construction taking place on the site, and he had agreed to create choreography for seventeen opera ballets (Shawn, 13).

After 1946, La Meri continued to be highly involved in the Jacob's Pillow school and performances, and often for the entire season. In the 1950 program, for example, she and di Falco were featured in the brochure as

"The Only Dance Artists to be Engaged"—probably meaning engaged for the whole six weeks since there were other dancers and choreographers on the different programs. During this season, La Meri performed every week in six of the programs—as a soloist in Gesture Songs (July 26–29), with di Falco in Spanish dances (August 2–5) and a Latin American program (August 18–19), and in a program of Indian and Near Eastern dances with St. Denis and Shawn (August 25–26). The whole group, including La Meri, di Falco, and Lilian, performed *Yaravi,* a dance-drama based on the culture of the Otavalo people in Ecuador, and a scene from *Scheherazade* (August 9–12) and a new work, *Danzas Fantasticas* (September 1–2). And, of course, all of this was in addition to intensive teaching. La Meri and di Falco continued to be full time during the Pillow's 1951, 1952, and 1953 seasons. And, in the fall of 1952, Shawn organized and led a nine-week Jacob's Pillow tour that had bookings in some fifty cities in the northeastern states (October 4 to December 5). The performers included Shawn, La Meri, modern dance artist Myra Kinch, ballerina Tatiana Grantzeva, and other regular Pillow artists (Jacob's Pillow 1952 Program, 6–7; newspaper clippings).

The last time La Meri was at the Pillow for the full season was 1953. During her ten weeks there, she was even busier than usual—teaching Spanish and Indian dance with di Falco and Lilian and performing and/or choreographing for four productions. And this year, a new development was on the program. As La Meri writes in her autobiography: "Besides a couple of weeks when I danced solos and duets with Di Falco, there was, for the first time in the history of the Pillow, a week of an all-ethnic program." Works included, besides single dances, her production of *El Amor Brujo,* with Shawn, Goya, Di Falco, Lilian, La Meri and the group, and the first production of *Drishya-kava,* with La Meri, di Falco, and six or seven other dancers (1977a, 184; see also *Chronology 1973,* 9). That was the summer when I was at the Pillow and met and studied with La Meri and the others.

There is no record of La Meri at Jacob's Pillow again until 1959, when she performed July 7–11, gave one lecture-demonstration, and probably taught a few classes. In the 1960 season, La Meri (now 61) performed three works on the June 30 –July 3 program: her Swan Queen solo from *Swan Lake*; a suite of two solos: "Recuerdo" and "Renacimiento," choreographed by di Falco to music by the Catalan composer Frederic Mompou (1893–1987); and a new work she had created for herself and four other dancers. In her writings and chronologies, she titles this *Escape*, but on the Jacob's Pillow program it is called *Variations on a Theme* and has four parts: "Resignation," "Play," "Work," "Defiance." The piano music was composed and played by Frederick Bristol.

This last work was based on La Meri's developing concept of what she termed "within techniques," which she says she had "discovered" in 1958 (1977b, 37). She defines the term as referring to "subtleties of body control that are an integral part of certain ethnic techniques" in contrast to specific steps, patterns, or rhythms. She gives as examples:

The delicate subtlety of emotional expression in Japanese dance.
The steady dynamic flow of Javanese dance.
The spiral line of Spanish dance.
The isolated controls of Indian dance.
The impressive ground contacts of the Amerind, flamenco, Kathak, and many others. (ibid., 23)

La Meri felt that such qualities could be taught in any dance context to increase students' understanding of movement and its expressive range, and she discusses the different types of techniques and how they might be used (ibid., 23–29, 37). She writes that in 1958, as part of her exploration of the concept, she had "made a series of short solos embodying the within techniques of certain ethnic forms to selected short pieces by western composers" and performed them at Jacob's Pillow, where "they were received pleasantly enough" (ibid., 37). This was not the high praise to which she was accustomed, but the response didn't discourage her from further experimental work in this direction. It is indicative of her never ending curiosity and her characteristic ability to muster focus and energy even amid disappointments that she began investigating this new direction after the devastating depression she had felt during the previous year. Unfortunately, however, the 1960 work did not create much enthusiasm among the public at the Pillow performances (ibid.), and La Meri apparently abandoned any further choreographic exploration of the "within techniques." She did introduce them, however, to some of her classes in Cape Cod (see chapter 8).

La Meri had brief engagements at the Pillow in 1961, 1962, and 1963. In 1964, she presented the revival of her *Swan Lake*, which she had staged in

June for the Dieman-Bennett Dance Theatre of the Hemispheres in Cedar Rapids, Iowa. Edna Dieman (1903–1999) had studied and performed with La Meri from 1943 or 1944 to 1951 when she returned to her birth city and with dancer and choreographer Julia Bennett (1916–2014), founded the school and company that would make innovative and important contributions to the culture of that city. In the *Swan Lake* revival—both in Cedar Rapids, June 11, and at Jacob's Pillow, July 21 to 25—La Meri again danced the role of the Swan Queen (now at age 66!) and other leading roles were performed by Matteo, and Julia Bennett. As usual, the work was greatly appreciated by the critics. Walter Terry, for example, praised the production and wrote that La Meri "beautiful of face, although a trifle matronly in build, gave a shining performance" ("Dance at Jacob's Pillow: Blending East and West" *New York Herald Tribune*, July 22, 1964). That summer, on August 23, La Meri also gave a lecture, "The Enrichment of Contemporary Dance through Use of Ethnic Source Materials" (news release).

In 1966, La Meri gave two lectures at the Pillow, and probably also taught. In her Christmas letter to Olivia Matteson, she writes that, while there, she and Shawn had discussed what they saw as a waning interest in ethnic dance in the United States, and that they planned to develop a program for the following summer that would begin to "build up the field." In 1967, La Meri spent six weeks at the Pillow, as head of the Ethnic Dance Department and was assisted by Rebecca Harris. Classes were also taught by Mariano Parra and other guest teachers, and the curriculum included classes in Spanish dance, Mexican and American folk dances, and other genres. Out of a total of twenty-four performing artists or groups, seven were in a field of ethnic dance: Mariano Parra and Matteo with their companies, Rebecca Harris, Maria Alba and her Spanish dance company, Olatunji and his group of African dancers and musicians, Sung Hae Oh in dances of Korea, and Edith McKenzie with the Jacob's Pillow Dancers in Polynesian dances directed by La Meri (1967 Jacob's Pillow Dance Festival Program). The ethnic dance emphasis that year was apparently not a great success, and it seems that La Meri had some problems with the administration at the Pillow. Several months after the Festival, on January 2, 1968, she wrote to Shawn that she would not be coming that summer. In subsequent years, however, La Meri did do some teaching and presentations at the Pillow, but her time was increasingly focused on her activities in Cape Cod.

Conclusion

Throughout her life, La Meri was very conscientious about documenting and keeping careful records of her activities, her travels and her dances. She asked Lilian to save for her the long letters she wrote while on tour, and these furnish an invaluable insight into those years and experiences. She also wrote detailed descriptions of the dances she had learned in different cultures and the dances and dance works she created herself. She made these notes for herself, using a system that she had devised, and they were surely very useful when she was restaging works. The notations, however, are difficult, if not impossible, for anyone else to decipher. The three productions of *Drishyakava (The Seasons)* that she staged were very separated in time, but with her notes and her memory, she probably had no trouble re-creating them, and undoubtedly changed some things along the way (just as those of us who write do with every draft of a text). It would be interesting to know how Matteo's restaging of that work was developed—and how close or far it was from La Meri's choreography. Matteo had performed in the original 1953 production, but that was twenty-five years before his company danced *The Seasons* in 1978. The printed program says the choreography is "after the original by La Meri, restaged by Matteo," but there is no indication whether she provided any assistance or even saw this production—or whether he used notes from her or notes he might have made when he danced in it. His *Seasons* could have been a new work that simply began with his experience of the original and some of its themes and movements and created from there. Or it could have been as close to the original as he was able to remember it. The lack of understandable notations of La Meri's works makes their reconstruction difficult, if not impossible. There are silent films of some of the works in the NYPL, SAPL, and JP collections, but the choreography is often difficult to figure out because the films are shot from such a great distance, the dancers and their movements are often not clear, and the musical accompaniment is, for the most part, nonexistent. One exception is the film that was made in 1960 of a studio performance of the Juilliard dancers in *The Seasons*. This was shown by Josie Neal at the 1989 Society of Dance History Scholars conference at Arizona State (see Neal, 1989).

We have seen that La Meri collected many traditional dances from cultures around the world and choreographed innovative and exploratory works on her own. The dances in her repertoire over the years number in the hundreds, and one could only wish that there were films of some of them. The hundreds of still pictures, however, provide a good sense of her movement and expressive skills and artistry. The range of her work was amazing—and unique within the world of dance.

V. Ethnic Ballets

38. *Gauba's Journey to Paradise* with La Meri as the Celestial Elephant.

39. La Meri as "Maja Deva" (the Abstract) in *Devi Murti*. Photograph by Lucas-Pritchard.

40. La Meri as "Dourga" (the Embattled) in the same work. Photograph also by Lucas-Pritchard.

41. *Swan Lake* debut, February 22, 1944, with (*left to right*) Aldo Cadena as the Prince, Gina Blau as the Sorcerer, and La Meri as the Swan Queen.

42. *Iberia* with La Meri as the Gypsy Wife.

8

New York, Cape Cod, San Antonio

New Transitions, 1956–1988

Last Years in New York City, 1956–1960

As noted in chapter 6, the last summer session of the Ethnologic Dance Center was June 18 to August 25, 1956. During that time, in addition to teaching and running the school, La Meri had two other time-consuming projects: she was packing her personal things to move from Queens, where she had lived with di Falco, to her own apartment at 400 East 55th Street in Manhattan (which she rented from June 30, 1956, to May 6, 1958); and, since the EDC was closing, she had to pack and store, sell, or discard all the school and performance equipment and costumes. While working on the latter, she would stay in the living quarters of the studio.

With the end of the EDC and her intensive activities there—and without her partner of so many years—La Meri seemed to be at a loss for focus in her life. In relation to the decision that she and Peter would live separately, she wrote: "Living alone takes some getting used to!" (*Chronology Notebook*, October 1956); and in the same source, which reports so much activity for other years, the 1957 entry only has: "Summer: Cape Cod Conservatory." Later La Meri wrote: "Very depressed, I just hung in there for two years doing whatever presented itself" (1977a, 187). As throughout her life, however, the anxieties and depressions she frequently suffered never seemed to prevent her from involvement in creative and educational projects. In the archives, there are no records of such activities for almost a year after the 1956 summer course ended, but then she again became involved in what had always been the center of her life and an important contribution to the world of dance.

The opportunity for La Meri to jump back into work was an invitation to direct the summer 1957 dance program at the Cape Cod Conservatory of Music and Arts,[1] which offered a range of courses in music and dance for children, teachers, and professionals at the Massachusetts Maritime Academy Building in Hyannis (*Cape Cod Yankee Times*, August 26, 1957; *Cape Cod Standard Times*, undated). An unidentified newspaper photograph shows (among other figures) La Meri as head of the dance program, Rebecca Harris as one of the teachers, and Lilian. There is no evidence of La Meri continuing to work for this school, but in 1968, she gave a lecture there for the Conservatory Guild, which is described in a news clipping as "a Cape-wide organization of women now in its second year of programs and activities designed to help the Cape Cod Conservatory" (*Register*, October 17, 1968).

Referring to the depressing year she had experienced in 1957, La Meri opens the 1958 entry in *Chronology 1973* with the declaration: "Well, you can't stop living just because the bottom drops out." There, and in her *Chronology Notebook*, she writes of current activities: choreographing for two of her former EDC students, Jerane Michel and Mariano Parra; writing articles; serving on the Fulbright Scholarship Board; teaching various places; and traveling to Cape Cod and elsewhere. She also notes that on May 6, 1958, she changed her residence in Manhattan to 233 East 70th Street, where she stayed until December 1960, when she and Lilian moved permanently to Cape Cod.

What was the most unexpected—and rewarding—event of 1958 was her invitation from Ram Gopal to perform with him in the Caribbean as his guest artist. As discussed in chapter 4, Gopal had complained bitterly in his autobiography about what he considered mistreatment and abandonment by Carreras and La Meri when he was touring with them in 1937 and had expressed disdain for La Meri's art (40–46). He might have felt more resentment toward Carreras than La Meri for what he describes as mistreatment, since Carreras was in charge of everything. However, La Meri's letters regarding his behavior and work with her—as well as long sections about him in her letters to Lilian—show that there were problems between them as well. There is no information as to what motivated him to reestablish his relationship with La Meri at this time. It may have been a realization that he had erred in his earlier evaluation of her work, or that he needed a well-known artist as collaborator for the Caribbean dates with repertoire that could be effectively combined with his.

Gopal contacted La Meri sometime in 1958 to join him in the performances he was giving in Trinidad (and perhaps elsewhere), and she lists rehearsals and other meetings she had with him in June and August of that year. In the San Antonio archive, there is a program for three performances (November 4, 6, and 9) at three different theaters in Trinidad with Gopal, La Meri, and Srimati Gina. The latter was Gina Blau (ca. 1906–1998), who had been one of the original Natyas and performed in La Meri's programs from 1943 to at least 1946. After studying in India, she took as her professional name Srimati Gina (Srimati, usually spelled *shrimati*, means Madame or Mrs.) and performed in the United States and elsewhere. Later, in the late 1960s and early 1970s, she would be engaged as guest artist and teacher at the Ethnic Dance Arts in Cape Cod (see below). On the programs in Trinidad, La Meri performed four solo dances (from Arabia, Japan, Java, and China) and "Radha Krishna, or Hunter in a Forest" with Gopal; Gina performed five Indian or Indian-themed solos; and, in addition to his duet with La Meri, Gopal performed six solos. La Meri was 59 by then, but apparently still had the energy and the desire to perform—and the ability. This continued to be the case as shown by her later appearances at Jacob's Pillow. There is no information in the archives as to any other performances she might have done with Gopal, but they did keep in contact. As mentioned in chapter 4, there is a letter from him (July 10, 1981) in which he refers to a recent conversation they had, and in contrast to the disparaging remarks in his autobiography, compliments her on her strengths during their tour in the 1930s.

While La Meri still felt discouraged and sad at times, she returned to her habitually busy life of teaching and writing, and still performed occasionally. In 1959, she gave workshops and master classes at various institutions and classes at a rented studio in New York for former students who wanted training in "specialized work (dynamic techniques, Japanese, Javanese, etc.)" (*Chronology 1973*). In her *Chronology Notebook*, she lists social and personal as well as professional activities during the year. Her summer schedule was particularly heavy. From June 8 to 12, she gave classes and a "lecture-lab" at the Oklahoma College for Women in Chickasha and spent a week (June 14–21) in San Antonio, Texas, visiting her old friend Olivia Baldessarelli, now Mrs. Barney T. Matteson. Then she drove to Denton, to teach "Ethnic Dance as It Relates to Modern Dance" at Texas Woman's University (June 22 through July 3). That course consisted of four sessions each day: "Fundamentals of Movement, Rhythm and Design" (7–8:30 a.m.), "Composition in Modern Dance" (8:30–10), "Folk Dance"(11:30–1 p.m.), and "Theory and Practice of Ethnic Dance as It Relates to Modern Dance" (8–10 p.m.) (TWU College of Health, Physical Education, and Recreation 1959 summer session brochure), and each of the sessions probably involved practical work as well as theoretical discussion. After what must have been a demanding two-week schedule for both La Meri and the students, she flew on July 4 to New York City, traveled to Jacob's Pillow for her July 7 to 12 engagements there, and after that to Boston for more teaching. Besides the necessity of continuing professional engagements to earn enough for living expenses, La Meri seemed to thrive, as before, on having a busy and purposeful life, and she continued intensive work throughout most of the rest of it.

In 1960, La Meri gave classes at New York University, Teachers College, and a few institutions in other states; she was also writing—for *Harper's Magazine* and other publications. As noted in chapter 7, a major event was her invitation by Antony Tudor to restage *The Seasons* at the Juilliard School, and she performed in the first Jacob's Pillow concert of that year. It was becoming more and more difficult, however, to live in New York City, so she decided to move to Cape Cod and began house hunting there in September and October (*Chronology Notebook*).

Regarding the decision to leave New York, La Meri writes "it was not from lack of energy, but because I found myself becoming bitter about my (lack of) recognition in the new Dance World . . . and bitterness I can do without" (*Chronology 1973*). And in her 1978 chronology in *Dancemagazine*, she remembers her last three years in New York, stating:

> Well, I struggled along . . . with a job here and a job there, much as I had done in the twenties, only I was now beyond the age of faith in the beautiful future. It was pretty grim. December 1960 I said the hell with this. I can't afford to pay New York prices any more, not with nothing ever coming in . . . so I moved to Cape Cod . . . selling all of my group costumes to pay for the move. I had so much that even selling saris for one dollar and Spanish dresses for five, I got close to $2,000. I still wonder where I got the money to buy that stuff in the first place. (64–65)

While she sold the group costumes, she kept the individual costumes she had bought for herself while touring internationally and donated them to the Duquesne University Tamburitzans in September 1977 (see below).

Another New Beginning—1960 through 1970

On December 17, 1960, La Meri and Lilian moved to their first Cape Cod residence at 46 Pearl Street, which she described in 1987 as "a two-story house with a big yard and all the amenities" and a rental cost of $60 a month (according to Pat Taylor, who interviewed La Meri in 1967). During the first four years at the Cape, La Meri continued writing—most notably, her book *Dance Composition: The Basic Elements*, which was published in 1965. She was also preparing entries for the *Encyclopedia Britannica*. In her 1978 chronology in *Dancemagazine*, La Meri claims that during the years 1961–64, she did not want to continue work in dance, but instead to focus on her beloved dogs and dog competitions. Eventually, however, she realized that giving up the dance "was a lost cause," and she wrote, "If you are stuck with dancing you're *stuck* with it. So in 1965, I *started all over again!*" (65). Despite what she wrote, however, La Meri was not totally inactive in the practice of dance in the early 1960s. Each year she did some work at Jacob's Pillow; in 1961, she gave workshops in Connecticut, Missouri, and Virginia; and in 1962 and 1964, she performed and taught at the Dieman-Bennet School in Iowa. As noted in chapter 7, her revival of *Swan Lake* was presented there in June 1964 and brought to Jacob's Pillow in July.

The end of 1964 was very difficult for La Meri because Lilian had become seriously ill with some kind of growth in her intestine and extreme loss of weight. In September she went through two operations and was supposed to get a third one. She developed other problems, however, and, although great efforts were made to bring her back to health, she died on January 19, 1965, at the Barnstable Hospital. There was an obituary the next day in the *New York Times* ("Mrs. David A. Newcomer, Dance Center Director"). Since the two sisters had been so close and shared so much throughout their lives, Lilian's death was, of course, a tragic loss for La Meri.

After this devastating event, La Meri gradually worked her way back into more and more dance activity by giving occasional lectures, allowing dancers to come from New York to study with her, and providing free dance lessons to members of the Barnstable Comedy Club (BCC).[2] She was working on a second, revised edition of her book *Spanish Dancing*, which was published in 1967. And she also began presenting an annual student workshop production at the Barnstable Village Hall that was sponsored by the BCC. For the April 12, 1966, performance, she restaged her Javanese dance drama of 1943, *Rama Breaks the Bow*, with twelve of her student dancers. In her 1966 Christmas letter to Olivia Matteson, besides writing about her plans with Shawn to promote ethnic dance at Jacob's Pillow, she also says that, in Cape Cod, she is teaching dance about seven hours each week and is "tickled to death to be busy and have no time to think about how I feel."

In the same letter, La Meri mentions two students who came in the winter of 1966 to study with her. One was William (Bill) Adams (1938–2015), whom she describes as a "young man who is mad for Spanish dance." After beginning as a student, he became a dancer in La Meri's company, taught in the school, and worked at times as administrative assistant. Later, he would be La Meri's companion and caregiver during the last four years of her life. The other, Uttara Asha Coorlawala, was a student at Smith College who had met La Meri at Jacob's Pillow that summer. She came to the Cape for ten days of intensive study in Spanish dance theory and practice, and returned the following year. La Meri worked with Coorlawala in the development of her undergraduate honors thesis at Smith, a paper and lecture-demonstration focused on Bharatanatyam and flamenco posture and movement in relation to Delsartean theory. Coorlawala finished her Bachelor of Arts at Smith in 1967 and her Master of Arts (1984) and Ph.D. (1994) at New York University. She is a highly respected contributor in research, choreography, dance performance, and university teaching.

As time passed, La Meri and her activities became increasingly known and appreciated by the Cape Cod community. In 1967, she continued teaching at the Comedy Club, and for the May 9 workshop program, nine students, including Bill Adams, performed dances of Spain, India, and Polynesia with La Meri's explanations before each dance. From June 6 to 8, 1968, she and her students performed what she termed the "first full-length dance show" (in contrast to the simpler "workshop productions") at the Barnstable Village Hall. Titled "La Meri and The Cape Cod Ethnic Dance Group in an Ethnic Dance Festival," the concert presented dances from India, Japan, other parts of Asia, Spain, the United States (including Hawaii), and Latin America. The

thirty-six-page printed program included, in addition to the actual performance data, lists of the officers, committees, and members of the Comedy
Club; La Meri's biography; the forty-member production staff; information
about the dances on the program; and advertisements of almost 100 businesses in the Cape Cod area. The latter must have paid for or contributed to
the costs of the performance, its promotion, and the printing of the program.
This "Ethnic Dance Festival" format, with student dancers performing a variety of dance genres, attracted audiences and was also offered in 1969 and
1970 with different programs each year. It is interesting that in her letter of
October 8, 1969, to Olivia, La Meri complains about losing dancers to professional companies—a problem that would continue. While such losses were,
of course, disappointing for La Meri, they attest to the continuing strength
and effectiveness of her teaching.

Ethnic Dance Arts, Inc.

The success of the student productions in attracting local audiences encouraged La Meri to bring professional ethnic dance artists into the area. To assist
with this, she developed a nonprofit organization, Ethnic Dance Arts (EDA),
which was incorporated in January 1970. From that year through 1979, La
Meri and the EDA staff organized and presented a "Summer Festival of Ethnic Dance" with professional dancers and companies performing in July and
August. For the first of these festivals, the printed program lists ten members
of the board of directors, including Russell M. Hughes, and nine members
of the production staff, including La Meri as artistic director, William Adams as administrative assistant and seven others working in stage and house
management, lighting, publicity, and box office. It is interesting that La Meri
put her name differently on the two lists. This document also includes the
names of thirty-five "Patrons and Friends" and encouragement for others to
join with that group. In her program "Letter," La Meri thanks, among others, "the Barnstable Comedy Club for their moral backing and practical aid,
particularly those Club members who are also on the E.D.A. Board of Directors." The first eight festivals were presented in the Barnstable Village Hall.

   As discussed in the article "Ethnic dance is visualized as embryo" (*Sunday Cape Cod Standard-Times,* May 17, 1970), there were broad aspirations
for the EDA. In addition to announcing the scheduled performances, the

author, Sherwood Landers, writes that the festival's "proceeds will pave the way for the development of a performing arts center on Cape Cod," which is "the dream of La Meri," and that she and the EDA board members were hoping that this "first introduction of professional ethnic dance companies to Cape Cod" would "spark interest in creating the arts center." There was even a preliminary plan for it: "a campus, two complete soundproof studios, showers and lockers for students, and later on, a dormitory," and the hope of financing the entire project by soliciting "state and federal aid plus a private corporate grant." This dream was never realized, but the ethnic dance culture and involvement on the Cape continued to grow with the annual festival and two other projects of the EDA: a performing company and a school.

EDA Festivals and Repertory Company

The 1970 festival included four programs: Mariano Parra and the Ballet Español, Nala Najan and his ensemble, Rhythms of India, Sung Hae Oh (from Korea) and Nobuko Shimagahi (from Japan) in "Dances of the Far East," and Matteo, with guest artist Carola Goya and members of his Ethno-American Dance Group. Three of the artists engaged for that year—Parra, Najan, and Matteo—had been students of La Meri's before embarking on further studies and their professional careers. In 1971, the second festival also included four groups: Luis Rivera and Company in Spanish dance, Sahoma Tachibana and Company in Japanese dance, Srimati Gina, with two guest artists, in dances of India, and the EDARC (see below), which performed a range of international dances. As was usual in her own performing and in projects such as this, La Meri's focus was on dance from Asian countries and Spain, but some of the later festivals (like some of her touring repertoires) also included dance from other cultures.

Sometime before 1970, La Meri had begun to organize her best student dancers into a performing company—as she had done before when teaching in Italy and New York City. In 1970 or later, a four-page brochure was distributed that advertised the Ethnic Dance Arts Repertory Company (EDARC), offered concert presentations, master classes, lecture-demonstrations, and assembly programs for schools and stated that the project was partially funded by the Council on Arts and Humanities of the Commonwealth of Massachusetts. The initial members of the group were William Adams, Barry

Edson, Jean Mellichamp, Suzanne Sausner, and Cynthia Small. On December 8, 1970, La Meri and the company gave what was termed a "Showcase Performance" of Indian dances at the Barnstable Comedy Club. In following years, EDARC performances would be included in the festival series, with the group variously identified as Ethnic Dance Arts or La Meri's Ethnic Dance Group.

The repertoire of the group must have started to develop in 1970, but there was still much to be added in the following years. In the 1971 entry in La Meri's *Chronology 1973*, she writes: "Working hard with E.D.A. Co. . . . Full repertory to teach and 70-odd costumes to make (A State grant in March helped some)" (13). And, in a mimeographed group letter that she sent to friends in February 1972, she apologizes for not writing individually but says, "I am working as hard as ever I did at 110 East 59th St. . . . some twenty years ago when I was twenty years younger! In a moment of aberration I started this Three-Pronged E.D.A-and I mean "Pronged," for I often feel the devil himself is poking me with his pitch-fork! The three prongs are the school, the company and the Festival." Then she gives some details about her heavy teaching and rehearsal schedules and the problems with making costumes for the company. Since it would have been too expensive to hire professionals to do the sewing, La Meri made samples of what was needed that could be "copied by whatever friends and students will take on the job" (ibid.). The group's first performance outside Cape Cod was at Quinsigamond State College in Worcester, and an article announcing that engagement also notes the partial funding the EDA had received from the state (Raymond Morin, "La Meri Opens Fete at Quinsig [*sic*] College," *Worcester Sunday Telegram*, April 18, 1971). For a few years, the EDARC continued to give performances in various locations, but by 1975, the group had lost too many members, and the last performance for which there is information is in the 1976 festival.

The 1972 festival departed from the pattern of the first two with eight different programs instead of four—each given once or twice rather than three times. Also new in this festival were genres from cultures that had not previously been represented: Polynesian dances by Taneo; a nonethnic work, "The Song of Sara," combining music, poetry, and dance by composer Daniel Jahn and Company; and a program by La Meri's former student, dear friend, and revered colleague Hadassah on "Dance Themes of Hassidism and Hinduism." Most surprising, there was a concert of African and Afro-American dance by dancer Charles Moore and musician Ladji Camara. As noted before, this is a cultural area that La Meri had usually ignored. The festival also included Mariano Parra's Spanish Dance Company, Ritha Devi in "Dances of India," and two programs in which the EDA Company participated—a Spanish concert of Dina Roman and her partner, and an Indian concert with Nala Najan.

While, during the 1972 festival, there was only one more performance (13) than there had been in the previous two festivals (12 each), the presentation of eight different artists or groups instead of four made for much more work—not only in dealing with the administration of twice as many contracts and lodging and transportation arrangements but also in having to schedule and complete twice as many technical setups and rehearsals in the theater. In addition, Dini Roman's originally scheduled partner, Salvadore Vires, suffered a knee injury, so extra rehearsals had to be scheduled with the fill-in partner, Roberto Cartagena. And La Meri says that she spent some six hours teaching Nala Najan the choreography of what had been her own solo in the *Bach-Bharata Suite* of 1946. Two sections of that were performed by Najan and the EDA Company in his concerts on the festival program in Barnstable (August 10 and 11) and later that month, at Jacob's Pillow. It is not surprising that in her June Newsletter, La Meri mentions feeling "twice as busy" organizing this festival. But, in her Autumn Newsletter, she writes that, although the festival "half-killed some of us," it was "brilliant, satisfying."

The fourth festival in 1973 with seven different artists or groups focused on the usual Asian and Spanish cultures with programs of dances from India (two), Japan (one), China and Korea (one), and Spain (two). In addition, La Meri presented EDARC in a restaging of her *Drishnakava* (Vivaldi's *The Seasons*), which had first been presented in 1953 at Jacob's Pillow, and in a new work, *Fifty Years of Spanish Dance*, which traced the developments in Spanish theatrical dance forms from the 1920s to the 1970s. The 1973 printed program includes an essay by La Meri, "What Is Ethnic Dance?" After a short discussion of the term, she writes, "it is my unalterable conviction that the study of ethnic dance, whether it be actively from the studio or passively from the audience, will inevitably produce a deeper understanding which will lead to the brotherhood of man," and she ends with: "May we never hate each other. Om! Peace, peace, peace." This reflects what she and others had written before—especially during World War II—about their belief in the potential for dance experience and understanding to work for the goal of intercultural and international understanding. This printed program includes almost fifty advertisements of local businesses—not as many as in 1968, but still, an important source of income and evidence of local interest.

The 1974 festival turned out to be the most successful of the ten that were held. As La Meri writes in the 1980 addendum to her *Chronology 1973*, "the EDA peaked in 1974" (23). Its eight weeks included the usual range of dance from Asia and related areas: China (Alan Chow and Company), Japan (Sachiyo Itō), India (Bhaskar), and the Philippines (Diwang Pilipino Company); and concerts by Luis Rivera and his Spanish dance company and by EDARC. There were also two unusual additions: the Ukrainian Dance Ensemble of Boston—the first time that a company specializing in European folk dance had been on the program—and the presentation of dance from the Caribbean by Jean-Léon Destiné and Company, which again gave attention to dance deriving from African cultures. It would seem that the international range of choices for the festival was gradually expanding and probably would have continued to grow if increasing financial problems had not prevented that.

As the summer festival tradition continued, La Meri was obviously as totally absorbed in this work as she had been in all her previous activities. Her life again had purpose, challenges, and the excitement and joy of accomplishment. This is illustrated on the first page of the 1974 festival program with a picture of La Meri throwing up her arms in an attitude of delirious joy, and her statement:

Hurrah! The paper work is behind us . . . six months of correspondence, lay-outs, articles, contracts, et.al.

We start before Christmas to get things lined up and from January first, onwards, it is a mad crescendo of counterpoint until the first curtain-up. Sometimes we wonder if we will live through it and we eye each other's long faces and short tempers with pessimistic alarm. But some way, somehow it gets done and, although all during the season there are minor "alarms and excursions," when the first artist appears we can sit back and savor the fruits of our labors. . . .

For all this work and confusion there is no one to blame but me, for I have an insatiable appetite for ethnic dance . . . and I am a "carrier" [of that "virus"].

With another successful festival underway, all indeed looked well—but problems loomed, and the next year, things began to go downhill. La Meri writes, "From 1974 on it was an easy slide down from the top of the rainbow" (*Chronology 1973*, 23).

From the beginning, the EDA and its festival and other activities were under financial strain, and La Meri had to deal with problems as severe as those she had faced in New York. The business advertisements helped pay for the printing of each summer's program, but not much more. La Meri requested tax deductible donations in every EDA newsletter, program, or announcement that was sent out, and in 1972 solicited donations for a "Barn Sale," subtitled "Trash & Treasures," that was held at the Barnstable Village Hall on May 27. Property donated for that included everything from large kitchen appliances to small pieces of jewelry. But, even with such efforts at money-raising, there was never enough. La Meri's April 14 letter announcing the program for the 1972 festival proudly tells of the interest the EDA and its activities were eliciting both in the United States and abroad. "But," she writes, "we must *find the money* to make it possible to keep up with our fast-growing reputation." She notes that the performing artists at the festival as well as the teachers in the school are either underpaid or not paid at all, and she begs for contributions, attendance at the performances, and the donation of items to the Barn Sale. She ends the letter: "In short. . . . Help! Help! Help! Help!" Beginning in 1972, a "boutique" was set up during the performance times to sell ethnic jewelry, shoes, textiles, and other items from St. Denis's and La Meri's collections. According to subsequent newsletters, that did bring in some income. But there was a continuing need to raise money, and things became particularly desperate after 1974.

In her June 1975 Newsletter, La Meri relates that "E.D.A. has been through a very rough storm since January '75. It looked for a time as though we might sink without a trace, but we have a pretty stubborn captain and crew and it seems we will ride it out if you will bear with our shortening of sail." There were many problems. One was that La Meri had lost many of the best dancers of her ensemble. As she writes in the March 1980 addition to her *Chronology 1973*, "several left to join professional companies; two left to get married; one left to go back to college (to specialize in Indonesian dance at UCLA); one left to open a school; . . . etc." Since these were young people and La Meri had been training them for professional careers, she knew that losing them was "to be expected" (23). The loss of dancers, however, was not the most serious problem. As she writes, "The worst knock was when a trusted employee stole us blind; and we did not even know it until we were called into Small Claims Court for bills unpaid which we thought we had paid. In our desperation to catch up financially we were forced to cut down the Festival shows to three" (ibid.). The employee had been hired in late 1971 to replace Bill Adams (see below), but there is no specific information about the alleged theft, and it seems that he was never prosecuted for it. What actually happened is not clear, but the EDA was definitely in even more dire financial straits than usual.

As a result of these problems, both the performances and the teaching had to be cut back. The main events of the 1975 festival were thus single concerts by only three groups. The first, on July 18, was the Charles Weidman Theatre Dance Company in modern dance works—a surprising choice for a festival of "ethnic dance." Weidman himself was scheduled to perform in this concert, but he died on July 15, a week before his seventy-fourth birthday and three days before the concert. Despite their loss, his dancers came and performed as a memorial tribute to him. A week later, the second concert featured dances mainly from India by Bhaskar with Cynthia Maddux, and the week after that, the EDA Repertory Company performed. To cope with the continuing financial problems, La Meri, always ingenious, initiated some programs that did not require funds, but could bring in a little cash. She termed these the "Little Shows" in her 1980 addition to *Chronology 1973*, and apparently, they were held in a studio in the Barnstable Village Hall. In her fall 1975 Newsletter, La Meri writes that these were informal evenings with the audience in chairs around the performance area and the main speaker of the evening explaining an aspect of dance art with one or two students illustrating. The ones presented in 1975 were "Talking Hands" (La Meri), "Spanish Dancing" (lecture-demonstration by Luis Olivares), and "Arabic Dance" (Nasrine and the Boston Oriental Dancers).

The festivals of 1976 to 1979 were also shorter than those of the first five years with just four single concert performances each. As in the past, the focus was usually on genres from Spain, India, and the Middle East and the visiting artists were mostly well known in the area as they had performed in previous festivals. The first 1976 concert was by "La Meri's Ethnic Dance Group," featuring three former members as guest artists: La Melodia (Melody Hall), Jean Mellichamp, and Amelie Hunter. This would be the last festival performance of that group. The other programs were by Pilar Gomez and Company, Bhaskar with Cynthia Maddox, and Mariano Parra and his Ballet Español. There were also three "Little Shows" in August: "Dance in Mexico" with Pilar Gomez, "Dance in India" with Bhaskar, and "Arabic Dances" by Madeline Dubrovsky.

A similar program was presented in 1977. Three of the concert artists had performed at the festival before: Dini Roman, who this year was with the Ramon de los Reyes company in a concert of Spanish dance; Bhaskar and two young dancers in Indian dances; and Roberto Cartagena, who had filled in as Dini Roman's partner in 1972. He and his company performed dances from both Colombia and Spain. In addition, an area of dance totally new to the festival was introduced. Identified on the program as "American Ethnic," this was "Razzmatazz Jazz," a combination of jazz and tap dance performed by Brenda Bufalino and her company. Bufalino (born 1937) had built her reputation as an innovator in these two genres. This last year of the "Little Shows" included Mexican dance by Dr. Josefina Garcia and her group, "Ethnic Departures" by Jean Mellichamp and La Meri, and Arabic dance by Martha Carr and her group.

By 1978, the Barnstable Village Hall had changed owners and the EDA could no longer rent space there for classes or for the "Little Shows." The performances could have continued in the 200-seat auditorium, but since the summer festival audiences had been growing considerably, the four July 1978 concerts were presented in the 750-seat Barnstable High School Auditorium in Hyannis (March 1978 EDA Newsletter; 1980 addition to *Chronology 1973*, 23). These included three separate programs of Spanish, Indian, and Polynesian dance artists and an evening of creative works based on Spanish and Asian dance forms by Jean Mellichamp and La Melodia, the two former members of the EDARC who had been guest artists with the group in 1976.

The 1979 festival was also at Barnstable High School with four concerts in July performed by the companies of Luis Rivera (Spanish), Bashkar (Indian), Jerane Michel (Spanish), and Ibrahim Farrah (Near East). As a celebration of the festival's ten years of history, the 1979 program booklet lists all the participants who had contributed to the festival in its previous nine years. There were thirty artists or companies on the concert programs and twenty artist/teachers in the workshop classes. Many of those listed had participated in more than one festival or workshop—as either performers or teachers, or both. There is a statement about the continuing fact that the EDA's projects were totally dependent on volunteer work and donations. That year, there was an additional event on August 12 at the smaller Barnstable Village Hall—a special performance by Uttara Coorlawala that included classical dances of India, modern dances of America, and creative works of her own.

In her EDA Newsletter of December 1, 1978, La Meri wrote that moving the regular programs to the high school auditorium was a good decision, since more people could fit into that larger hall. But later she would write and complain about the severe problems there—referring to the hall's rundown condition and its high cost. While the greater capacity was a definite advantage for the 1978 and 1979 festivals, the hall's physical condition was terrible, as elaborated in La Meri's letter of August 30, 1979, to the chair of the Barnstable School Committee and in reporter Fred Bodenslek's article in the the *Barnstable Patriot* ("La Meri rips open curtain on Barnstable HS Auditorium," October 20, 1979). Besides discussing what La Meri wrote to the committee, Bodenslek tells of complaints made about the same problems by the school's faculty and others. There were serious risks for the audience members from the loose tiles in the ceiling (many of which had already fallen). And the holes in the carpeting on the aisles and the many missing seats could both lead to falls—especially for those arriving after the lights were down. The stage area was also in shambles—the curtains, wings, lighting fixtures—and the technical staff provided minimal service and, in La Meri's opinion, was "impudent." La Meri also wrote that she could not understand why John Vetorino, who had been skillfully running the lights and contributing equipment at the Village Hall auditorium since 1968, was "expressly forbidden to have anything whatever to do with the lighting at Barnstable High School." On top of all the problems, the EDA was being charged almost $1,000 for the use of the auditorium and its staff for four performances, and she found this excessive in relation to the state of the facility and what was being provided. All these problems were a heavy burden for this seventy-nine-year old artist who was trying to share culture with the community. And La Meri was puzzled by the fact that the school board and faculty had apparently no interest at all in the festival programs or in the mission of the EDA's work as something of benefit to the community.

In her February 1980 EDA Newsletter, La Meri writes that she had received "a most courteous letter" from the school superintendent, Edward Tynan, saying that the auditorium was to be repaired—so she was already planning the 1980 festival. But in the June Newsletter, she informed her readers "with the greatest regret," that the festival had to be canceled because the high school auditorium would not be ready by July, and she had not been able to find another location. It turned out that 1979 was the last Ethnic Dance Arts festival in Cape Cod.

Ethnic Dance Arts—The School

La Meri had been teaching to some extent since she moved to the Cape in 1960, and in 1970, she and William Adams taught a five-day workshop in Spanish dance as part of the first year's festival. In 1971, however, she began two educational endeavors as major components of EDA. The first was a summer session of classes as part of each year's festival. Its length was six weeks in 1971, two weeks in 1972, and three weeks in each of the following years. The second was a regular fall-winter-spring schedule of ethnic dance classes. The special sessions in the summer provided the year-round students as well as the summer participants with opportunities to experience teaching methods of the performing artists they were seeing on the festival programs and different approaches to the various techniques and genres. The summer sessions continued for two years after the last festival—until 1981.

The 1971 summer session included Spanish dance taught by Mariano Parra, Jerane Michel, and Manolo Vargas, East Indian by Srimati Gina, and Javanese and Thai by La Meri. Of course, focus on the dance genres of Spain and Asia would be the norm every year. As in this first session, dancers who had studied and performed with La Meri in the 1940s and 1950s in New York City were often teachers in the summer program and—except for Rebecca Harris and Josefina Garcia—also in performances.[3] As students of La Meri, their approaches would have been to some extent in line with her own teaching, but also incorporating what they may have learned from study abroad and their own developing ideas and strategies. As noted above, in 1978, the new owners of the Barnstable Village Hall would not (or could not) continue to provide space for the classes. Since no other local facility was available, the summer classes were then held in La Meri's small home studio, which limited the number of students; and for the 1978 and 1979 workshops, there were only two teachers: La Meri and Rebecca Harris.

During most of the summer sessions, La Meri did some teaching, but basically, her role was as administrator of the entire festival project including the

EDARC performances. For the summer of 1978, however, she decided to offer classes as they had been taught at the EDC in New York so many years ago. As she writes in the EDA Newsletter of December 1, 1978, she engaged Harris to teach Hindu and Spanish dancing using the "tried and true system" that she had developed there, and La Meri herself worked with the "approaches" that she describes in her book *Total Education in Ethnic Dance*. The classes were limited to a maximum of seven, and the students were "hand-picked for seriousness and dedication." At the end of the letter, she expresses her deep satisfaction with her work that summer: "I had more joy in teaching than I have for many years!" The 1979 three-week summer session included East Indian and Spanish taught by Harris while La Meri taught dance composition and "within techniques," the approach she had been developing since the late 1950s and had presented at Jacob's Pillow in 1959. It is amazing that at seventy-nine and eighty years of age, La Meri still had such dedication to and passion for her field. It was also very fortunate for her that she had the strength and good health to continue the work that she loved.

With some exceptions, there is little information about the year-round classes that La Meri began in 1971–72. An unidentified report, probably from some time in 1971, states that the school "offers 20 to 30 hours a week in techniques and historical backgrounds in Spanish and East Indian dance" and that more will be scheduled "once the school and organization is housed within its own buildings." Unfortunately, that never happened. During these regular sessions, La Meri would sometimes do all the teaching, but at times, EDA dancers or guest artists also taught. For example, in April 1971, an EDA flyer announced that the regular classes and teachers would be Spanish dance taught by La Meri and William Adams, Hindu dance by La Meri, and ballet classes by Barry Edson and Suzanne Sausner, both of whom had backgrounds in that genre and performed with La Meri's repertory company. In the fall 1973 semester (October 8 to December 14), there were only fifteen hours of classes a week, but the students were expected to practice every day (as La Meri had done throughout her career). During that term, in addition to the regular Hindu, Spanish, and ballet instruction, there were also classes in Javanese techniques and background culture, Vedic literature (of ancient India), and costume construction (EDA Newsletter, December 1973). La Meri's emphasis on cultural studies as well as dance training dated from the EDC curriculum that she had developed in New York City in the 1940s and 1950s. And no one knew better than she how important it would be for an ethnic dance artist to be able to produce the necessary costumes.

According to an announcement for 1976–77, La Meri was available for private lessons in techniques, including East Indian, Spanish, Javanese, and Arabic; to teach any of fifty-seven solo or group works from her own performance repertory; and for classes in "Dance Composition, Program Counseling, Coaching, etc." Attached to the announcement is a list of the fifty-seven repertory works. Prices are given for the private lessons, classes, and repertory works; the students could also purchase music tapes for the dances, photographs of the costumes, and some actual costumes. To be accepted for any of this, however, a prospective student had to submit a recommendation from "someone established in the dance field" or pass an audition with La Meri—who obviously no longer wanted to take on beginners.

While La Meri continued her teaching both in the summer and during the rest of the year, she gradually did less and less. In 1977, she cut her winter schedule to two days a week, and in 1978, limited her work to private lessons. In October 1978, she added something new—she began to teach classes in the work of Michio Itō, with whom she had studied so many years before. In the addendum to *Chronology 1973*, she writes: "After 30 years of teaching ethnic dance, I decided to offer classes in Michio Itō work. The work of this amazing artist has been kept alive in Japan and recently has been again introduced into the USA. I studied with him in the 'twenties, danced in his works all over the world and still remember much of it" (22). One can wonder how she remembered his teaching method after such a long time. Unfortunately, there is no information about what of Itō's technique or dances she taught nor about who might have studied this with her, and if or how they might have used it.

Apparently, by at least 1971, the Cape Cod community had developed an appreciation for La Meri's educational endeavors as well as the EDA festivals. For example, an article by the music critic of the *Worcester Sunday Telegram,* opens: "Even the most stoic and skeptical Cape Codders are beginning to accept La Meri's Ethnic Dance Arts as an important addition to the area's cultural life." He then goes on to trace in some detail the history of the EDA, La Meri's life and career, and that of William Adams as dancer and administrative assistant in the organization (Morin, 1971b). An article published the following year, "Dance on Cape Cod: Cultural Asset," focuses on three prominent schools of dance with professional companies that are "firmly based on Cape Cod" (*Cape Cod Standard Times*, October 15, 1972). The author, Evelyn Larsen, gives most attention to La Meri's school and company, and some to Barry Edson's (the section on the third school is missing from La Meri's clipping). The long section on the EDA and La Meri's work illustrates the community's interest in and respect for her contributions to their culture. Enthusiastic press coverage of La Meri's life and work would continue throughout her years in Cape Cod.

The Ruth St. Denis Award

In 1977, to continue her promotion of ethnic dance and its visibility, La Meri established an annual award for outstanding accomplishments or innovations in the field. The first year it was titled the "Award for Creative Ethnic Dance"; after that, the "Ruth St. Denis Award for Creative Choreography in the Ethnic Field," in honor of that pioneer in ethnic dance. The awardee would receive a certificate and a check for $1,000, and there would be a festive award dinner to which many guests were invited. One can only wonder how such a large amount of money for the award and the dinner was possible with the constant financial problems of the EDA. Perhaps La Meri had found a dedicated supporter to underwrite this endeavor.

The first artist to be honored was Jean-Marie Mellichamp, who had begun her studies with La Meri in 1970. She was a member of the EDA Repertory Company from its beginning, and after her marriage in 1974, she continued coming to Cape Cod as guest artist and teacher. She had also studied in Spain and had experimented with the creative uses of ethnic dance techniques, which is what earned her the award. Subsequently honored were Bhaskar (1978), Ibrahim Farrah (1979), Mariano Parra (1980), and Nala Najan (1981). In 1982, for the sixth annual award, La Meri went in a new direction. Instead of choosing an established professional to be honored, she announced a competition for the award in New York City with the purpose of encouraging creative work by young dancers in the ethnic field. In October of that year, four awards were given to developing artists. There is no information about the amounts awarded, but it seems likely that the $1,000 was divided among the four. Again in 1983, there was a competition, and four winners were chosen. Another competition was announced for 1984 but didn't take place since La Meri had moved back to San Antonio in July of that year.

William J. Adams (1938–2015)

Adams was a major collaborator with La Meri in Cape Cod, cared for her during her last years, and was the executor of her estate. While he had experiences outside of dance, such as two stints in the navy (in the late 1950s and again in the 1960s) and skills in various kinds of work to earn his living, the focus here will be on his involvement with dance and his relationship with La Meri and the EDA—drawing mainly on his own memories as communicated to me.[4]

What first stimulated Adams's interest in dance was seeing a 1959 performance of the famous Spanish dancer José Greco (1918–2000). He began classes in Spanish, ballet, and modern dance with Eleanore Thompson, a teacher in Worcester, Massachusetts, the city of his birth. Thompson encouraged him in the direction of ballet and also told him about La Meri and her work. Adams said that he performed "briefly" with the Boston Ballet in 1959 and during its 1960–61 season.[5] During his second service period in the Navy, he apparently had also had time for some dance activities in places where he was stationed, which included Guam and Spain, among others.

Adams was a student at Jacob's Pillow in 1961 and 1962, and in 1964, he saw the revival of La Meri's Hindu *Swan Lake* there. He moved to Cape Cod in September 1966 to continue training with La Meri and performed in the May 9, 1967, workshop program. After that, he left Cape Cod and spent about two years in New York City studying Spanish dance with Mariano Parra and other teachers, and perhaps performing with some of them.

Probably in June or July 1969, Adams returned to Cape Cod, where he performed, first with La Meri's student group and then with the Ethnic Dance Arts Repertory Company when that was established. He earned his living, $50 a week, by doing different kinds of work for La Meri and the EDA; and on the 1970 and 1971 festival programs, he is listed as "Administrative Assistant." Adams also taught in the school two or three hours a day, rehearsed the company, made costumes, props, and headdresses, and dealt with various problems that arose. Sometime after August 1971, he decided to leave Cape Cod and the EDA. As he wrote to me on March 2, 2012, "All I can say is that I was terribly overworked and exhausted." Since La Meri herself was used to an overload of work, she undoubtedly didn't realize what might be an extreme strain on someone else. Of course, Adams's departure put more load on her shoulders: she had to find another administrative assistant and replacements for Adams's dance roles and other work with the company—and train the new people.

For the next few years, Adams lived with his parents in Massachusetts, earning money from various jobs and performing at times. In 1975, after some correspondence with La Meri, he returned to Cape Cod, rejoined the EDARC, and danced in their last two summer festival programs of 1975 and 1976. While there is no indication that he did any more administrative or teaching work, he did help with the advancement of the 1976 festival. He told me that he left Cape Cod again in 1978 since his father had had a "massive heart attack" (letter of March 12, 2012). That could have been the year before, however, as there is no record of him at the Cape in 1977. According to his memories, he returned to Cape Cod in the spring of 1980, worked as a waiter for his living, "rejoined La Meri to help her with various dance projects," and, under the name José Sorillo, performed in partnership with La Melodia (Melody Hall) (ibid.).

Apparently, it was in 1980 that Adams began working with La Meri as her assistant and caregiver. And, when she decided in 1984 to return to San Antonio, she asked him to help her with the move and to stay there with her, which he did. He ended up caring for her during the last years of her life, and, after her death, he was the executor of her estate.

La Meri's Personal Life and Recognition: 1970 and Beyond

By the end of 1970, La Meri's spirits seemed to have totally recovered. Her Christmas letter was a humorous poem, with names of dances in each verse. Some excerpts:

Now Christmas time has come again.
O, dance a rigaudon!
(And Christmas cards must be addressed and Christmas seals stuck on.)
[two verses are omitted here]
A piney wreath adorns the door.
Step out a gay gavotte!
(The last few shopping days will come, whether you like or not.)
[two verses also omitted here]

The turkey steams: the egg-nog flows.

The multidanzak trips!

(Candy lies on every side. What's *happened* to my hips?)

Christmas 'seventy is here.

A bouncing Jota's fun!

(And just about next month you'll find it's Christmas 'seventy-one!)

From then on, until her energies began to flag in the early 1980s, La Meri was again committed to being an energetic promoter of dance and of knowledge about it. While she might have felt discouraged at times and did have some health problems, the positive aspects of her life seemed to prevail now that she was back on a demanding schedule. As discussed above, in her February 1972 group letter, she wrote about her heavy schedule of teaching, choreographing, rehearsing, and organizing the summer festival. And, of course, with Adams gone, there was even more work as she trained a new administrative assistant and made necessary changes in the EDA company repertory and casting. But she apparently had the energy to manage it all—and to enjoy her life.

In the 1970s, La Meri received recognition and appreciation of her work from a number of sources. In 1972, she was chosen for the twenty-first annual Capezio Dance Award[6] along with Reginald and Gladys Laubin, specialists in Native American dance. The ceremony was held on April 19 at the St. Regis Roof in New York City. The booklet for the event includes five pages on each of the awardees with sixteen pictures of the Laubins' work and twenty-four of La Meri's. The introduction states that this year's award "salutes the oldest and most universal dance expression in the world, ethnic dance, the dance art accomplishment not of persons but of peoples." The award of $1,000, of course, went to these "persons" who were furthering ethnic dance. In her February 1972 group letter, La Meri notes that this prestigious award "should be a shot-in-the-arm for ethnic dance and my own small E.D.A." The following year La Meri was awarded a citation from the Commission of Texas Arts and Humanities, which was presented sometime in January 1973 at the First Southwest Conference of the Dance in Austin. She was not able to travel there to receive it since, as usual, she was very involved in the school and company, and planning for the next summer festival. In addition, around the same time, she was scheduled to teach Mariano Parra and his company a three-movement choreographic work that she had prepared for them.[7]

During this decade, La Meri was also invited to contribute to programs in New York City. For example, to commemorate "International Women's Year," the Dance Theater Workshop, Inc. (DTW) presented her in "An Evening with La Meri: The Life of a Woman in Dance" at the American Theatre Laboratory on December 8, 1975. This was announced as "an open discussion" and was moderated by dance critic Deborah Jowitt and Mariano Parra (DTWnews release, November 19, 1975). There is a short review of the event by editorial staff member Lois Draegin in the March 1976 *Dancemagazine* (10, 14). And in 1979, she was engaged by American Ballet Theatre to restage her work, "The Meeting," for their April 30 gala performance at the Metropolitan Opera House in New York City. This dance, identified as "Arabic" and set to a poem by Ibn-el-Fared from 1220 CE, was first presented with that name in 1944. Forerunners of "The Meeting" were the "Chethat-al-Maharma," versions of which were presented from the late 1920s, and "Chethat-al-Selah," which entered La Meri's repertoire in 1943. For the gala, it was danced by ballerina Marianna Tcherkassky, and in her *New York Times* review, critic Anna Kisselgoff writes that "Miss Tcherkassky looked beautiful in 'The Meeting,' a sensual whirling solo with overtones of Indian Kathak dance, that was La Meri's sophisticated abstraction of a 13th-century Arabic love poem, recited in English during the performance" (May 2, 1979).

Major evidence of the respect La Meri had gained in the field of dance is the August 1978 issue of *Dancemagazine* where sixteen pages with numerous photographs are devoted to her life and work. There are three parts (titles all in lower case): the first, "i remember . . . ," written by La Meri (55–62); the second, "a chronology of learning, labor, and life," edited and with a foreword by Walter Terry (62–65); and the third, "a lifetime in ethnic dance," a review by Jane Sherman of La Meri's two 1977 books (see chapter 9). Other examples of interest in and respect for La Meri's work include articles in the *New York Times,* the *Contemporary Dance News* of Boston, and the magazine *Arabesque*—and her election to the advisory boards of Jacob's Pillow and the Western Massachusetts Dance Company.

Throughout her life, La Meri had been committed to being a teacher, an "explainer," and a promoter of ethnic dance in addition to her work as an artist, and she continued such activities to some extent during her last years in Hyannis—some there and others outside the Cape Cod area. On

April 27, 1980, assisted by Cynthia Small, she gave a lecture-demonstration and taught a "smorgasbord ethnic dance master class" at the Ballet Theatre School in Springfield, Massachusetts, presenting examples of dance cultures from around the world (Richard Conway, "Humanity Missing in Dance," *Springfield Daily News,* April 29, 1980). Shortly after that, on May 5, in New York City, she was a special guest and speaker at the annual Capezio Award, which honored Walter Terry. A 1981 announcement in the *Sunday Cape Cod Times* says that La Meri would be choreographing and directing a production of Ravel's *Bolero* that spring for the Cape Cod Ballet (March 22). And in June of the same year she was the keynote speaker for the Dance Critics Conference in New York City.

A particularly notable event in 1981 was arranged by Ibrahim Farrah (1939–98), noted Middle Eastern dance artist and publisher of *Arabesque,* a magazine dedicated to Middle Eastern and related dance and music. Farrah and his company had performed at the 1979 summer festival in Cape Cod, and he was the recipient of the St. Denis Award that year. In 1978 and 1979, La Meri's work as a specialist in Middle Eastern and other world dance cultures had been featured in *Arabesque* articles by Adam Lahm, one of the magazine's staff members. She was later invited to be one of its contributing editors, a post she held from 1982 until her death in 1988, and her articles were published in issues from 1982 to 1986. In 1981, to open a National Dance Week in New York City, Farrah organized a Festival of Ethnic Dance (April 4–5) featuring La Meri and held in the facilities of the Dance Education Department of New York University (NYU). There were two days of workshop classes, and the January 25 *Arabesque* news release announced that La Meri would "highlight the weekend classes" and that there would also be teaching by Farrah (Middle Eastern), Mariano Parra (Spanish), and Carolyn Kay, a former member of the Bhaskar company (Indian). On April 5, at the University Theatre, a program titled "A Salute to La Meri" included performances by Farrar, Parra, Kay, and other dancers.

Recognition and appreciation of La Meri and her work was also evident in other publications and events. In March 1980, an article, "La Meri: The High Priestess of Ethnic Dance" by Bhaskar Roy Chowdhury (1930–2003), was featured in the first issue of a new publication: *IN-STEP: The Dance Newspaper of New York City.* Chowdhury gives an overview of La Meri's life and work, tells of his first meeting with her in 1955, and highly praises her contributions to dance.[8] Also in 1980, she was honored at the New England Regional Conference of the American College Dance Festival with the establishment of a scholarship for ethnic dance studies in her name and a citation praising her contributions to dance. The citation was written and presented by noted modern dance innovator and educator Gertrude Lippincott (1913–1996) on April 19 at the Boston Conservatory of Music. And in 1982, Adam Lahm's article, "La Meri: Ethnic Dance's Living Legend," was published in the November–December issue of *Dance Teacher Now,* which introduced her work to the dance studio culture, which may have been unaware that there was such a thing as "ethnic dance."

During her last two years in Cape Cod, while La Meri was still involved in the St. Denis Award competitions and a few other things, it was clear that her health and energy were decreasing. The heavy winters and her advanced emphysema were making life less and less comfortable. In an August 23, 1983, letter, probably to John Igo,[9] she writes, "I have come to a momentous decision! To wit . . . if I can hold myself together until then, I am determined to go to San Antonio for bluebonnet time next Spring." She achieved that wish in early April, accompanied by Adams, and soon after their arrival, Igo arranged a homecoming party for her. After that event, Olivia Matteson expressed appreciation in a letter to "dear capable talented and charming John Igo" with the message: "Please know it was deeply and lovingly appreciated and your praises will continue to be sung. The whole affair was gracious and sparklingly charming, so worthy of a true artist—one whose talent you and I appreciate and celebrate" (April 11, 1984, letter in SAPL archive). In San Antonio as well as other parts of the world, La Meri had many loving friends who greatly valued her.

The San Antonio press also responded with enthusiasm to the return of this former society girl who had become a world-famous performing artist, teacher, and author. The articles discuss her life, career, and publications and particularly note her visit to the former Hughes home on Courtland Place that had become a Catholic Student Center near the San Antonio College campus. One by Igo in the *North San Antonio Times* mentions that during her visit to the center, La Meri was "trailed by a corps of press photographers and reporters." It includes pictures of her from both the past and present and information about her visit, her interviews, and the demonstration of gesture songs that she gave ("La Meri visits childhood home here," May 10,

1984). In the *San Antonio Express*, the arts writer John Phillip Santos provided an overview of La Meri's entire career, drawing on the memories of
Olivia Matteson as one of his sources. And he noted that La Meri was cur-
rently "a resident of Cape Cod" ("She's danced across the globe," April 15,
1984). That residency would not continue for long, however. Adams reported
to me that "within two weeks after her return to the Cape, [La Meri] decided
she wanted to move back to San Antonio . . . she asked if I would go with her
and continue to work for her. I agreed" (email, July 21, 2012). Adams packed
up the things from her house and from his apartment that they wanted to
take with them, and in early July 1984, they flew to San Antonio where they
would live for the rest of La Meri's life.

There is not much in print about La Meri after her return to San Antonio.
The May–June 1985 issue of *Arabesque* includes a section on her in Valerie
Baker's article, "Ethnic Dance, U.S.A. (11/1: 8–9, 21), and a San Antonio article by Josie Neal, "Tamburitzans, La Meri share love of dance, 5/26," announces a performance by that group but focuses mainly on La Meri and her
accomplishments (May 19, 1985, unidentified publication in SAPL archive).
In 1977, La Meri had donated all her original costumes to the Tamburitzan
costume collection.

As noted in the preface, Josie Neal had decided to research La Meri's life
and work and write her biography, and, in support of the project, La Meri
gave her a large collection of archival materials. In addition, during the last
several months of La Meri's life, she and Neal met for interview sessions—
sometimes once or twice a week, with Adams assisting. After La Meri's death,
Neal contacted everyone she knew about and could find who had had any
professional contact with La Meri over the years. From the Neal files, it looks
like there were between 150 and 200 people to whom she sent letters with
questions they might be able to answer. It was all this material that was transferred to me in 2014.

La Meri died on January 7, 1988, in a San Antonio hospital. There were
appreciative obituaries in many publications, including the *New York
Times, Los Angeles Times, Arabesque, Dance Magazine, San Antonio Light*,
and *San Antonio Express-News*. The ones in *Dance Magazine* and *San Antonio Light* were written by Josie Neal. Most of the obituaries give her birth
year incorrectly as 1898—as she does in her autobiography. Information in
archival collections such as those of the New York and San Antonio Public

Libraries give her correct birth year of 1899, but some say she was 89 when she died, an age she would not have reached until May 1988.

La Meri's Legacy through Donations to Institutions

Over the years, La Meri had amassed an enormous number of items related to her professional and personal life. These included performance costumes and paraphernalia; concert announcements, programs, and reviews; articles about her life and work; legal documents; correspondence with a range of people from her beloved sister to unknown fans who had seen her perform; photographs; and, of course, her own writings. What is probably the largest La Meri archive is in the Jerome Robbins Dance Division (JRDD) of the New York Public Library for the Performing Arts. According to Adams, La Meri had been sending items there over many years, and after her death, he sent others that were appropriate for that collection. The La Meri archive at the JRDD is divided into three parts: personal and professional letters and other documents, La Meri's own writings in both draft and final forms, and what is termed Oversized Materials, which includes photograph albums and miscellaneous items.

At least by 1977, La Meri had begun to make careful plans for the donation of her possessions and archival materials to various institutions. Prominent on the list were her international costumes, jewelry, and related items, which she gave to the costume collection of the Duquesne University Tamburitzans (DUT) in Pittsburgh, Pennsylvania.[10] In September 1977, that institution sent David Kolar, son of DUT's managing director, to Cape Cod to index and pack the materials they were to receive and transport them to Pittsburgh. On September 18 and 19, Kolar and La Meri worked together to organize the collection and record information about its contents. Before packing each item, Kolar would briefly describe it, and La Meri would give specific information about its identity, where it was from, how she had used it, and any alterations she had made to accommodate the quick changes in her solo concerts. This was all taped and then transcribed onto sixty-six typed pages. When I visited the DUT center in May 2003 Susan M. Stafura, director of the Costume Department, allowed me to examine everything in the collection and gave me a copy of the transcript. At the end of the transcript (67), Kolar notes that the total of the collection was "about 12 or 13 major trunks and about as many small boxes worth of costumes, artifacts, jewelry—those three categories primarily." La Meri writes that altogether, the items in this collection were worth $29,847 (1980 addition to *Chronology 1973*, 21). It is clear from this—and from examining the collection—that she had certainly not sold her personal costumes when she left New York for the Cape.

In 1977, about seven years before her return to San Antonio, La Meri wrote to John Igo about donating materials to the Theatre Archive there. In his September 26 response, he wrote that he had "decided to include ALL STAGED performance in the archive," which "opened it up to opera, ballet, and, of course, La Meri." And he said that for many years, he had been "an awed follower of the legendary La Meri" and had contacted her friend Olivia Matteson to see what relevant materials she might be able to provide. Since La Meri had spent most of her childhood and youth in San Antonio and felt a strong connection to it, she was very happy to contribute to this archive. On November 5, Igo wrote that he had received the two packages of photographs, writings, and other items that she had sent, and he suggested also setting up an archive for Lilian's materials, which was done. Over the years La Meri contributed other documents to the San Antonio archive, which I visited in September 2001. The collection is very extensive and divided into five parts. The largest consists of articles, reviews, correspondence, programs, and brochures. The others are La Meri's writings (including the detailed section about her family and early life that the publisher of *Dance Out the Answer* refused to include in the book), photographs and albums, scrapbooks, and "Ephemera."

Since Kentucky had been the original home of her family, La Meri donated "family memorabilia" to the Kentucky Historical Society (KHS), and, in May 1978, someone was sent to Cape Cod to transport the items to the institution. La Meri writes that what she gave them consisted of "family portraits, flat silver, Father's fine photos, several pieces of furniture, etc., etc." with an approximate value of $16,000 (1980 addition to *Chronology 1973*, 22). It is interesting that she estimated the monetary worth of some of her donations—perhaps to take them as deductions from her income tax. One can wonder how she managed to keep all these things with her over the years—if she had room for them in her living or teaching quarters or had placed them with friends or students or in public storage units.

Another important collection is the La Meri archive at Jacob's Pillow, which contains documents from her activities there and the originals of the materials that Josie Neal had collected, that her daughter sent to Bill Adams, that he sent to me—and that, after making copies, I sent to the Pillow. This collection includes the large number of letters that La Meri wrote to her sister and others, the three-volume travel journal she gave her mother for Christmas 1924 (describing their 1922 travels in Europe), her dance and choreography notations, letters that La Meri received from various people, programs, and press clippings. This collection is indeed a treasure to be carefully studied for insights into the work and personal life of this artist and the world around her.

VI. Cape Cod

43. La Meri walking one of her dogs.

44. La Meri teaching flamenco.

45. William J. (Bill) Adams.

46. La Meri teaching Bill Adams and Cindy Figge in her basement in 1981. Photograph by Ulrich Figge.

47. *Jota Aragonesa*. Performed by Ethnic Dance Arts dancers at Clark University, Worcester, Massachusetts, June 14, 1973.

48. Mariano Parra and Jerane Michel in a Spanish dance. Photograph by Roberto Sandoval.

49. St. Denis Award 1981, with previous recipients (*left to right*) and the years of their awards: Ibrahim Farrar (1979), Jean-Marie Mellichamp (1977), La Meri, Nala Najan (1981), Bashkar (1978), Mariano Parra (1980). Photograph by Ulrich Figge.

50. La Meri and her beloved dogs at home in Cape Cod. Photograph by Dave Murdoch.

9

La Meri's Writings

There is much evidence of La Meri's lifelong commitment to writing, which seems to have been as central to her life as dance. Fortunately, her thoughts, feelings, and insights survive not only in her published poetry, articles, and books but also in the hundreds of notes and notebooks, dance descriptions, letters, and other materials in her archives. At an early age La Meri began publishing her poetry and, later, works about her own life experiences and about dance and its many manifestations. Information about her life and work can be found in articles from the 1920s on and in her autobiography of 1977. Most important, in six other books and many articles, she presents information about numerous dance genres and their cultural contexts, histories, and notable practitioners—information she obtained from a variety of written sources plus her practical experience in studying and seeing dance around the world. In her dance writings she also sets forth her theoretical, aesthetic and pedagogical conceptions and ideas. A brief consideration of her poetry will be followed by discussion of her books and a survey of her articles.

Poetry

When Russell Hughes was still a teenager, her poems began appearing in local Texas publications and in national journals and magazines such as *American Poetry Magazine*, *Literary Digest*, and *Poetry Journal*. And when she was touring as a concert dance artist, examples of her verses were sometimes printed in news articles about her—especially in Latin America. Between 1917 and 1925, she published five books of poetry under her birth name—the first two in Texas, and later ones in Boston and Philadelphia. *The Star Roper* of 1925 was republished in 1927 and 1928 with sketches by Carreras, and her last collection, *Songs and Voyages* came out in 1938 in Italy under her professional name. The latter includes poems from her previous collections as well as new ones.

Many of the early verses of the young woman were inspired by her summer 1917 stay on a Texas ranch, sharing work and play with the cowboys and becoming fascinated by their culture (see chapter 1). Participating in that life was a romantic journey into a world totally different from anything she had known before. The first section of *Songs and Voyages* consists of fifteen "Cowboy Songs," many presented in a humorous vernacular—supposedly, the "cowboy" language. For example, the first of the six verses of "Give a man a horse" reads:

> Th' Sargent wuz a cowboy from th' Big Bend 'fore he jined,
> He could ride th' meanest bucker an' roll a cigarette.
> He could gentle up a green hoss, ride him easy, treat him kind,
> In a day or so, That feller savvied hosses, you can bet. (1938a, 10)

In addition to her published cowboy poems, she also wrote a tongue-in-cheek travelogue in the cowboy lingo—a take-off on experiences she had during her Latin American tour of 1928–29. Titled "The Traveling Cowboy (South America)," it consists of fifty-eight typed pages, and is very humorous. The original is in the Jacob's Pillow archive.

The second and third sections of *Songs and Voyages* contain eighteen "Love Songs" and sixteen poems on travel. The love songs are poignant and moving, and some of them refer to Carreras. For example, in "Appassionata," she writes:

> Once your kiss was a precious thing,
> Sweet to dream of again.
> Now your kiss is a vital thing,
> A promise, a hungry pain.
>
> Ivory white on a purple couch—
> (Life is so short to live!)
> Heaven holds nothing as sweet as this!
> All that I have I give! (1938a, 45)

The poems on travel give glimpses or probing descriptions of what she saw in the places she visited, or they address her fascination with travel itself and some of her experiences. For example, in the section, "Voyages," the first poem (57–61), which also has the title "Voyage," contains single verses on the West Indies, Panama, Peru, Chile, Argentina, Uruguay, Brazil, Venezuela, Colombia, Costa Rica, and Mexico and ends with:

> Silver light;
> Stars catch on the mast and crest
> The blowing foam.
> Hearth light;
> A dog barks and a door-key clicks,
> And I am home! (61)

Her focus on travel in these poems reminds one of both the extensive report of the 1922 European trip she made with her mother and her detailed letters to Lilian while touring Australia, Asia, and Latin America. La Meri's poems provide insights into her character, imagination, dreams, sense of humor, and sensuality. But poetry, along with the other "horses on her carousel" did not continue as a life focus for her. As we know, she committed herself to dance, although occasionally she would write a new poem for a Christmas letter or other communication.

Writings on Dance

In the beginning of her career, La Meri's time and energy were dedicated to the practice of dance—on developing her skills as a performing artist and choreographer and on learning new dance languages and adding them to her repertoire. Her first published writings on dance were articles that were probably encouraged by Carreras as promotional material—to stimulate interest in her concerts. The earliest of these appeared in 1926 in a Mexico City newspaper, and from then until the 1980s she wrote more than thirty pieces for special interest publications such as *The American Dancer, Dance Magazine, The Dancing Times, India Newsletter, Educational Dance,* and *Arabesque*—and occasionally articles for publications with a general readership.

As La Meri's reputation became established and her expertise recognized, the articles came to address dance and related issues in some depth rather than simply presenting attractive fodder for prospective audience members. Throughout her life, La Meri was teaching through her writing as well as through her studio classes, choreography, lecture-demonstrations, and dance concerts. And, as noted earlier, she identified herself as an explainer. The full statement on this is in her preface to *Total Education in Ethnic Dance*:

> For some reason known only to Siva, who orchestrated the Cosmic Dance of the Universe, all the facets of my career seem to have been preparing me for the role I have found myself playing during the past fifty-odd years. It seems I have been cast in the character of explainer, and it is my destiny to reduce to a common denominator the complicated techniques and backgrounds of the various aspects of many dance arts and dance sciences." (1977b, vii)

And most of her writings were geared to this task of teaching and explaining.

Over the course of forty-four years La Meri completed seven books: *Dance as an Art Form: Its History and Development* (1933); *The Principles of the Dance-Art* (1933); *The Gesture Language of the Hindu Dance* (1941; republished 1964, 1979); *Spanish Dancing* (1st edition 1948; 2nd revised edition 1967); *Dance Composition: The Basic Elements* (1965); *Dance Out the Answer: An Autobiography* (1977); and *Total Education in Ethnic Dance* (1977). After a separate discussion of each book, there will be some general information about her working process, research, and results.

Dance as an Art Form: Its History and Development (1933)

La Meri says that she began writing this book in the summer of 1931 while she and Carreras were on their "honeymoon" in the village of I Ronchi on the Tuscany coast in Italy (1977a, 71). She doesn't say what possessed her to take on such a project—if this was something she had been planning for a while, or if the previous touring in Europe, seeing important dance artists perform and meeting Pavlova, had spurred her to the effort. One wonders if, in addition to their huge collection of performance costumes and equipment, La Meri and Carreras were also traveling with an extensive library—it seems unlikely that all her citations in this book could have been from memory. There is no information as to exactly when she finished writing the book or if there was any difficulty finding a publisher. In any case, a contract was signed with A. S. Barnes on May 12, 1933, and the book came out that fall.

In her foreword (chapter 1), La Meri states that the book is not designed for "the finished artist" or "the philosophic aesthete," but rather "to help the experienced professionals of the intellectual dance by teaching those who watch them, who study with them, and who write about them to appreciate more fully their art" (4). She does not define what she means by "intellectual dance," but says that her goal is "to present to the reader a concise view of the basic principles upon which rests the technique and spirit of the different types of dancing now being presented by serious artists for aesthetic judgement" (5). Her second chapter, drawing on the writings of Havelock Ellis, John Martin, Ananda K. Coomaraswamy, and others, defends the art of dance as a fundamental and important component of human culture and argues for a welcoming acceptance of the variety of forms it takes. The third chapter surveys the history of "the Occidental Dance-Art" and each of the next seven focuses on a different genre or area of world dance: ballet, the "free dance," ethnologic dance, Eastern dances, Spanish dance, European national dances and American dances (including North American Indian, Latin American, and Caribbean dance). She notes in the foreword that she is omitting discussion of dances from cultures where they have not yet developed into theatrical dance arts (5), referring to dances of sub-Saharan Africa that had not yet entered the arena of Western theatrical dance performance. While the book relies heavily on written sources, La Meri's personal experiences also contribute substantially to her sections on Latin American, Caribbean, Spanish, and Middle Eastern dance.

After chapter XI, "A Final Word," there is a "Table of Dances Mentioned in the Text" and "Glossary of Terms Used," as well as a bibliography and an index. La Meri was typically considerate of the reader in providing such reference tools. In the process of writing this book (and later ones as well), she obviously realized that the reader could have trouble making sense of a text that included unfamiliar terms or dances. The six-page table lists the dances in alphabetical order and for each gives the page(s) where it is mentioned or discussed, the country or province where it is or was located, its form as a solo, couple, or group dance, its place of origin (if known) and a short descriptive comment. Notably missing from the list are any specific dances from India, although some fourteen Indian dance terms appear in the glossary. By this time, she had come into contact with Uday Shankar and the writings of Coomaraswamy but had not yet studied dance techniques or learned traditional dances in India itself. The glossary includes general dance terms, names of genres or categories of dance, and terms specific to one or another dance culture. The bibliography items, organized in relation to chapters, lack full names of authors, years of publication, and sometimes other information—showing that La Meri was not trained in academic writing and referencing. But the three addenda, along with the text, demonstrate her knowledge about and conception of the world of dance, her thoroughness in tackling a project, and her commitment to being an explainer.

There were many positive reviews of the book beginning in November 1933 and continuing into 1934. They appeared in publications such as *Research Quarterly* and the *Journal of Health and Physical Education*, and in newspapers of New York, Boston, Hartford, and California. In the December–January 1933–34 issue of *Mind and Body*, for example, reviewer Frances Sellers Williams writes: "La Meri has her own unique way of telling the story of dancing in many countries. It is not often that a book primarily of textbook quality falls into the category of interesting and exciting reading. This new contribution may be classed as such." And she goes on to praise La Meri's knowledge, her style of writing, her sources, and the importance of this work.[1] The only somewhat negative comment on the book came from Ruth L. Murray (1900–1991), of the College of Education at Wayne University. Her review is analytical and generally favorable, but she complains that the "modern dance" (what La Meri refers to as the "free dance") is not covered adequately or accurately (*Research Quarterly* V/2, May 1934).

Since the early 1930s when La Meri was writing this book, dance history has developed as an academic field of study, and much research and theoretical analysis has been accomplished. Therefore, from the perspective of 2019, there is much that is incorrect or questionable in this work, but in 1933, it was a ground-breaking contribution, providing a volume of information and discussion that had not been previously available.

The Principles of the Dance-Art (1933)

Later in 1933, this small book (fifty-eight pages) was published as number V in the Channing Useful Pocket Series (London: Channing Press).[2] The first chapter, with the same title as the book, defines "dance-art" and identifies three different "schools" of practice: "the Ballet, the Free, and the Ethno-logic" with explanations of each (11–19). The second chapter, "The Origin of the Dance-Art," traces dance's earliest history (20–25), and the third, "The Development of the Dance-Art," discusses the continuing history from the ancient Greeks to the twentieth century (26–38). The final chapter, "Aspects of the Dance-Art To-day," addresses the situation up to the early 1930s in the United States, Latin America, and Europe (39–48). The appendix at the end includes a bibliography (again with incomplete information), a page announcing the first book, *Dance as an Art-Form*, a few term definitions, an index, and information about three dances referred to in the text.

One can wonder where this interesting compilation of information was marketed and sold. It is also curious that there is no mention of it in any of La Meri's writings or archival materials.

Gesture Language of the Hindu Dance (1941, 1964, 1979)

By the time La Meri began work on this project, she had had actual training in Indian dance forms to add to the knowledge she had previously gained from her readings and her contact with Uday Shankar. As discussed in chapter 4, while touring India in the first three months of 1937, she was able to devote some time to studying Bharatanatyam and Kathak with respected masters of those genres, and she also acquired more literature on the dance and related topics. She apparently didn't have time to begin work on this book, however, until her "enforced layoff" in the midst of the 1939 Latin American tour when she injured her ankle during a performance in Rio de Janeiro and was in a cast for two weeks (probably July 6–21). As she writes, she "whiled away the long hours, bereft of even practicing, by starting on a book about the gesture language of Indian dance" (1977a, 149, 152). This initial writing must have been totally from memory, as it is unlikely that she would have been carrying sources such as Coomaraswamy's books with her during her travels. Some time, probably late 1940 or early 1941, she completed the manuscript in New York, and the book was out by the end of 1941. This was an unbelievably speedy completion of an ambitious endeavor that, like many of her writings, she managed to accomplish alongside her busy schedule of performing, choreographing, and teaching.

Three others also contributed to this project. Carreras photographed La Meri's hands illustrating each of the thirty-six *mudras* (hand-gestures) and her full figure with double hand gestures in 200 combined poses.[3] Coomaraswamy checked La Meri's text for accuracy and wrote the short foreword (vii–viii), and Sanskrit scholar Henry R. Zimmer[4] corrected Sanskrit terms in the text and wrote the introduction (xiii–xviii). The support and involvement of these two leaders in Indian cultural studies attests to the respect they had for La Meri's work—as do statements in their sections such as "we cannot but congratulate her upon the devoted care and real learning that have gone into the making of a book at once attractive and informative" (Coomaraswamy, viii); and "By her acting and teaching she is exceptionally qualified to transmit one of the most precious lessons Old India has treasured up for modern civilization" (Zimmer, xviii).

Coomaraswamy and Zimmer both discuss the philosophical, historical, and religious foundations of Indian dance as the context for understanding the technical material shown in the illustrations. Coomaraswamy compares the sacred nature of the dance of India with that of the ancient Greeks, quoting Plato's *Laws* to illustrate his points, while Zimmer discusses the origins of Indian dance in relation to the Hindu religion, referring to ancient and revered texts such as the *Nāṭya Śāstra* and the sacred *Vedas*. La Meri's text, "Hindu Nāṭya," begins with an introduction that includes a comparison of "occidental" and "oriental" dance arts (3–6). This kind of strategy is typical in La Meri's writing—a way to help the reader comprehend the subject—to find a way into it. She continues with four sections: "Religious Background," "Legendary History," "Characteristic Schools," and "Technique." Under "Characteristic Schools," she goes into some detail about Kathakali, the male dance-drama of Malabar, and Sadir Nautch, or Bharatanatyam, the well-known female dance form of South India—and discusses briefly some of the other traditional schools and new dance forms of the twentieth century.

With the section on technique, the book moves from the historical and philosophical contexts to the actual practice of the Indian dance language. It provides an overview of the training and an introduction to the hand gestures and poses that are shown in the rest of the book. The photographs are further discussed in La Meri's "Introduction to Plates," where she explains her choice of poses and their identifications. For each hand gesture, several meanings are provided, and for each full body pose (such as "elephant," "river," "grief," "meditation," "laughter"), an explanation is given. The book ends with a glossary of terms and "The Viniyoga of the Hasta Mudrās" which lists the various meanings depicted in the illustrations with the figure or page number where each can be found. One could learn these gestures and poses from the book—or, if one studied them in classes (as I did with La Meri in the 1950s), the book would provide a means of reviewing and memorizing them. It can serve the same purpose for the Hindu gesture language as a French or Spanish grammar serves for learning those verbal languages.

It is interesting to compare La Meri's book with *The Mirror of Gesture*, the 1917 translation by Coomaraswamy (1877–1947) and Duggirala Gopâlakrishnâyya (1889–1928) of the ancient Indian work, *Abhinaya Darpana* by Nandikeshvara. In his introduction to that, Coomaraswamy states that it is a "shorter compendium" of the full treatise on "Dramatic Science," the *Nāṭya Śāstra* of Bharata, and that it "may be of use as an introduction to Indian method" (15). This translation of a nineteenth-century publication of the work includes sections on terminology, on the performance and performers and, also, on gestures and movements of the head, neck, eyes, eyebrows, and hands. This was obviously a useful resource for La Meri as she began to study Indian dance. In her book, however, she doesn't cover all the elements that are in *Mirror of Gesture*, but rather focuses on the single and combined hand gestures (*hasta mudras*) and their ranges of meanings.

The reviews that began to appear early in 1942 expressed deep admiration and appreciation for this work—from both the Indian cultural community and Western scholars and critics. In the journal that had published the text of La Meri's 1939 lecture-demonstration in London (see chapter 5), there is a four-page review by British artist and writer W. G. Raffé, who discusses it in the context of the twentieth-century renaissance of Indian arts, which he believes was "stimulated somewhat from Europe." In relation to dance, he mentions the 1900 Paris Exposition and the work of Diaghilev, St. Denis and Shawn, and Uday Shankar. His review is detailed, analytical, and positive, and he states his belief that

> Madame La Meri's book will certainly be welcomed in all schools of dance; not only those working on Indian dance, moreover, will find it of value for its fund of visual gesture. Much devoted labour has gone into

its compilation, and in the United States it should do much to extend a wider comprehension of the aesthetics of the art of Hindu dance.

At the end, however, he mentions a few misprints and one possible error (*Indian Arts and Letters* XVI/1 (May–June 1942).

In the United States, appreciative reviews appeared in journals devoted to Indian and other Asian cultures, such as *India News Letter, India Today, Asia*, and the *Journal of the American Oriental Society*; in dance magazines, such as *American Dancer* and *Educational Dance;* and in newspapers, such as the *Christian Science Monitor* and the *New York Herald Tribune*. Interest in this book continued into the 1960s and beyond with a republished edition in 1964 and a reprint of that in 1979. A review of the 1964 edition was published in *Ethnomusicology,* the professional journal of the Society for Ethnomusi-cology. Written by Frances B. Wright, it praises the work as "a book, a text, beautiful and full of enlightenment, for those who would understand the dance of India in all its exotic excellence. It is written clearly for those who will bother to read carefully" (233). And this book is included, along with other writings by non-Indians, in the bibliography of Enakshi Bhavnani's *The Dance in India* (1965), a major study tracing Indian dance's history from earliest times to the 1960s.

The continuing respect and appreciation for La Meri within the Indian culture is demonstrated by the fact that, after her death in 1988, the Indira Gandhi National Centre for the Arts in New Delhi purchased a large archive of her letters, diaries, and books and commissioned scholar and dancer Usha Venkateswaran to write a monograph on her life and work that the centre published in 2005 (Kapila Vatsyayan foreword in Venkateswaran, vi).

Spanish Dancing (1st edition 1948; 2nd revised edition 1967)

Since the 1920s when she first studied dance in Spain, La Meri had also been collecting materials that would be useful in her practical work and in later writings. Her publications on Spanish dance began to appear in the 1930s with one chapter in *Dance as an Art-Form* and a few articles; and in 1946, A. S. Barnes and Company commissioned her to complete a book on Spanish dance. As discussed in chapter 7, she was so busy with her performance and teaching responsibilities in New York and Jacob's Pillow that she could not work on it until the Pillow season ended in late August. And then she had only ten days free until the beginning of the fall season of the EDC. She writes that she worked nonstop to finish the entire manuscript in that short time (1977a, 164–65). In her introduction to the second edition of *Spanish Dancing*, La Meri writes that the book had been "long in the making" and that she had begun to collect the materials that she used for it when she first visited Spain in 1922 (1967, 7). Obviously, what she did in the ten days in 1946 was the typing into final form of what she had been working on for many years. But it was a hurriedly finished manuscript, in any case, and had, as she herself recognized, many problems. She welcomed the opportunity to correct the weaknesses and update information for another edition, and fortunately, she was able to spend a year on that revision (1967, 7). It was Ted Shawn who contracted La Meri to produce the second edition under the auspices of Jacob's Pillow, and he had it printed by the company in Pittsfield, Massachusetts that, in 1940, had produced the first edition of one of his books, *Dance We Must*.

The first edition of *Spanish Dancing* was published sometime before April 15, 1948, when a book signing was held at the famous Kamin's Dance Bookshop in New York City—and it received much praise. In the La Meri archive at NYPL, there are clippings from twenty-nine publications in twenty-one states that refer to this first edition, including both notices of its publication and reviews. Seeing this massive amount of press coverage, one is reminded of the efforts of Carreras, always industriously promoting La Meri's work. Carreras, however, had been out of the picture since their break-up in 1944, so the successful marketing of this book must have been due to the efforts of the publisher with La Meri's assistance.

A comparison of the two editions of *Spanish Dancing* shows great improvement in the writing, depth, and detail of the second. Besides rearranging the chapters to some extent, La Meri rewrote much of the text and added information from new sources that had not been available before. Each of the editions has an appendix with "Technical Terminology" (names of dances and dance steps) and a "Glossary of Terms" (Spanish words sometimes associated with dance, sometimes not). The 1948 edition also has an index and "Table of Dances Mentioned in the Text," which gives a dance's name, its type, the province it is from, and other useful information. However, for some unknown reason, both the index and the table were omitted from the revised edition.

The sources in the bibliographies and textual citations in both editions are remarkable for their historical range—with the oldest reference dating from 1642. Many of these sources are in Spanish, and one wonders how advanced La Meri's knowledge of that language might have been. She gratefully acknowledges the assistance of Guido's niece Juana "for her translations of rare books which are in the library of the Hispanic Society of America"— translations that were apparently done for the first edition (1967, 7). From that statement, one might assume that La Meri's knowledge of Spanish was minimal. For both editions, she draws very heavily on her study with José Otero in Spain and his *Tratado de Bailes* and on the writings of Havelock Ellis and many other sources. By the time she was working on the 1967 edition, there was also important new material such as *Andalusian Dances*, the 1959 translation into English of Spanish scholar José Manuel Caballero Bonald's *El baile andaluz* (1957), books by the originally American flamencologist Donn E. Pohren, and other relevant publications.

As with most of La Meri's books and articles, her writing in *Spanish Dancing* has the purpose of "explaining," of providing information about the range of dance forms that have been and are important in Spain. As usual, she begins with the historical background and goes on to describe the various categories of dance in the culture. In Spain, these include traditional dances indigenous to the different regions (what we might loosely call "folk dances"), flamenco, "school dance" (traditional and newly choreographed dances that were part of the repertoire taught in dance schools such as that of Otero), and what she terms "renaissance" or "neo-classic" (creative works for the concert stage that drew on or were developed from the traditional dance forms). She briefly refers to the bolero school (*escuela bolera*) in her historical overview (1967, 20–21) and occasionally in her chapter, "Neo-Classic Dance and the Ballet Españole" [*sic*], but does not go into depth about what is now an important genre in the spectrum of Spanish dance.[5] Both editions of *Spanish Dancing* include chapters on dance technique, castanets, and La Meri's experiences while studying in Spain. In a short review of the revised edition for *Ethnomusicology*, noted dance anthropologist Gertrude P. Kurath (1903–1992) summarizes the contents of the book, mentions some of the changes from the 1946 edition, and concludes: "The release shows how little Spanish dance has changed within the past twenty years and how dependable La Meri's account remains" (XII/2, May 1968, 294–95). This, coming from a scholar of Kurath's stature, was praise indeed.

Dance Composition: The Basic Elements (1965)

By the 1960s, La Meri had had decades of experience with choreography of all kinds. She had performed dances created or taught by others—from her early days as a young student through her mature work with teachers in India, Spain, and other lands. And she herself had created a massive number of solo and group works for herself and members of her companies. In addition, she taught choreography to students at the EDC in New York and EDA in Cape Cod, and occasionally at other institutions. I have found no information about when or why she decided that she should write an instructional book on dance composition—or whether it was Shawn who encouraged the endeavor with plans to publish it from the beginning. Her draft was completed by late 1964, and she sent copies to Shawn, Walter Terry, Labanotation specialist Ann Hutchinson Guest, and others.

Shawn praised it highly and arranged its publication by the Jacob's Pillow Dance Festival. In a promotional statement, Walter Terry notes that La Meri's book "effectively fills a long-existing gap in the literature dealing with dance education" by providing "a sort of guideline approach to dance composition" and writes: "The book is practical, simple, eminently usable for the novice dancer who would like to create a program, for the teacher, who must build a showcase for a students' recital, for the town-theater-group director who suddenly finds he must choreograph as well as direct. . . . as an extra dividend, it is eminently readable" (Jacob's Pillow announcement). Terry's words reflect clearly La Meri's purpose in developing this book—to assist beginners and those with little experience in choreography to be aware of its many aspects and to provide strategies for learning and mastering the art.

The manuscript was sent to Ann Hutchinson Guest sometime in the late fall of 1964, and in her November 8 letter to La Meri, she expressed her deep appreciation for it: "You write beautifully, and indeed inspiringly, with so many quotes from timeless sources. What I find most satisfying of all is that you are able (as no one else can) to draw on examples from the ethnic field which lifts it immediately onto a broader and less local or personal plane. I feel I have gained so much just by reading it." Regarding Guest's praise for "examples from the ethnic field," the book includes references to ethnic dance forms on almost fifty of its pages. In her letter, Guest also asked if she should submit the manuscript to a British publisher, discussed some of the terms in the book, and wondered if a sequel dealing with more advanced work was being planned. She did send the manuscript to a London publisher, but it was rejected on the premise that there would not be a substantial market for it there (letter to Guest from general editor of Sir Isaac Pitman and Sons Limited, March 30, 1965).

This 152-page lesson-book consists of two parts. The first, "The Craft," begins with an "Introduction" and continues with ten separate sections: "Floor-Design," "Air-Design," "Music-Design," "Dramatic Design," "Dynamics," "Theme," "Movement," "Process," "Accessories," and "Group Choreography." Each section ends with a list of "Suggested Lessons" or "Suggested Assignments," making it clearly a handbook to be used for instruction by a teacher or for self-instruction by a student. Part II also begins with an "Introduction," and has four sections: "To the Student," "To the Teacher," "To Parents," and "To the Audience"—with advice to each group.

The book ends with a suggested reading list of twenty-two items on dance history, ethnic dance, choreography, and movement theory and practice. La Meri was, as always, committed to drawing on written sources for information and insights, and it is significant that she included recent works on dance composition and on nondance movement theory. The sources on choreography that she recommends are *Dance Composition and Production* by Elizabeth R. Hayes (1955), *Dance: A Creative Art Experience* by Margaret H'Doubler (1940), *Modern Dance Forms* by Louis Horst (1961), and *The Art of Making Dances* by Doris Humphrey (1959). The ones listed on nondance movement and theory are *Expression Gymnastics* by Rudolf Bode (1931), *Eurythmics* by Émile Jaques-Dalcroze (1931), and *Every Little Movement*, Shawn's 1954 book on the Delsarte System. (It should be noted that some of the items on her list are incomplete or with errors.)

In her *Dance Magazine* review of this book, critic and editor Doris Hering (1920–2014) begins by expressing gratitude for being introduced to and gaining knowledge of world dance forms from La Meri. And while she found the book to some extent "uneven, sometimes lofty and penetrating in its viewpoint, sometimes resorting to esthetically irresponsible statements," she also found much to recommend, saying "as a whole it is a sound and thoughtful contribution to the gradually widening shelf of dance composition texts." Hering considered "one of the delights" of the book to be La Meri's "use of ethnic dance imagery" and gives a few examples of that. However, she criticizes what she considers "questionable statements"—generalizations about Western dance that La Meri related to certain ethnic dance principles or practices (XXXX/3, March 1966, 23–24).

It would be interesting to know if any teachers or students have ever used this book as a text for their classes or for independent study. I think it has value as an overall general view of the components of dance composition and teaching it—all the elements are clearly defined, and exercises are suggested for work on each of them separately and in combination. In my opinion, however, her curriculum is too rigid and reflective of half a century ago to be effective in a choreography class of today. I believe that the most useful value of the book now is the insight it gives into (1) La Meri's concepts, processes, and values in regard to, not only choreography, but also the relationship of dance to the world at large; and (2) her own ethics and values in relation to life and art. She generalizes about many things—those that Hering mentions and others, and while some are questionable in relation to fact, they provide valuable insight into La Meri's thinking. For example, her statement that "Choreography is a series of pictures, a painting come to life" (14), suggests the concept she may have used for her own work, but one can argue that not all choreography fits that definition.

In 1975, a Javanese translation of this book was published in Yogyakarta, Indonesia.

Dance Out the Answer: An Autobiography (1977)

In her acknowledgments at the beginning, La Meri states that the "vast welter of material" that she had initially planned for her autobiography was first brought together and edited by a reader named Carolyn Stagg in 1965 (vii). However, she had begun working on this project by 1956 or earlier since, in her archives, there is a summary of eleven chapters covering her life up to that year with comments by an unidentified reviewer. Also, in a typed statement dated May 18, 1957, La Meri writes: "Well, my autobiography is finished . . . or will be, if I can get around to re-writing the last chapter. . . . And it is not an autobiography at all, but the story of a career . . . not of a person." Further on, she says that she "resents" that and goes on a diatribe against her own lack of ability to write about herself and about some of the disappointing and hurtful aspects of her life. Of course, she did not really lack that ability. She demonstrated it consistently in her correspondence with Lilian.

It was not until 1975 that she received a contract for publication of the work from Marcel Dekker, Inc. In her original plan, the book was to include far more information about her childhood and family up to 1920 than Dekker was willing to publish.[6] The editors were apparently mainly interested in the glamorous aspects of her life as an international performing artist, so this early period (to the age of twenty-two) is only briefly covered in the sixteen pages of the first chapter. Chapter 2, on her beginning professional career, 1920–1927, is also short (nine pages). The next seven chapters are devoted to her international touring, and the tenth begins in Peru in 1938 and continues through the beginning of La Meri's wartime years in the United States, when she was establishing herself and her work in New York City. The eleventh continues that history to 1949, with focus on the Ethnologic Dance Center and her performing in the city and on tour. The final chapter, "An End and a Beginning," is a short nine-page summary of her life and work from 1949 to 1970, which ends with a poem, "The Star Roper" (from San Antonio, 1920). Throughout the book, there are bits of information about family, personal experiences, and her feelings in relation to her professional and personal life, but the book is mainly a narrative of adventures and accomplishments while touring, learning new dances, and performing.

The work received mixed responses in *Dance Research Journal, Dancemagazine, Dance Chronicle, Dance Scope*, and other publications. Some of the problems noted may have been due to Dekker's demands rather than La Meri's own decisions. For example, in her review for *Dance Research Journal*, dance historian Christena L. Schlundt (1922–2004) states that the book provides "a vivid account" of La Meri's life as a "traveling artist" and of her "point of view toward such a life," but very little about her personal life or the world events that affected it. Schlundt compares La Meri's coverage of the personal and professional aspects of her life, writing: "Personal grief, imminent tragedy, global war: all are off-stage, merely noted by her 'art-insulated consciousness'" (La Meri's phrase from 1977a, 148). On stage center throughout the account is only the joy, the gaiety, the hectic pace, the upbeat of her life" (50). And, while Schlundt appreciated much about the book, she lamented that it lacks any descriptions of the dances "to bring them to life for the reader" and concluded that "little of the substance, and only the exterior of the great artist La Meri was, shines through these reminiscences" (51).

In her evaluation for *Dance Chronicle* of both *Dance Out the Answer* and *Total Education,* Asian specialist and writer Renée Renouf considers both books "essentially one, for the style and development in the second [*Total Education*] are inextricably linked to La Meri's own experience" (67). In appreciation of La Meri's discussions in the autobiography of touring and performing around the world, Renouf writes that "they reflect several different levels of awareness, all of which I find quite admirable. She writes with the performer's reactions, the professional's capacity for public relations and diplomacy, . . . and her perception of the 'world at large' to whom she presented herself—an eager world, somewhat naive, but essentially generous" (69). In this very positive review of the autobiography, Renouf compares some of La Meri's experiences with her own in India and elsewhere.

For its August 1978 issue that featured La Meri, *Dancemagazine* had Jane Sherman (1908–2010), a leading Denishawn dancer and noted writer on Denishawn and other subjects, review the two 1977 books. After summarizing the contents of *Dance Out the Answer,* Sherman writes: "This record of a rich life is written in a breezy, simplistic style that constantly reminds the reader of La Meri's Texas background. At times it seems more a travelogue than an insight into her philosophy." She also notes that the book contains "some errors in La Meri's memory, some inaccuracies an editor should have corrected, and some statements to which this reviewer takes exception" and gives a few examples of those. Sherman's criticism is similar to Schlundt's in regard to La Meri's apparent lack of attention to the extreme political situations and conflicts during which she lived. Sherman writes: "I find it strange that this sensitive human being could have had a home for many years in Mussolini's Italy—have lived through the era of the Civil War that devastated her beloved Spain—and have survived as a performer throughout World War II—without writing her reactions to these momentous events and times" (66). However, while La Meri does not mention the Italian or Spanish events, she does write (briefly) of the looming World War II in relation to their touring and lost home in Italy (1977a, 148–50). She may not have considered discussion of the political situations in Italy and Spain relevant to the focus of the book. Despite Sherman's questions and criticism, however, she writes that "this autobiography is one that serious students of America's disparate dance innovators will want to read" (69).

Total Education in Ethnic Dance (1977)

La Meri's lifelong interest was "ethnic dance." She claims in this book that she herself introduced that term, and that it "came into general usage during the 1940s as a way to differentiate among ballet, modern, and ethnic in theater-dance presentations . . . a convenient means of quick identification of the ethnic art dance" (1). Of course, ballet and modern dance are single genres, and as she writes, "Ethnic dance . . . covers an unwieldy majority of the world's choreography" (ibid.), in other words, many genres. In *Total Education in Ethnic Dance*, La Meri sets forth her concepts, principles, and practices in relation to the learning, teaching, performing, and understanding of dance from a variety of cultures. The book contains ten chapters: 1. "What is Ethnic Dance? 2. "Total Education in Ethnic Dance," 3. "Why Study Ethnic Dance?" 4. "Creative Ethnic Dance," 5. "*Swan Lake* and *Bach-Bharata*," 6. "Ethnic Dance Appreciation," 7. "The Spine," 8. "Exoteric and Esoteric Origins," 9. "Spanish Dance," and 10. "East Indian Dance." At the end there are twenty-four recommended readings and an index. One can see from the titles of the chapters that La Meri was, as usual, investigating her topic in breadth and depth. We will consider some parts of this volume.

In her first chapter, "What Is Ethnic Dance?" La Meri defines the term as designating "all those indigenous dance arts that have grown from popular or typical dance expressions of a particular race" (1); and she makes a distinction between folk dance and art dance, with her own work focusing on the latter (3–4). As discussed in my introduction, in contrast to predecessors such as Ruth St. Denis and Maud Allan, who used non-Western ("exotic") themes in their dance creations but did not (for the most part) learn actual dances from other parts of the world, La Meri assiduously worked to understand and master traditional dance techniques and choreographies from different cultures. As we have seen, to further that goal, La Meri studied with many teachers from various cultures—during the brief times she had while on tour—and she would read whatever written sources she could find.

There is no evidence that La Meri ever questioned her right to learn and perform foreign dance arts or to create original works using aspects of the traditions. She did, however, insist on knowledge of the cultural contexts of the dances and awareness of (and honesty about) how they were being presented "in transplantation to the stage." Rather than insist that duplication of traditional dances and dance languages was the only acceptable way to present such material, she wrote that, for the stage, "the ethnic dance arts may take, loosely, any one of five forms" (4). On the next two pages (5–6) she explains her definitions of those forms (I have quoted or paraphrased her words and put my comments or explanations in brackets).

The Traditional—Presentation of a dance exactly as done in its own culture—with the original dance movement, choreography, music, and costumes. [Of course, within most cultures, there is usually not only one way of performing a dance or musical form—individual artists will bring their own understandings and creativity to their renditions (when the tradition does not forbid that). And all arts change over time. What La Meri means here, I assume is duplication of a dance exactly as she learned it.]

The Authentic—Work that would incorporate "the traditional costumes, music, and techniques, but might take certain liberties with the form." [Examples could include the shortening of a dance for stage presentation, rearranging the stage design or other aspect of the choreography, or setting a repeatable choreography for a dance that would normally be improvised.]

The Creative Neoclassic or Renaissance—A work retaining the movement techniques, style, and motivation of the original genre or specific dance, but with the costuming, music, and/or choreography altered to some extent. La Meri mentions the work of Uday Shankar and La Argentina as examples of this approach.

Creative Departures—In these, the choreographer would take more liberties with the original dance material than in the previous category.

Applied Techniques—Using any aspects of the traditional dance practices in the creation of original works. [Examples would include La Meri's 1944 staging of *Swan Lake* using the gesture language, movement vocabulary, and costumes of East Indian dance with the Tchaikovsky music, and her 1946 *Bach-Bharata Suite*, in which she set abstract South Indian Bharatanatyam technique to Bach's music.]

La Meri developed a precise pedagogical approach to teaching what she had learned of Spanish, East Indian, and other dance traditions, and she sets forth these principles in the book. Convinced that someone outside of a culture requires a kind of training different from that received by students within the culture, she developed movement exercises for the Spanish and East Indian dance vocabularies that could be taught in technique classes comparable to those of ballet or modern dance. As noted previously, this is a departure from the practice in many cultures where dances are traditionally learned from imitation or taught as whole choreographies.

A fundamental principle of her approach to teaching was her belief that posture is the primary element of any dance practice, with the movements and steps secondary. This is discussed in chapter 7, "The Spine," a part of the book unanimously praised by the reviewers. As La Meri explains, "Of first importance is the placement and control of the spine and its adjuncts—the neck, the shoulders, and the pelvis . . . In many cases the dance techniques of two different peoples will differ more in the spine carriage than in any other part of the anatomy" (65). She then discusses the postures of dance practices from various cultures, including those of Spain, Latin America, Asia, and the Middle East (65–74), and illustrates several of them with drawings of stick figures (68–69).

La Meri realized that posture and movement vocabularies do not evolve in a vacuum, but as part of a total cultural complex, and in her writing and teaching she stressed the importance of understanding the cultural elements that contribute to the nature of a dance language. These include the historical context of the dance form; its connection to religious beliefs or practices; the social customs of the culture (what is acceptable or promoted in terms of gender differences, for example); the traditional site of the dance activity— its physical characteristics as well as its function (as a temple, palace, theater, park, or other setting); who does the dance (professional dancers, members of a religious organization, or community members) (75–79).

In developing her approach, La Meri also used the theoretical system of the French teacher and theorist of acting and singing, François Delsarte (1811–1871). His theories had become popular in the United States in the late nineteenth century and adapted for use in physical culture and expression (Ruyter 1979; 1999a). La Meri was particularly interested in Delsarte's division of "being" into three elements: the intellectual or spiritual, the emotional, and the vital (physical), and in his categorization of parts of the body in terms of this triune conception. She discusses his theory and applies it to the genres of Spanish flamenco dance and East Indian Bharatnatyam (80–83).

While La Meri had no formal training in ethnographic research, movement analysis, cultural studies, or pedagogy, she developed her own ways to research and learn foreign dance languages, to analyze them, to study them in their historical and cultural contexts, and to teach them responsibly and effectively. And, as I note in chapter 6, students at her Ethnologic Dance Center were required to take a broad curriculum that included classes not only in the practice and staging of dances from various traditions, but also in their history and culture.

Total Education in Ethnic Dance received coverage in major dance publications, sometimes (as noted above) along with La Meri's *Dance Out the Answer*. All the reviews were mixed. The most positive evaluation was that of Jane Sherman in *Dancemagazine*. While she criticizes some of La Meri's information and the lack of a glossary of foreign terms, she appreciated the book as a whole, particularly La Meri's broad coverage of different world dance cultures and techniques and her emphasis on the spine. She concludes that reading the book would be beneficial to the dancers of the time, since they "are often called upon to perform all kinds of dancing," and "the technical benefit alone [of reading this book] should prove enormous." And what she considered "an even more important benefit would be the increased respect for the ancient and honorable world-wide art of the dance that one is bound to acquire from a study of this book written by a woman of real integrity" (69). The pages of this review also include historical photographs of La Meri—in portraits, performing, and in a 1955 meeting with Walter Terry and a photographer.

Renée Renouf's review of *Total Education* is more critical, demonstrating her broad knowledge of Asian dance and its literature and the field of ethnomusicology. Renouf had traveled to India for the first time in 1966 and was active in organizations related to Asian or international arts. While she finds much to question in the book, she also appreciates La Meri's section on posture, writing, "When La Meri discusses the differences in the use of the spine for the various dance styles, she is at her best" (71). In addition, she praises La Meri's "attempts to create a curriculum and to provide a historical and cultural background" as "admirable" (ibid.). On the negative side, Renouf compares La Meri's short and superficial study of many traditional dance arts with the experience and depth of knowledge of Western ethnomusicologists, who would spend two or three years living in and focusing their research on the art or arts of one culture (70–71). She also criticizes other problems, including that the reading list at the end lacks many important works relevant to topics in the book (73–74). There are other reviews with similar objections.

In 1976, Dekker had asked Walter Terry to evaluate the manuscript and make suggestions, which he did—by phone to La Meri and in a September 29 letter to the publisher. In the letter, he identifies the work as "without question the finest book on ethnic dance studies that I have ever seen. As a dance professor at the University level, I would make it recommended and even required reading for my students taking dance history and criticism courses." He also appreciated the section on the spine, writing, "One of the most brilliant and revealing chapters of a brilliant and uniquely informative book is that on the spine (and its related stances, poses, posture, etc.)." And it was his suggestion that the postures be illustrated with line drawings. Later, in Terry's foreword to the book (v), he repeats his praise of the work as "the finest" in its field and his statement about the section on the spine.

La Meri's Articles—An Overview

Of the thirty-eight articles that La Meri published from 1926 to 1986, about half focus on one or more of the international dance forms she had studied; the others discuss ethnic dance in general, particular dance artists, or other topics (see bibliography for details). From 1927 on, her articles appeared in various publications dedicated to dance, and in 1939, 1940, and 1950, in ones focusing on Indian culture. There were also a few in publications of general interest, such as *Bright Scrawl* (the magazine of the Junior League of San Antonio), *Harper's Bazaar*, and the *Boston Sunday Globe*.

She was recognized as a specialist—perhaps the only one—on "ethnic dance," and, as such, was invited to write "Theatrical Ethnic Dance" for the survey, *25 Years of American Dance* (1951a) and "The Ethnologic Dance Arts" for Walter Sorell's collection, *The Dance Has Many Faces* (1951b and 1966). That last article, however, was among ten not included in the 3rd revised edition of Sorell's work (1992), which contained many new pieces on post-1966 developments. Perhaps Sorell no longer considered her work or ethnic dance relevant in the 1990s. However, important as evidence that she and her work were still recognized and valued in the dance world into the late

1970s was the 1978 *Dancemagazine* publication of her biographical article, "I remember . . ." and "A chronology of learning, labor, life (edited and with a foreword by Walter Terry), both of which provide information not included in La Meri's autobiography.

Conclusion

While La Meri's performance, choreography, and teaching have been very important to the history of dance and the spread of knowledge about and experience of world dance forms, in my opinion, her books and articles have also been a significant contribution. From the time she was a young girl in San Antonio, she had demonstrated an insatiable desire to search for information about whatever caught her interest, and this yearning for more and more knowledge never abated. Throughout her life, she assiduously sought and used a variety of sources for her writing as well as her creative work. While La Meri's short stints in higher education had given her little or no formal academic training in scholarly study, from the beginning of her dance writing, she created publications that draw on a range of sources, provide useful information, and encourage further exploration and research. And, in each book, except for *Dance Out the Answer* and *Gesture Language of the Hindu Dance*, La Meri included a bibliography of the published works that she had used.

The number and quality of sources La Meri consulted for her work and shared with her readers is impressive. The bibliography of *Dance as an Art Form* contains twenty-nine items, and there are at least fifteen additional works cited in the text. *Gesture Language of the Hindu Dance* has no bibliographic list, but in the text there are citations of eleven sources. The first edition of *Spanish Dancing* has a bibliography of forty-six items, which is expanded to fifty-four in the second edition. *Dance Composition* has twenty-two "Suggested Readings," and a number of other sources cited in the text. Finally, *Total Education in Ethnic Dance* has twenty-four works listed as "Recommended Readings." Most of the publications cited are in English, with some in French or Spanish.

The bibliography in La Meri's first book, *Dance as an Art Form*, is a treasury of writings well known and respected in the early decades of the twentieth century. Works that she both cites in the text and lists in the bibliography include *The Dance of Life* (1923) by Havelock Ellis; *The Dance: Its Place in Art and Life* (1914) by Troy and Margaret Kinney; *The Art of the Dance* (1928) by Isadora Duncan; and books on ballet by the prolific Cyril Beaumont and others. Also on the list are *Dance of Siva* (1924) and *Mirror of Gesture* (1917), two major sources on Indian culture and dance by the respected scholar Ananda K. Coomaraswamy—works she first learned about from her contact with Uday Shankar. And the bibliography also includes books on the "free dance," Dalcroze Eurythmics, Spanish dance, Japanese dance, European folk dance, and American Indian dance.

La Meri continued her search for information and insights throughout her life. As new publications appeared, she would update her lists. For example, in the first edition of *Spanish Dancing*, she has sources dating from 1642 to 1941; in the second edition, she added works published from after 1941 to 1964, including two important texts by the noted flamencologist Donn E. Pohren. The works cited in *Total Education in Ethnic Dance* go up to 1967 and include not only writings specifically on dance but also important publications on theater such as *Theatre in the East* (1956) and *Japanese Theatre* (1959) by Faubion Bowers; *Theatre in Southeast Asia* (1967) by James R. Brandon; and *Introduction to Chinese Theatre* (1958) by A. C. Scott. In La Meri's text citations and in some of the bibliographies one also finds writings on the cultural and historical contexts of the dance arts she is "explaining." On the other side, as noted above, Renée Renouf had found the recommended reading list of *Total Education* to be totally inadequate, and she lists numerous sources that were relevant to the topics in the book—and available when La Meri was writing it—and severely criticizes their omission. Renouf concludes, "The absence of these texts leads me to surmise that perhaps La Meri is summarizing her experience and her beliefs as much as presenting material for other people to utilize (73–74). I think that is a fair conclusion since La Meri was never writing traditional scholarly works.

Despite the criticism by reviewers such as Renouf, however, I am continually impressed by the range and depth of La Meri's research and study for both her practical work—performing, choreographing, and teaching—and her writing projects. It is clear that she was continually seeking source materials—both for her own enlightenment and for that of her students and her readers. And while her writing is full of her own opinions (sometimes expressed in a humorously combative manner), the information she gives is from the array of respected materials that she consulted. Her writing, of course, was that of an untutored enthusiast, so there are problems if one considers it in relation to academic standards. They include the following: (1) she usually does not specify the sources of paraphrased information; (2) she sometimes omits the page numbers of citations for quotations or paraphrased opinions; (3) she rarely questions or compares what sources have said; (4) she often names someone in the text without identifying who it is—assuming that the reader is familiar with the person and his or her significance; and (5), as Renouf notes, her reading lists are limited. One could also fault her for not addressing the kinds of theoretical and ethical questions in relation to cultural borrowings and fusions that have come to the forefront in scholarship in recent years, but she was living, working, and writing in a different era. Overall, her writings, even with their flaws, are significant contributions to our knowledge and understanding of dance and its various manifestations—and of La Meri and her work.

10

Final Words

Overview

During her life as an international dance artist touring the world, and the long and equally active years when she was based in New York City and Cape Cod, La Meri was an avid practitioner and promoter of world dance arts and a firm believer in their importance to human life, culture, and understanding. As noted in my introduction, her work carried on traditions of cultural borrowings and sharing that began in the Western world at least as early as the Renaissance and have continued up to the present day. The phenomenon of one culture drawing on another has occurred within various contexts and with differing goals. While often sponsored by governments or organizations with specific purposes in mind, in some cases, such as that of La Meri, it has been the result of individual curiosity and interest. She was not working on behalf of any established hierarchy or institution, but on her own—as a solo artist, student, and researcher who had developed interest in gaining knowledge about and fluency in the performance of dance from a broad range of traditions around the world. During her main touring years (1926 to 1939), she was learning dances from different cultures and introducing them to audiences in other cultures, who, for the most part, probably had no prior knowledge or experience of any of the foreign dance arts she presented or their social and cultural contexts. It is important to note that she did not simply take non-Western dances and introduce them to the West; she also performed a variety of both Western and non-Western dances in the non-Western locations where she gave concerts. Whenever possible, she would perform one or more of the dances from the culture where she was appearing, which always elicited great appreciation. After La Meri settled in the United States, she performed her international repertoire to American audiences, most of whom also would have known little or nothing about the foreign cultures whose dances she introduced. While the responses here were usually positive, it took time for some of the critics to appreciate these "alien arts."

One might ask to what extent La Meri managed to accurately master, perform, and teach any of the dance arts with which she worked. From my experiences studying with her and with native teachers of Spain and India, and seeing performances of artists from those cultures, I think she did amazingly well. I found no discrepancies between what I had learned from her and what I was later taught by the native teachers or saw in their performances. I think she was unusual in having the ability to become fluent in a number of movement languages with sometimes very little intensive training. And I believe she served an important function in fostering international cultural experience and understanding for all.

An analysis of La Meri's stage presentations as well as her life's work is difficult, because of their many facets and developments. She became deeply interested in the cultures whose dances she studied and in the complex process of understanding and acquiring new dance languages and then teaching and performing them. Of course, the brevity of her time and studies in so many countries suggests that any expertise she displayed could be considered superficial. And she was a woman from Western culture who had grown up with perspectives on life and the arts that were very different from those of the populations where she learned native dance practices. During her travels in Latin America, Asia, the Pacific area, and Europe she entered each culture as an outsider—both from her own point of view and from that of the local members of the societies—so one can ask to what extent she was able to gain a deep understanding of each culture.

Both the briefness of La Meri's actual training in the various dance forms and her minimal or nonexistent knowledge of any of the local verbal languages would have limited her understanding of the foreign cultures whose dances she studied, performed, and taught—and about which she wrote. She could have nothing approaching the depth of knowledge gained by a researcher who spends months or years in the field, living in one culture, learning its language, and participating in its life and practices. La Meri did not have that kind of experience anywhere. To gain understanding of the dance traditions and practices that fascinated her and their cultural contexts, she read as many relevant writings as she could find, and she used the knowledge she gained in all aspects of her career. Important sources specifically on dance included those of native scholars such as Coomaraswamy (Indian dance) and Caballero Bonald (Spanish dance) that were available in English translations. She also read English language works: general studies of the history and culture of the areas of her dance interests and publications specifically relevant to the performing arts such as those on Asian dance and theater by Faubion Bowers, James Brandon, and Claire Holt. In addition, La Meri consulted writings by or about theorists and educators such as François Delsarte, Émile Jaques-Dalcroze, and Rudolf Bode. She was an avid reader and learner throughout her life, and she used the knowledge she gained in her creative work, teaching, and writing. La Meri added significantly to international knowledge of the world's dance arts; she also stimulated her many students to study broadly and to develop their own contributions to the field.

La Meri's Work in Relation to Theoretical Issues

In recent times, issues such as appropriation, commodification, cultural imposition, orientalism, and objectification have become concerns within the academic community, and it is clear that La Meri's entire life's work was based on what today some might criticize as the questionable appropriation of dance material from cultures not her own. During most of her life, however, the theoretical and ethical questions that are now asked about such practices were not even considered, and reviews and articles generally praised her for introducing treasures from unfamiliar cultures and providing knowledge about them. Furthermore, although she lacked sophisticated academic education, La Meri was concerned with investigating and developing an understanding of the historical and cultural contexts of the materials with which she worked and theoretical principles for the performance and teaching of these foreign dance languages. She always showed the utmost respect for the cultures and arts that she studied, performed, taught, and wrote about. In her time, La Meri had the allure of a glamorous and exotic artist, but her primary goal was to render the dance arts she performed in a seriously authentic way—or to use them creatively—but not simply to exploit them for popular consumption.

It is interesting to consider La Meri's work in relation to some of the concepts that have been investigated in gender and cultural studies. For example, in her article "Embodying Difference: Issues in Dance and Cultural Studies" (*Meaning and Motion*, 1997, 29–54), choreographer and cultural theorist Jane C. Desmond writes of "dance as a performance of cultural identity and the shifting meanings involved in the transmission of dance styles from one group to another" (31). In the section "Appropriation/Transmission/Migration of Dance Styles" (33–35), she points out that it is important to study not only the "pathway" by which a cultural element travels from its original setting to a new one "but also the form's reinscription in a new community/social context and resultant changes in its signification" (34). Of course, La Meri acquired her knowledge of various dance languages not as a member of the communities in which they had developed, but as an outsider hiring teachers to impart to her some elements of their traditions. In this primary transition, there was certainly a transfer, and perhaps one could say a reinscription of a dance form into a new social context: that of a native imparting aspects of the culture's dance to a foreigner—for a fee. La Meri then created other reinscriptions: her performance of the form as an outsider for members of the source culture (which she did frequently), her performance of it outside of its home culture on international concert stages, and its further migration when she began teaching it to students in Europe and the United States.

Without a doubt, any of the forms would change to some extent along the "pathways." The native teachers with whom La Meri studied would have chosen certain aspects of their art to teach this person who, in addition to being an outsider, was on a concert tour and had limited time for study. After learning a dance, La Meri would adapt it for the concert stage and for teaching students outside of its culture. Major changes that she made included shortening long dances for concert presentation and setting choreography for originally improvised dance forms. And, as discussed before, instead of teaching students only entire dance compositions, as native teachers did in many of the source cultures, La Meri would begin with separate technical elements of the dance, then put those into combinations, and finally teach the complete dance.

In discussing gender in relation to dance, Alexandra Carter, dance historian and theorist, urges consideration of "what kinds of images of femininity are represented in and by dance, and how these images reflect the beliefs and values of specific cultural situations" (1996, 44). Exploring such questions regarding La Meri's work is complex, since she was presenting what she had learned of images and movement styles from a large variety of cultures—to a large variety of audiences in many parts of the world. And, of course, the way any specific cultural image and style will be understood depends not only on the characteristics of the performance and performing artist, but also on the setting and culture where it is being shown and the values and tastes that prevail there. Today, most of the world's urban populations have the opportunity to see an array of internationally touring performing artists from many foreign countries and cultures. However, when La Meri was performing on tour in the 1920s and 1930s and later in New York, she was introducing dances that had rarely, if ever, been seen outside their own culture areas. While she learned and added to her repertoire a few male dances, most of her repertoire consisted of dances traditionally done by women, so she was also introducing her audiences to many different "images of femininity," each of which was connected to the "beliefs and values" of its source culture, which may have been in line with those of the audience—or totally different. Carter also asks, "How can the movement vocabularies of non-Western dance forms be read out of their cultural contexts where different notions of gender may exist?" (1998a: 249). One could ask the same thing about the "movement vocabularies" of populations in the West (for example, Andalusian Gypsies, Romanian peasants, American Mormons) who follow traditional ways that differ significantly from those of other Western cultural groups. Replicating the dances of such groups is also a challenge for someone outside the culture. A detailed analysis of La Meri's presentation of feminine (or masculine) images and dance vocabularies would require a very close study of writings about each genre, the international reviews of her performances, the large collection of her photographs in costumes and dance positions, and her own writings about the dances and their reception in different cultures and contexts.

Conclusion

Throughout her life, La Meri demonstrated a fervent commitment to do the very best that she could in all her work. Like any conscientious dance artist and choreographer, she would rehearse hours every day, continuously revise choreography, improve technical details, and rethink what she was doing. In her teaching, she was equally committed to excellence, carefully considering and planning what and how she would teach her various levels of students. In writing, La Meri, with her untutored scholarship and voracious desire for knowledge and understanding, addressed difficult subjects and sought answers to questions of culture, aesthetics, and learning. Her writings demonstrate imagination, a sense of humor, skill in organization—and a commitment to her never-ending search for knowledge and understanding of her life and professional field. A reader may disagree with some of what she states—either because more recent research has provided other information or understanding or because something may seem otherwise off base. However, La Meri's writings always provide insights into both her subject and her own values, goals, and insights.

Unfortunately, there is considerable evidence that, in her last years, La Meri felt her life's work was no longer appreciated or considered important in the world of dance. Some of those who studied with her in the 1940s and 1950s and went on to become professional dancers and teachers also felt that the entire field of "ethnic dance" had lost prestige and interest. While that term has, for the most part, fallen out of use, I would argue that La Meri opened the door to a broad awareness of international dance arts and practices that are now presented in both popular and concert venues and written about extensively by dance scholars. The term usually used today, however, is "world dance" instead of "ethnic dance."

During the decades of her career, La Meri performed, taught, and wrote about dances from many traditions that had previously been unfamiliar to most Western urban populations. Today, dancers and companies from an array of cultures, including our own, tour internationally and provide knowledge and experience of dance from one culture to another. In addition, specialists in various genres, such as Spanish flamenco, Indian Bharatanatyam, Brazilian Capoiera, Mexican *ballet folklórico*, and Middle Eastern belly dance, provide training in those arts in many different countries. Many, of course, are from the country that is the source of the dance tradition they teach. But more and more, there are also specialists who have trained in a foreign dance genre and teach it in their own culture, and perhaps also perform and have a company. La Meri is a prime example of that—with many world genres in her repertoire. In addition to the work of private artists and teachers spreading knowledge and experience of international dance traditions, university dance programs in the United States and parts of Europe sometimes include world dance forms in the curriculum as well as the more traditional ballet and modern dance. This spread of world dance that we have today owes much to the pioneering work of La Meri.

Appendix A

Chronology of La Meri's Life of Travel

1899 Born Louisville, Kentucky (May 13).

1900–1910 Resided partly in Louisville and partly in San Antonio, Texas.

1910 Settled in San Antonio, began performing dance and music, saw notable dance artists: Pavlova, Denishawn, La Argentina.

1919 Traveled to New York City with her mother (probably September). Engaged in academic and performance studies.

1920 Returned to San Antonio (March). Began performing professionally there (June).

1922 Returned to New York City with her mother in the spring; then they traveled in Europe (early July to late September).

1923 Performed in San Antonio and other parts of Texas.

1925 Arrived in New York (late July) after performing on a "prologue circuit" in Texas and other states.

1926 In Mexico City (ca. June 11 to July 22), performing and learning about the culture and its movement genres. After time in San Antonio, returned to New York City (probably by late August).

1927 Toured in Cuba and Puerto Rico with "Teatro de las Artes" (June 30 to mid-August). In San Antonio (late October until after Christmas).

1928 Performances in New York. Latin American tour (June 1928 to August 1929): Venezuela, Colombia, Panama, Costa Rica, Peru, Chile, Brazil, Uruguay, Argentina, Paraguay.

1929 Sailed to Europe (September). In Spain (late September to early November, except for five days in Morocco). In Italy (November 12 to early 1930).

1930   Touring Europe for most of the year: Italy, Austria, Germany, Sweden, Norway, Denmark, France. Contact with Anna Pavlova in Oslo (April) and saw La Argentina performance in Paris (probably May 30).

1931   A few concerts in Paris, Lyon, Brussels (January–May). Saw performance of Uday Shankar in Paris (probably March 3). After marriage to Carreras in London (June 24), living in Italy. Began teaching at the Accademia dei Fidenti in Florence (fall 1931).

1931–1935   Stayed in Italy teaching at the Accademia, performing some, and developing a student group of dancers. Two months in the United States (late August 1931, to late October 1932).

1936   Performances in London (February–March). Touring Australia and New Zealand (June–November). In Ceylon (Sri Lanka) (December).

1937   Performing and learning new dances in India (January–April); Malaysia and Singapore (April); Java, Indonesia (May); Philippines (June); Hong Kong (July); Japan (arrived July 15) and gave a few performances (in September); Hawaii (October). Returned to New York City (probably November), with one performance (December).

1938   Concerts in New York (January), San Antonio (February), and six cities in Mexico (February–April). Second Latin American tour (May–July): Peru, Chile, Argentina. Returned to Italy (August). Performances there (November–December).

1939   Performances in London (January). Toured the United States (February–April). Third Latin American tour (May–September): Venezuela, Brazil, Uruguay, Argentina. Returned to New York City (October), her base for the next 20 years.

1940–1960   Teaching, performing, and choreographing mainly in New York City and at the Jacob's Pillow summer sessions. After World War II ended, performances in the United States, sometimes on long tours—and one foreign tour. States or countries visited are listed below.

1940–1947   Performance locations in alphabetical order: Alabama, Connecticut, Florida, Georgia, Louisiana, Maine, Massachusetts, New Jersey, New York State, North Carolina, Ohio, Pennsylvania, South Carolina, Tennessee, Texas, Virginia, West Virginia.

1948   Touring with di Falco and others: Michigan, Iowa, Missouri, Illinois, Minnesota, New Jersey, New York (January–March). Latin American tour with Rebecca Harris: Mexico, Panama, Ecuador, Peru (ca. April 20 to July 24).

1949   With di Falco and others: Wisconsin, Illinois, Missouri, Colorado, Utah, Florida, New York, California, Iowa, Pennsylvania, Rhode Island (January–July?).

1950   Solo or with ensemble: Indiana, Illinois, Wisconsin, Illinois, New York, Illinois, Virginia, Delaware, Iowa, Illinois, Connecticut (January–May).

1951   With di Falco: Indiana, Louisiana, Nebraska, and other locations (January–June?). (There is very little archival material from this year.)

1952   With Ted Shawn and Jacob's Pillow Dance Festival Company: 48 cities in New York, New Jersey, Michigan, Pennsylvania, Maryland, Illinois, Ohio, West Virginia, Vermont, Massachusetts, Connecticut, and Washington, D.C. (October–December).

1953–1956   Some touring with di Falco until May 1955. Then her "Little Show," from July 1955 to sometime in 1956).

1958   With Ram Gopal, performances in Trinidad (November).

1959–1960   Teaching some in New York, Oklahoma, and Texas.

1960   Moved to Cape Cod with her sister, Lilian (December).

1961–1980s   Lived and worked in Cape Cod with some travel to New York for special events. Visited San Antonio (April 1983). Moved back there (July 1984).

1988   Died (January 7).

Appendix B

La Meri's "Ethnic Ballets" and Other Works

In addition to many single dances, La Meri choreographed longer works using the movement languages she had learned abroad in various creative ways. Most of them incorporated Spanish or Indian techniques and had a story line and characters. Each entry here includes the work's title, the composer or source of music (if known), the theme or other information, the place and date of the first performance and, in some cases, later history. The information comes from archival sources, which are often incomplete.

Alborada del Gracioso. Music by Maurice Ravel with the title translated as "Morning Song of the Jester." It was performed by La Meri and five other dancers and included the reading of one of La Meri's poems. Presented in 1944 in New York City.

El Amor Brujo ("Love, the Magician"). Music by Manuel de Falla. Parts were created and performed in Europe, Tokyo, Latin America, and New York (1933 to 1943), and the entire work premiered in New York City, April 11, 1944. A revised version was presented at Jacob's Pillow, August 1953.

Bach-Bharata Suite. Music by Johann Sebastian Bach. This was a nonnarrative work choreographed with the movement vocabulary of the Bharatanatyam genre of India. It premiered in New York City, May 20, 1946, and was performed until at least 1952. It was revived for presentation at Jacob's Pillow, August 22–26, 1972.

Bosquejos Ibericos (Iberian Sketches). Performed to Spanish traditional and popular music played on the piano, this was a Spanish collection of dances in eleven scenes choreographed for thirty students and three lead dancers and presented at Jacob's Pillow, September 4–5, 1953.

Chitra. Music unknown. A one-act play by the Indian writer, musician, and artist Rabindranath Tagore (1861–1941) that was staged by La Meri and Gina Blau and presented in New York City, December 19–20, 1944, and again sometime in 1945. The choreography was by La Meri.

Devi Murti. Music by Vishnu Dass Shirali and Wana Singh. In this work, La Meri portrayed five manifestations of the Hindu "Supreme Goddess" assisted by members of her company. It premiered in New York City, August 26, 1941, and was presented several times in and around New York until the end of December 1947. La Meri also performed one of the manifestations, Dourga (the Embattled) as a solo in the 1940s in New York City and elsewhere and in 1952 at Jacob's Pillow.

Drishyakava (tone poem). Music: sections of "The Four Seasons" by Antonio Vivaldi. Performed by La Meri with six or more other dancers, aspects of each season were portrayed through movement vocabularies of Bharatanatyam and other Indian dance genres. It premiered at Jacob's Pillow, August 11–15, 1953, and was also presented at the Juilliard School of Music, New York City, April 9 and 12, 1960; and in Cape Cod, July 26–27, 1973. It was restaged by Matteo Vitucci for his company in New York City, February 16–19, 1978.

Ea Mai Hawaiinuiakea (Legend of the Birth of the Islands). Accompanied by recordings of traditional Hawaiian music and chants. A work by this name was presented in New York City, at Jacob's Pillow, and in Jutland, New Jersey, in 1942. However, the New York City presentation of February 2, 1943, is listed as the "first public performance," so the others were probably earlier versions. Sections of this or the entire work continued to be performed until at least 1947, and it was revived in Cape Cod in 1969.

Estampes. Piano music by Claude Debussy. This work had three sections: (1) "La Soirée dans Granade" (Evening in Granada), danced by La Meri, di Falco, and Matteo Vitucci; (2) "Pagodes" (Pagodas), danced by five of the female dancers in La Meri's company; and (3) Sarabande," danced by La Meri. It was performed December 1, 1951, in New York City.

Gauba's Journey to Paradise. Music by Vishnu Dass Shirali and Wana Singh. This comic work was based on a popular Hindu folk tale published by Baba Trinco and featured La Meri in the role of the "Celestial Elephant." After its premier in New York City, August 12,

1941, it was presented about eight times more in and around New York. The last performance was probably in 1948.

Iberia. Music by Claude Debussy. The tale of a young Gypsy woman married to an elderly duke during the time of the artist Francisco Goya (late eighteenth–early nineteenth centuries) and leaving him to participate in a village festival. La Meri created the libretto as well as the choreography. The first scene was presented in New York City, May 17, 1945; then the entire work (with three scenes) premiered there, May 22–23, 1945—with a cast that included a Portuguese and a Spanish dance group. It was also presented at Jacob's Pillow, August 23–24, 1946.

Krishna Gopala. Music by Vishnu Dass Shirali. This was based on a story from the book *Gita Govinda* by the twelfth-century Indian poet, Jaidev (or Jayadeva) and depicted the Hindu god Krishna on the banks of a stream with his devoted *gopis* (milkmaids). With La Meri in the role of Krishna, eight members of her company in other roles, and readings by Ruth St. Denis, it premiered in New York City, November 2, 1940. There were a few other performances in and around New York until at least 1947, and it was presented at Jacob's Pillow, July 30, 1942.

Krishna and Radha. Music by Vishnu Dass Shirali. This humorous portrayal of the relationship between the Hindu god Krishna and the goddess Radha was jointly choreographed by La Meri (who portrayed Radha) and Ted Shawn (who played Krishna). Also cast were members of La Meri's company. Premiered in New York City, August 23–25, 1945, and presented at Jacob's Pillow, August 9–10, 1946.

The Pradakchina of Ganesh (The Circumambulation of Ganesh). Music unknown. This was a dance-drama based on an ancient legend of the elephant-headed Hindu god, Ganesh (or Ganesha) and his belief in the power of encircling. The cast included La Meri as the Hindu goddess Parvati and fifteen of her Cape Cod dancers in the roles of gods, devotees, and others. Movements from the various genres of Indian dance were used for the different characters. This was presented in Cape Cod, June 12–14, 1969.

Rama Breaks the Bow. Music unknown. Based on the *Ramayana*, the Sanskrit epic about the Indian prince, Rama, and his wife, Sita, this was choreographed by La Meri as a Javanese dance-drama. At this time, there were no men in her group, so La Meri danced the role of

Rama, and the other male roles were also performed by females. The work premiered in New York City, March 30, 1943, and was presented again in June of that year. Excerpts were on programs in New York in 1946 and 1947.

Scheherazade. The music by Nikolai Rimsky-Korsakov is based on four scenes from *One Thousand and One Nights,* the collection of ancient Middle Eastern folktales first published in English in the early eighteenth century. La Meri choreographed these scenes using Indian dance movement and gesture. This work premiered in New York City, March 6–7, 1945, and the entire work or excerpts continued to be performed until at least 1951.

Swan Lake. Music by Pyotr Ilyich Tchaikovsky. La Meri "translated" this famous ballet story into the language of Indian dance culture, and it was presented for press review in New York City, February 19, 1944, and had its official premier on February 22. The full work or excerpts continued to be presented until at least 1952.

Appendix C

La Meri's Dance Students and Colleagues

La Meri taught, performed and/or collaborated with hundreds of individuals around the world. This list includes those with whom she had the longest contact and the most significant relationship. Most of them began as her students and progressed to other levels.

Adams, William J., Jr. (1938–2015). At Cape Cod, in the 1960s and 1970s, Adams worked with La Meri off and on as student, then dancer, teacher, and office worker. In the 1980s he served as her caregiver, and after her death, he was the executor of her estate. More information in chapter 8.

Blau, Gina (Srimati Gina) (ca 1906–1998). Performed and choreographed with La Meri's company in New York 1940–1946. Then, as Srimati Gina, she performed with La Meri and Ram Gopal in Trinidad in 1958 and taught at the EDA summer sessions in the late 1960s and early 1970s.

Carreras, Juana. See Jurgeas, Joanna.

Dieman, Edna (1903–1999). From 1943 through 1949, she studied, performed, and taught with La Meri at the EDC. In 1951, she returned home to Cedar Rapids, Iowa, where she and Julia Bennet established a dance school and company. They invited La Meri to give master classes there and presented some of her choreography. Their June 11, 1964, concert included a revival of *Swan Lake* with La Meri dancing the role of the Queen and Matteo Vitucci as the Prince. This production was repeated at JP, July 21–25 of that year.

di Falco, Peter (1924–2017). With La Meri from 1946 until the mid-1950s. For information about their relationship and work together, see chapters 6 and 7.

Epstein, Spira (Hadassah) (1909–1992). Dance artist. Student and then colleague of La Meri from the 1940s on.

Garcia, Josefina. Dancer, university professor, and scholar specializing in traditional dance practices of Mexico and other cultures. Archival materials show that she was active in the EDC school and company from January 1947 to the spring of 1951. She completed doctoral studies and obtained a faculty position at Oklahoma College for Women. She has published books and articles on ethnic dance and participated in programs at JP. She also taught in the EDA summer workshops in 1974, 1975, and 1977.

Gina, Srimati. See Blau, Gina.

Hadassah. See Epstein.

Harris, Rebecca (1907–2004). Worked with La Meri from 1945 through 1979. In the 1940s and early 1950s she was a member of the EDC company and taught at the school. For some of La Meri's solo concerts, Harris performed as a "ladies maid" helping with the costume changes between dances as La Meri talked about the next dance she would perform. She apparently taught at Stephens College in Columbia, Missouri, in the early 1960s and she was a guest teacher at the EDA summer sessions from 1975 to 1979.

Jurgeas, Joanna (Juana Carreras). Niece of La Meri's husband Guido Carreras. In the 1940s she lived with La Meri and Guido and studied and performed with La Meri and her company. La Meri always referred to her as "Jo."

Michel, Jerane (now Costanza). Began dancing as a child. In the early 1950s, she went to the EDC in New York and completed the four-year program. Her first study of Spanish dance was there with La Meri, and later, she trained with some of the most respected teachers in Spain. She was a lead dancer in Marianno Parra's Spanish Dance Company and performed in other contexts as well. She is also known for her teaching of Spanish dance.

Miller, Charles (or Carlos) (1915–2004). With La Meri in the mid-1940s. For information about their relationship and work together, see chapter 6.

Najan, Nala (b. Roberto Rivera) (1932–2002). Studied Indian dance with La Meri in the mid-1950s and then went to India and trained there for five years. After returning to the United States, his first full concert was in New York in February 1961. In the late 1960s and 1970s he sometimes taught or gave performances at the Ethnic Dance Festival in Cape Cod. In 1981, he received the St. Denis Award.

Parra, Mariano. Began dancing after graduating from high school. He then attended the summer sessions at JP in 1952 and 1953. Since La Meri offered him a scholarship to study full time at the EDC, he moved to New York and entered that program. Besides training there, he also studied with other teachers in New York and began to perform. He and Jerane Michel worked together, and he formed his Spanish Dance Company. In the 1960s and 1970s, he was teaching, performing, and choreographing. He was given the St. Denis Award in 1980.

Notes

Preface

1. This multicultural music and dance company separated from Duquesne University, July 1, 2016, and is now the Tamburitzans, supported by the Pittsburgh International Folk Arts Institute (PIFAI).

Introduction

1. Fuller began performing professionally in 1878; St. Denis in 1894; and Allan in 1903.

Chapter 1. Russell Meriwether Hughes: The Early Years, 1899–1920s

1. In her autobiography and most of her obituaries, La Meri's birth year is given as 1898. It was actually 1899, as evidenced by the following documents in the NYPL archives: (1) the list of U.S. citizens on the ship, SS *President Garfield*, on which she and her mother returned from Europe (October 1–11, 1922); and (2) the U.S. Social Security Death Index of 1935–2014. On both her name is given as Russell Hughes.

  Most of the biographical information comes from archival materials in the New York Public Library, San Antonio Public Library, and Jacob's Pillow; from La Meri's autobiography *Dance Out the Answer*; from Terry, 1978; and from the following unpublished writings: La Meri's *Chronology Notebook*, which she began in 1957 and which goes to 1973; her *Chronology 1973*, which is separate from the *Chronology Notebook*; the sections for *Dance Out the Answer* that the publisher chose not to include—cited as *Draft 1977*; and her letter to Hadassah providing information about her family—cited as *Letter 1979*. In addition to these sources, there are also earlier drafts of her autobiography that include more details about her family and early life. There are often conflicting dates within these sources and incorrect or questionable dates for performances of various artists whose work she saw.

  2. There are two different dates for Russ Hughes's birth: La Meri gives 1857 (*Letter 1979*) and the Kentucky Historical Society 1860. There are also different dates for his death: La Meri writes May 15, 1914, in 1977a; and May 16, 1914, in *Draft 1977*. KHS has May 14, 1914.

3. According to KHS documents, Lily Belle Allan was born in 1855 in Trimble County, Kentucky, and died in March 1927 in New York City.

4. See "The Influenza Pandemic of 1918" http://virus.stanford.edu/uda/; and https://www.cdc.gov/features/1918-flu-pandemic/index.html.

5. The system of expression developed by French artist, teacher, and theorist, François Delsarte (1811–1871) had been brought to the United States in the late nineteenth century and adapted to performance forms such as statue-posing, song and poetry interpretation, and quasi-dance. It was very popular from the 1870s to the early 1900s as a form of training in physical culture and expression (see Ruyter 1999a).

6. In her autobiography, La Meri writes that she saw Pavlova perform in San Antonio in the winter of 1912 and two months later began ballet training (1977a, 2). However, it must have been in 1913 that she both saw Pavlova and began her own training. That year the Pavlova Ballet toured the United States for six months, performing in 146 cities (see Lazzarini 1998, 124; and Money 1982, 111–26, 179–89); and, in an archival source, La Meri states that she began ballet training in 1913 (*Chronology 1973*, 1).

7. La Meri gives April 1, 1915, as the date she saw Denishawn (*Draft 1977*, 34–35; 1977a, 6). However, there is no record of Denishawn touring at all in the month of April 1915. The company was in San Antonio at the Opera House, November 18–19, 1914 (which is probably when she saw them), and at the Majestic Theater, February 17–23, 1918 (Schlundt 1962, 22, 30).

8. La Meri implies that she saw the performance of La Argentina sometime in 1915 (*Draft 1977*, 35; 1977a, 6), but according to one source, La Argentina toured in the United States in 1916 and 1920 (*Homenaje*, 169, 171); and another says 1917 and 1920 (Bennahum, 186, 187).

9. Simmions was a singer and musician who had been teaching in New York since 1911 and was known for his invention of a device called the "Vocalscope," a machine for testing the vocal production of singers and speakers (see *Norwalk Hour*, March 3, 1933; and *Musical Courier*, May 11, 1922).

10. Ottokar Bartik (1868–1936), was born in Prague and trained there and elsewhere in Europe. He served as ballet master and choreographer for the Metropolitan Opera in New York City from 1908 to 1932, when he retired and returned to Prague ("Ottokar Bartik, Dance Expert, Dies," *New York Times*, July 28, 1936).

11. In the *Dancemagazine* chronology, the teacher is identified as Doña Rosa of the Barcelona Opera (Terry 1978, 62).

Chapter 2. Early Professional Work and Touring, 1920s

1. Information about her professional work comes from La Meri's writings and other sources listed in note 1 of chapter 1. The dates and places of some of Russell's engagements are unclear since La Meri's chronologies, drafts, and published writings often have conflicting information—or data that are inconsistent with historical records.

2. The Texas Cotton Palace was revived in 1970 and continues to operate today. Information is from *Handbook of Texas Online*, Roger N. Conger, "Cotton Palace" http://www.

tshaonline.org/handbook/online/articles/lbco2; and Texas Cotton Palace Records #792 www.baylor.edu.

3. Information about this annual celebration is taken from "Fit for a Queen: Each spring for 85 years San Antonio society has entertained itself with an extravagant game of dress up" by Jan Jarboe Russell www.texasmonthly.com/articles/fit-for-a-queen/; and "History of Coronation; Coronation is steeped in long, rich tradition" by David Uhler, on *mySA*, the news and entertainment site of *San Antonio Express News* (April 8, 2015). Also, on the Internet are other relevant sites with information and pictures of the queens in their costumes.

4. Most of the information in this paragraph is from the article "Magic Hours with Famous Painting on Monday Eve," *San Antonio Express* (April 22, 1923); the printed program for the April 23 event; www.satmc.org/about-tuesday-musical-club; and "Sigmund Spaeth" on Wikipedia. Russell was also engaged for many other Tuesday Musical Club events according to an unidentified clipping, "Tuesday Musical Octet," a review of the club's February 27, 1924, program, which included four dances by Russell—*Passapied* (Delibes), her peacock dance, and two Spanish dances. See "La Chauve-Souris" in Wikipedia for information on that company.

5. Maria Montero (1901?–1928) was a Spanish dance teacher as well as performer in New York City and Europe. Tragically, she was murdered in her studio in 1928 by a spurned lover who then shot himself (*New York Times*, May 17, 1928).

6. The "subway circuit," which existed until the 1950s, consisted of theaters in Brooklyn and other boroughs of New York where touring companies occasionally tried out new productions and frequently performed them after their Broadway runs.

7. In both her *Chronology Notebook* and *1973 Chronology*, La Meri gives December 1925 as the time of the meeting while the chronology in the August 1978 *Dancemagazine* says the summer of 1926 (62). The latter is incorrect because by then she was performing in Mexico under Carreras's direction. Regarding Carreras's age, on the birth certificate sent to Paris in 1931 and the marriage certificate in London, his birth year is given as 1880. In her autobiography, however, La Meri says that he was twenty-five years her senior (76); and in *Chronology 1973* that he was fifty-nine years old in 1932. If these statements are correct, his birth year would have been 1873 or 1874, not 1880.

8. In 1977a, La Meri writes that the auto show performances preceded those at the Regis (28–29), but her statement in *Spanish Dancing* (1967, 130–31) and the Mexican newspaper clippings show that the Regis performances were first. See "Auto Show Opens This Evening in Theater," *Excelsior: English Section* July 10, 1926, which says that it will run for eight days or more.

9. *El Universal Ilustrada* (Mexico City), 37, 57. The date at the end of the article is July 1926, and it was probably published in the July 29 issue of this weekly literary magazine. Page 37 has a half-page photograph of La Meri, identified as Meri Hughes, sitting in Chapultepec Park in Mexico City.

10. Itō dances in La Meri's repertoire (and composers of the music) included: "Golliwog's Cakewalk" and "Passapied" (Claude Debussy), "Empress of the Pagodas" (Maurice Ravel), "Tango in D" (Isaac Albéniz), "Preludes" (Alexander Scriabin) and "Danse Arabe" (Pyotr Ilyich Tchaikovsky) (La Meri 1986, 12; and programs).

11. What was the Teatro Municipal (dating from 1824) is now the Teatro Alejandro Tapia y Rivera, or Teatro Tapia (Wikipedia).

12. This letter is postmarked Havana, October 27, and originally addressed to Carreras at his San Juan hotel. However, there is another postmark from San Juan, November 10, when the letter was forwarded to him c/o Russel M. Hughes at the San Antonio address.

13. In her autobiography, she writes that as soon as Carreras had arrived in San Antonio, he began planning for a concert. However, as noted above, she was already making the plans on the ship from San Juan.

14. In her autobiography (45), she dates this concert incorrectly as May 6.

Chapter 3. Life in Italy and Beyond, 1929–1936

1. The full title of Otero's book is *Tratado de bailes de sociedad, regionals españoles, especialmente andaluces, con su historia y modo de ejecutarlos* (Treatise of society dances, Spanish regional dances, especially Andalusian, with their history and method of execution). It includes descriptions of twenty-five dances from urban social contexts and thirteen Spanish regional dances, with music notations for five of the latter.

2. In her autobiography (61–62) and in *Spanish Dancing* (1967, 137), La Meri writes of the meeting with "Murcillo Laborda" and refers to him later as "Laborda." His full name was Mariano Morcillo Laborda. In the Spanish culture, the first family name, in this case, Morcillo, is from the father and is used in references. The second is from the mother.

3. One wonders if her reference here to "gitanas" (female Gypsies) was intentional—if she was only referring to the dance of the women and not that of men, or if this was an error.

4. Felix Cleve was an Austrian music and literary critic and a scholar of pre-Socratic philosophy. La Meri writes that he was editor of the *Neue Frei Presse* when she performed the January 19 concert in Vienna (1977a, 66). In 1938, Cleve and his family, who were Jewish, fled Austria because of the arrival of the Nazis. They settled in New York City in 1940, where Cleve continued his work as scholar and critic and his association with La Meri.

5. La Meri writes that it was after the Scandinavian tour ended when "Dallapiccola went back to Italy" and "Lilian returned to the States" (1977a, 68), but there is no mention of either of them in the few documents I have from this tour.

6. In her autobiography, La Meri writes about this meeting as occurring during her first visit to Oslo (67), which was in March 1930. Then, in the January to July 1930 section of her chronology in *Dancemagazine* (August 1978, 63), she writes, "I think it was on this tour that in Oslo, I played matinees and Pavlova gave evening shows." So she herself was not sure of the date. I have been in contact with the organization, Dance Information Norway, and they have no record of a Dance Week in Oslo that year. However, they sent me information about a dinner held during Pavlova's 1930 performance time in Oslo (April 8–12) where the two met, and there is a picture of the group in the La Meri archive. The meeting was probably April 10 or 11 when La Meri had returned to Oslo after performing in Stavanger (*Chronology Notebook*). There is no record, however, of her giving matinee performances then.

7. Writing in 1977, La Meri uses the term "ethnic" in relation to her discussion with Pavlova about dance traditions from different cultures (1977a, 67), but in 1930, that word would not have been used—or probably even known.

8. In her book, *Modern Dance in France: An Adventure 1920–1970*, Jacqueline Robinson gives c. 1907 to 1947 as the years of Gregory's life, which would mean he was about twenty-three years old in 1930. However, in her letter to Lilian of September 20, 1930, La Meri writes that, while he appeared very young, he was a thirty-four-year-old widower with a young daughter.

9. The father's full name was Hendrik Willem van Loon. Born in Rotterdam, he completed an undergraduate degree in the United States and a doctorate in Munich. He became a U.S. citizen in 1919 and taught briefly in American universities. His main activity was historical research, and he published many books from 1913 until his death. His son's full name was Gerard Willem van Loon.

10. In December 1931, she had given a presentation on Indian dance for the British Institute of Florence, according to an English-language newspaper article promoting a performance to be given at the Accademia in April 1932. The article remarks on "the extraordinary success obtained by the famous dancer La Meri at her conference on the Philosophy and Technique of Hindu Dancing which was organized by the British Institute last December" (*Italian Mail and Tribune*, April 2, 1932).

Chapter 4. Australasia and Asia, 1936–1937

1. According to the contract, the tour of Australia and New Zealand would begin ca. July 1936; the management would provide round-trip boat fares between Italy and Australia (four first class and one third class), first-class hotel accommodations, and living and production expenses during the tour; the pianist would be paid 1,000 lira per month, the assistant one English pound per week, and the artist 60 percent of the net profits.

2. From the programs and articles I have seen, I count something under eighty. However, there may have been performances for which no records exist in the archives.

3. Information about the visit to Rotorua comes from her August 31 and September 20, 1936, letters to Lilian; her pre-December 16 Installment Letter; and her autobiography (1977a, 85–87).

4. Information about the time in Kandy and the Kandyan dances comes from her autobiography (1977a, 94–95), her letter to Lilian of December 29, 1936, and Kotelawala 1998, 647–49.

5. Bharatanatyam is one of the major genres of Indian dance. It is a solo dance form that developed from the ancient temple dance tradition of the *devadasis* (temple dancers) in southern India. Today, it is performed and taught internationally. The title appears in different forms in different sources.

6. *Mudra*: "stylized hand gesture; also referred to as *hasta mudra*." *Rasa*: "The overall mood of a piece; emotional sentiment." *Bhava*: "Mood or tone; emotional expression." *Mudras* are used in both dramatic and abstract Bharatanatyam dance forms (O'Shea, 199–200).

7. There is no Internet site on G. K. Seshagiri himself, but in sites focused on various film and arts events, he is identified as a "rich impresario, fine-arts lover, and talent scout" who financed various film and stage events. He also was the financial backer of and wrote some articles for the English language Chennai magazine, *Sound and Shadow*, which was published monthly with news and articles about movies and fine arts.

8. In her autobiography, La Meri writes that she gave three concerts in Rangoon (112), but there is no evidence for a third in either the clippings or the letters.

Chapter 5. Here and There in a World of Turmoil, October 1937 to October 1939

1. When La Meri was in Latin America and Italy, one can assume that she was writing frequent letters to Lilian—just as she had done during her previous long tour in the East. Unfortunately, no such letters have been located, so the information here is from her autobiography, her Fourth and Fifth Installment Letters (which cover her activities until mid-August 1938), and archival materials. There are also two letters that Lilian wrote to La Meri and sent in August and September 1939.

2. This would have been Francis Charles Coppicus (1880–1966) who had founded the Metropolitan Music Bureau in 1916 and, in 1930, merged several small concert bureaus into Columbia Concert Corporation, which later became Columbia Artists Management (CAM).

3. In the program for the Little Theater concerts on January 30, 1938, the management is identified as the Metropolitan Musical Bureau, Inc., a Division of Columbia Concerts Corporation of Columbia Broadcasting System.

4. In her Fifth Installment Letter, La Meri writes that when Lilian left, "Olivia came down from San Antonio to take her place," but there is evidence that Olivia was with them from the time they all left San Antonio in February.

5. The *cueca* has a long history as a folk/social dance in Chile and other parts of Latin America. This energetic dance humorously portrays the courtship of a chicken and a rooster. In 1979, it was designated as the national dance of Chile.

6. On page 146 of her autobiography, La Meri writes that they had been away from Italy for twenty-seven months. However, they actually left in January 1936 (1977a, 77; programs and clippings), so they were out of Italy for about thirty-two months. There is no information as to who was taking care of the house or the dog during that time.

7. This was a national organization of student groups in universities and other educational institutions. It began in 1920 and was restructured in 1927 under the totalitarian regime. Under the *Scuola de Mistica Fascista* (School of Mystic Fascism), they engaged in political and cultural activities, and the *Teatro Sperimentale* was one of their venues (Wikipedia: "Grupi Universitari Fascisti").

8. Her birth name was Joanna Jurgeas, but she is at times referred to as Juana Carreras or Jo Carreras. In her letters to Lilian, La Meri always referred to her as "Jo."

Chapter 6. A Reinvented Life in the United States as a Teacher, Innovator, and Woman, 1939–1956

1. This was "Devi Dja and her Bali and Java Dancers," who had given a series of performances at New York City's Guild Theatre in late October. Reviewers had noted that this group gave more of a commercialized "show" than a serious presentation of the cultures represented (see, for example, John Martin, "East Indies Troupe in American Debut," *New York Times*, October 28, 1939; *Time*, November 6, 1939), but one wonders what motivated Carreras's passionate diatribe. He doesn't mention La Meri but compares the work of Devi Dja and her dance with that of La Meri's first Indian dance mentor, Uday Shankar—of course, praising the latter. This was probably an effort to indirectly support the values and aesthetics of his wife's work.

2. The Museum of Costume Art was formed in 1937 under the direction of Irene Lewisohn (1886–1944), who was known for her work as cofounder of the Neighborhood Playhouse (an off-Broadway theater) in 1915 and its director until 1927. In 1946, it became a part of the Metropolitan Museum of Art as the Costume Institute ("The Metropolitan Museum of Art—Works of Art—The Costume Institute" http://www.metmuseum.org).

3. The Master Institute of United Arts (MIUA) was founded in 1928 by Louis L. Horch as the Roerich Museum. It was a twenty-nine-story edifice uptown, at Riverside Drive and 103rd Street, that housed one of New York's earliest contemporary art museums, a 300-seat theater, a nonprofit school of fine arts, and living quarters for artists ("Louis L. Horch, 90, Founder of Museum; Set up Master Institute of Arts—Foreign-Exchange Expert" *New York Times*, April 16, 1979).

4. Sometime before the 1947–48 season, the theater was redecorated and the chairs put on raised levels for better visibility ("Ethnologic Dance Theater Redecorated," *Musical Courier*, October 15, 1947).

5. In February 1944, Lilian's husband, David, had been transferred to Europe for overseas duty, and on August 25, he lost his life on a mission in Southern France. Lilian and La Meri lived and worked together from the time David left the United States until Lilian's death in 1965.

6. By "percussives" she probably meant the castanet, clapping, and rhythmic footwork of Spanish dance forms and the drumming and footwork of the Indian genres.

7. *Escuela Bolera*: The genre of Spanish dance in which regional dance forms (such as *sevillanas*) were balleticized for performance in theatrical contexts. It began to develop probably in the late eighteenth century, and during the nineteenth century it became codified and established as a specialized form that still exists today. There was also a social dance version of this genre in the nineteenth century.

8. During World War II, the United States government had become concerned about the future of veterans returning home after their experiences in the war zones of the Pacific or Europe and developed a program, the Servicemen's Readjustment Act, that became law on June 22, 1944. Familiarly known as the G.I. Bill, it provided educational costs and a year of unemployment compensation for the returning veterans.

9. Information on di Falco's life comes from an interview in person with him (March

26, 2003), various phone conversations and email communications, and archival materials that he sent me.

Chapter 7. Performance and Choreography in New York and Beyond (1940 to 1956) and Jacob's Pillow (1940s to 1970s)

1. Beaucaire Montalvo had been a student of Otero's and a professional dancer in Spain until the 1920s, when he retired from performing and opened a studio in New York. La Meri first met him when she was working with Maria Montero, and she continued her contact with him until his death in 1945 (La Meri, 1946a).

2. In her autobiography, La Meri states that the Exotic Ballet began in January 1946 (1977a, 163), but in newspaper articles, the debut of the company under that name was announced as October 1, 1947.

3. Rebecca Harris (1907–2004) was a performing artist and teacher. She began her work with La Meri at the EDC in the fall of 1945 and continued collaborating with her until the late 1970s in Cape Cod. Harris performed and taught at the EDC and Jacob's Pillow; she also taught for several years at Stephens College in Columbia, Missouri.

4. With that film and the incredibly strong and time-consuming help of Jerane Michel (Costanza), who had danced in the 1953 production as one of the Gypsies, we did a restaging of this work at the University of California, Irvine, in June 2008.

5. The music for the five sections of the *Bach-Bharata Suite* was: "The Art of the Fugue" (1st movement), "Two Part Inventions," "Air on the G String," "Come, Sweet Death," and "Concerto in D Minor" (Allegro).

6. Most of the historical information about Jacob's Pillow is taken from Shawn, 1953, which will be cited in this section as Shawn, without the year, but with the specific page numbers.

Chapter 8. New York, Cape Cod, San Antonio: New Transitions, 1956–1988

1. The Cape Cod Conservatory of Music and Arts (later titled the Cape Conservatory) was established in 1956 and still exists today. Its advertisement in the program booklet of La Meri's first Ethnic Dance Festival in 1968 announces that classes are given in Falmouth, Barnstable, and Orleans. The Conservatory's 2018 website gives its location as Falmouth.

2. The Barnstable Comedy Club (BCC) was founded in 1922 as Cape Cod's first amateur theatrical organization, and it gave performances in the Barnstable Village Hall and other locations. In 1961, the BCC purchased the Village Hall from the Barnstable Women's Club, the original owner, and in 1975, obtained tax-exempt status as a nonprofit corporation. It still exists today with an active theater program (BCC website; and communication from Rachel Kenneally, BCC webmaster and historian, February 28, 2012).

3. Those who had been a part of the New York EDC and the years they taught in Cape Cod summer sessions: Srimati Gina (1971, 1972), Mariano Parra (1971, 1972, 1974, 1976), Jerane Michel (1971, 1972, 1973, 1976, 1977), Nala Najan (1972, 1973), Josefina Garcia (1974, 1975, 1977), Rebecca Harris (1975, 1976, 1977, 1978, 1979).

4. My information about Adams is from our written communications, phone interviews, and discussions when I visited him in Putnam, Connecticut (2011 and 2013), and from Norton Owen, director of preservation at Jacob's Pillow.

5. It would be surprising if Adams had developed enough technique to perform that soon—but perhaps he was cast in minor character roles—and perhaps the company had a dearth of male dancers. The actual name of the company when he performed with it was the New England Civic Ballet, founded in 1958 by E. Virginia Williams (1914–1984). It became the professional Boston Ballet in 1963 (information provided by the staff of the Boston Ballet, July 17, 2017).

6. Capezio is a well-known provider of shoes, apparel, and other items for the field of dance studies and production. In 1952, the Capezio Dance Award was created to honor major figures in the professional dance world; the next year, the Capezio Foundation was established to administer the award and operate a grant program (Wikipedia).

7. This was *Las Danzas Fantásticas* to music by the Spanish composer Joaquín Turina and demonstrates that her creativity had not abated over the years. The work was first performed January 26, 1973, in Buffalo, New York, with a full symphony orchestra.

8. Chowdhury, under the single name Bhaskar, performed a variety of Indian dance genres in the EDA festival programs in 1974 as a soloist, in 1975 and 1976 with EDARC dancer Cynthia Maddux and in 1977 with two young dancers—probably his students. Later that year, he was crippled in a fall that left him wheelchair-bound. In 1978, he was the recipient of the St. Denis Award (see Wingfield, 2013). His group performed in the 1979 EDA festival.

9. John Igo (1927–2016) was known as a poet, theater critic, historian, author, and photographer. For forty-seven years he taught English literature at San Antonio College, and, at some time before 1977, he created the Theatre Archive at the San Antonio Public Library (John MacCormack, "Igo was San Antonio's genial literary uncle," *San Antonio Express-News*, August 10, 2016).

10. This organization, which dates from the 1930s, is devoted to presenting performances of traditional music and dance forms from the Balkans and other parts of the world. From 1937, it had been connected with Duquesne University. In 2014–15, it transitioned to an independent nonprofit organization, which, since 2016 has been supported by the Pittsburgh International Folk Arts Institute (Sara Bauknecht, "Tamburitzans embrace change as group separates from Duquesne University," *Pittsburgh Post-Gazette*, November 10, 2015).

Chapter 9. La Meri's Writings

1. This was taken from the book *Mind and Body: A Monthly Journal Devoted to Physical Education* vol. 40, which includes all the issues from April 1933 to March 1934, 235–36.

2. The acknowledgment, signed by La Meri, Italy, 1933, says: "The four chapters relating to the Dance-Art are reproduced with kind permission of the Editor of 'Home & Abroad' (The English Illustrated Review), published in London." And one page in the appendix advertises *Dance as an Art Form* and identifies La Meri as dance editor of *Home & Abroad*. I have not been able to find any information on the publisher or this review.

3. There are actually 204 photographs of the poses, as four of them are given in two versions. The double hand gestures are known as *samyuta* and depict everything that could be part of a story being told through the gesture language (such as deities, actions, emotions, places, relationships, and animals).

4. Zimmer (1890–1943) was a German Indologist and historian of South Asian art who had moved to the United States in 1940. His name is originally and usually given as Heinrich Robert Zimmer.

5. As noted previously, the *escuela bolera* dates from the late eighteenth century and combines regional dance forms and vocabularies with ballet technique. Today, there are schools and companies that specialize in this genre.

6. As stated in the bibliography, I obtained a copy of the draft of this section (fifty-three typed pages) from the San Antonio Public Library Archive.

Bibliography

Abbreviations

JP   Jacob's Pillow Dance Festival and Archive. Becket, Massachusetts
KHS   Kentucky Historical Society
NYPL New York Public Library. Usually referring to Jerome Robbins Dance Division, New York Public Library for the Performing Arts
SAPL San Antonio Public Library

Archival Materials

The Hughes, Russell Meriwether (La Meri) archives in JP, NYPL, and SAPL have newspaper and magazine articles and reviews. Some lack volume, issue, and/or page numbers. If such information is missing in a citation, it could not be found. The archives also include letters, official documents, pictures, films, etc. Particularly important are the letters La Meri wrote to her sister Lilian when they were not together and those she wrote to her agent/husband Guido Carreras. With the items below, the locations are in parentheses.

Chronology Notebook, which she began in 1957 and continued adding to until 1973. It documents her life and activities from birth through the first part of 1973 (JP).

Chronology 1973 (JP and SAPL).

Draft 1977. Draft sections for *Dance Out the Answer* (1977) that the publisher chose not to include in the book (SAPL).

Journal. Written 1952–1982. Mostly from 1940s and 1950s (JP).

Letter 1979. "Letter to a Friend," unpublished information about her parents that had been requested by Hadassah (SAPL).

Travel 1924. Three-volume account of travels in Europe with her mother in 1922 (JP).

"Charles James Miller Papers 0333." *Online Archives of California,* California Digital Library.

Recorded interviews with Josie Neal in 1984–87 (JP).

Recorded interviews with Patricia Taylor in 1987.

La Meri's Publications

Published under Her Birth Name

Hughes, R. M. (1917a). *Poems*. San Antonio: Passing Show Printing.

——. (1917b). *Marching to France, and Other Texas Rhymes*. San Antonio: Koenig and Amos.

——. (1921). *Mexican Moonlight*. Boston: Richard G. Badger, Gorham Press.

——. (1922). *Poems of the Plains*. Boston: Cornhill Publishing.

——. (1925). *The Star Roper*. Philadelphia: Dorrance. Republished in 1927 and 1928 with sketches by Guido Carreras. N.p.: Longacre Press.

——. (1926). See first item under next section.

——. (1931). "Dancing in Mexico." *Bright Scrawl* (magazine of the Junior League of San Antonio). (March): 5, 13. (Middle name misspelled as Meriweather).

R.M.H. (1934). "Congress in Vienna: A Report of the International Competition and Folk Dance Congress." *American Dancer* (August): 7, 24.

Published under Her Professional Name

La Meri. (1926). "Nueva Visión de México." *El Universal Ilustrado* (Mexico City). (July 29 or later): 37, 57. Author given as both La Meri and Meri Hughes.

——. (1927). "South of the Rio Grande: Where Dancing Is Unaffectedly Mexican." *The Dance* 7 (March): 20–21. With sketches by Matias Santoyo. Also see introduction, "Allow Us to Present," on p. 8.

——. (1931a). "The Gypsy Dancers of Granada." *Dance Magazine of Stage and Screen* 15 (March): 14 (photo), 16–17, 56 (text).

——. (1931b). "South American Dances." *Dancing Times*, New Series, No. 250 (July): 332–35; No. 251 (August): 421–24; No. 252 (September): 514–16.

——. (1932). "Broadening the Art of Dancing." *Bright Scrawl* (Magazine of Junior League of San Antonio) (January).

——. (1933a). *Dance as an Art Form: Its History and Development*. New York: A. S. Barnes.

——. (1933b). *The Principles of the Dance-Art*. London: Channing Press (Number V of Channing Useful Pocket Series).

——. (1934). "The Dance Art Today." *American Dancer* 7 (July): 9, 18.

——. (1936). "The Story of the Spanish Gypsy Dancers." *Dancing Times*, New Series, No. 304 (January): 513–15.

——. (1938a). *Songs and Voyages*. Livorno (Italy): Arti Grafiche S. Belforte & C. Anthology of poems, some of which had been published earlier.

——. (1938b). "Dances of the Maoris." *Dance Magazine* 12 (October): 9, 28–29.

——. (1939). "Dancing in India." Lecture-Demonstration on Indian dance. Reprinted in *Indian Arts and Letters* 13. London: India Society, 6–21.

——. (1940a). "The Indian Dance." *India News Letter* 1 (July).

——. (1940b). "A Lesson in Bharatya Natya." *India News Letter* 1 (October).

——. (1941a). *The Gesture Language of the Hindu Dance*. New York: Columbia University Press. Republished 1964, New York: B. Blom; reprinted 1979, New York: Arno Press.

———. (1941b). "Contrasts—Choreography, East and West." *Educational Dance* 3 (March): 8–9.

———. (1941c). "The Dance WEST and EAST in Contrast." *Dance* 9 (March): 18.

———. (1941d). "So You Want to Be a Dancer?" *Dance* 10 (October): 19.

———. (1946a). "Exit an Hidalgo: A tribute to JUAN BEAUCAIRE MONTALVO." *Dance* 20 (January): 18, 53.

———. (1946b). Statement in "Symposium on the American Dance" in which "twelve renowned artists set forth their views on trends of the dance world." *Dance* 20 (November): 14, 41–43.

———. (1948). *Spanish Dancing*. 1st ed. New York: A. S. Barnes.

———. (1949a). "Sevillanas—A Teaching Film about Spanish Dance." *Dance Magazine* 23 (April): 26–27.

———. (1949b). "The Children of Inti." *Dance Magazine* 23 (June): 30–35.

———. (1949c). "Dance in Review." La Meri's review of performance of Nona Kapua and Hawaiian Concert Dancers on August 8. *Dance News* 15 (September): 11.

———. (1949d). Contributed to the first edition of Anatole Chujoy's *The Dance Encyclopedia*. See 1967b for her sections in that revised edition.

———. (1950a). "Exotic Dances." Notes to Folkways Album No. FW 8752, music for international dances, many of which were in La Meri's repertoire.

———. (1950b). "*Why* did I ever become a dancer? A lament by La Meri." *Dance Magazine* 24 (December): 16–17.

———. (1951a). "Theatrical Ethnic Dance." In *25 Years of American Dance*, ed. Doris Hering. New York: R. Orthwine, 176–84.

———. (1951b). "The Ethnological Dance Arts." In *The Dance Has Many Faces*, ed. Walter Sorell. New York: World Publishing, 1951. 2nd edition: New York: Columbia University Press, 1966, 3–11.

———. (1952). "Jacob's Pillow: Haven for Dancers." *Dance Magazine* 26 (September): 22–23, 43.

———. (1956). "Antonia Mercé: La Argentina." *Dance Magazine* 30 (December): 26–28.

———. (1960). "¡Flamenco!" *Harper's Bazaar* (May): 183.

———. (1961). "Learning the Danse du Ventre." In "A curious and wonderful gymnastic . . ." *Dance Perspectives* 10 (Spring): 42–47.

———. (1965). *Dance Composition: The Basic Elements*. Lee, MA: Jacob's Pillow.

———. (1967a). *Spanish Dancing*. 2nd rev. ed. Pittsfield, MA: Eagle Printing and Binding Co.

———. (1967b). In the revised edition of *The Dance Encyclopedia*: "Ethnic Dance," 338–39; "Hawaiian (Hula) Dance," 445–47; "Hindu Dance," 456–59; "Oriental Dance," 689–94; and "Spanish Dance," 855–57. See Chujoy and Manchester in the next section (Other Publications).

———. (1972). "Shawn's love for a woman of magic." *Boston Sunday Globe*, Theater/Arts section (May 21): B15, 16. (memorial article after his death).

———. (1974). "Let Me Fold My Hands in the Anjali He Taught Me." In S. Durai Raja Singam, *Ananda Coomaraswamy: Remembering and Remembering Again and Again*. Petraling Jaya, Malaysia, 61–62; illustrations on 60.

———. (1975). *Komposisi tari; elemen-elemen da sar [oleh]*. Yogyakarta, Indonesia: Akademi Seni Tari. Translation of La Meri's 1965 *Dance Composition: The Basic Elements*.

———. (1977a). *Dance Out the Answer: An Autobiography*. New York: Dekker.

———. (1977b). *Total Education in Ethnic Dance*. New York: Dekker.

———. (1978). "La Meri." Part I. "I remember . . ." *Dancemagazine* 52 (August): 55–58, 62; Part II. "A chronology of learning, labor, life," edited and with a foreword by Walter Terry (62–65).

———. (1982). "Possibilities for Presenting Ethnic Dance," *Arabesque* 7 (May–June): 16.

———. (1982–83). "Elements of Dance Composition." Excerpts from La Meri's book *Dance Composition: The Basic Elements*. In *Arabesque* 8, nos. 2–6 (1982–83); and 9, nos. 1–3 (1983). Each excerpt is 2–3 pages.

———. (1983). "Encounters with Dance Immortals: Ruth St. Denis." *Arabesque* 9 (November–December): 14–15.

———. (1984a). "Encounters . . . : Anna Pavlova; Jack Cole." *Arabesque* 9 (January–February): 16–17, 22.

———. (1984b). "Encounters . . . : Ted Shawn." *Arabesque* 9 (March–April): 14.

———. (1984c). "Dance Quest." *Arabesque* 10 (May–June): 18–19, 32. About her studies in Fez, Morocco, in 1929.

———. (1984d). "Uday Shankar." *Arabesque* 10 (July–August): 12–13, 20–21.

———. (1985a). "Encounters . . . : La Argentinita and Carmen Amaya." *Arabesque* 10 (January–February): 8–9, 21.

———. (1985b). "Encounters . . . : Balasaraswati and Ragini Devi." *Arabesque* 11 (November–December): 12–13, 25.

———. (1986). "Encounters . . . : Three Free Dancers: Michio Itō, Mary Wigman, and Grete Weisenthal." *Arabesque* 11 (March–April): 12–13.

(La Meri was Contributing Editor for *Arabesque* from May–June, 1982 (issue 8/1) until her death in 1988.)

Other Publications

Adair, Christy. (1992). *Women and Dance: Sylphs and Sirens*. New York: New York University Press.

Albright, Ann Cooper. (1997). *Choreographing Difference: The Body and Identity in Contemporary Dance*. Hanover, NH: University Press of New England.

———. 2007. *Traces of Light: Absence and Presence in the Work of Loïe Fuller*. Middletown, CT: Wesleyan University Press.

Arkin, Lisa C., and Marian Smith. (1997). "National Dance in the Romantic Ballet." In Garafola, 11–68.

Armstrong, Alan. (1964). *Maori Games and Hakas: Instructions, Words and Actions*. Wellington, New Zealand: A. H. and A. W. Reed.

Aulestia, Patricia. (1995). *La Danza Premoderna en México (1917–1939)*. Caracas: Centro Venezolano Instituto Nacional de Teatro-UNESCO. Edición especial XXVI congreso mundial, junio 1995.

Aulestia de Alba, Patricia, and Orlando Taquechel Mederos, eds. (1992). *Quién es quién en la danza mexicana*, vol. I. Mexico City: Cenidi-Danza "José Limón."

Baker, Valerie. (1985). "Ethnic Dance, U.S.A." *Arabesque* 11 (May–June): 8–9, 21.

Balme, Christopher B. 2007. *Pacific Performances: Theatricality and Cross-Cultural Encounter in the South Seas*. New York: Palgrave Macmillan.

Barba, Eugenio, and Nicola Savarese. (1991). *A Dictionary of Theatre Anthropology: The Secret Art of the Performer*. Trans. Richard Fowler. New York: Routledge.

Barlow, S.L.M. (1944). "With the Dancers." *Modern Music* 21 (March–April): 186–88.

Bassoe, Henriette. (1941). "Flights beyond the Horizon with La Meri." *American Dancer* 14 (April): 11, 32.

Benedicto. (1928). "Meri, La Gloriosa," in "La Información," column of unidentified newspaper (Maracaibo, Venezuela, 7 July).

Bennahum, Ninotchka Devorah. (2000). *Antonia Mercé "La Argentina": Flamenco and the Spanish Avant Garde*. Hanover, NH: Wesleyan University Press.

Bhaskar, see Chowdhury, Bhaskar Roy.

Bhavnani, Enakshi. (1965). *The Dance in India: The Origin and History, Foundations, the Art and Science of the Dance in India—Classical, Folk and Tribal*. Bombay: D. B. Taraporevala Sons.

Blasis, Carlo. (1820). *An Elementary Treatise upon the Theory and Practice of the Art of Dancing*. Trans. Mary Stewart Evans. New York: Kamin Dance Gallery, 1944.

———. (1828). *The Code of Terpsichore: A Practical and Historical Treatise, on the Ballet, Dancing, and Pantomime; With a Complete Theory of the Art of Dancing; Intended as Well for the Instruction of Amateurs as the Use of Professional Persons*. Trans. R. Barton. London: James Bulcock. Reprint, Brooklyn, New York: Dance Horizons, 1976.

———. (1847). *Notes Upon Dancing, Historical and Practical*. Trans. R. Barton. London: M. Delaporte.

Bode, Rudolf. (1931). *Expression Gymnastics*. Trans. Sonya Forthal and Elizabeth Waterman. New York: A. S. Barnes (from *Ausdrucksgymnastik*. Munich: Beck, 1925).

Bodenslek, Fred. (1979). "La Meri rips open curtain on Barnstable HS Auditorium," *Barnstable Patriot* (October 20).

Bose, Mandakranta. (1998). "Gender and Performance: Classical Indian Dancing." In Goodman, 251–54.

Bowers, Faubion.(1956). *Theatre in the East; A Survey of Asian Dance and Drama*. New York: Thomas Nelson and Sons.

———. (1959). *Japanese Theatre*. New York: Hill and Wang.

Brady, Erika. (1999). *A Spiral Way: How the Phonograph Changed Ethnography*. Jackson: University Press of Mississippi.

Brandon, James R. (1967). *Theatre in Southeast Asia*. Cambridge, MA: Harvard University Press.

Brodie, Joan (J.B.). (1948). "La Meri." *Dance Observer* 15 (February).

Buset, Jorge. (1926). "'Meri,' la Bailaora [*sic*] Americana." Revista de Revistas (a section of the Mexico City newspaper *Excelsior*), June 20, 1926, 31.

Caballero Bonald, José Manuel. (1959). *Andalusian Dances*. Trans. Charles David Ley of *El baile andaluz.* Barcelona: Editorial Noguer, 1957. In the bibliographies of her 1967 and 1977b publications, La Meri gives the name as Bonald, Caballero, which is incorrect.

Cahan, Alfonso. (1928). "La Meri y nuestra danza aborigen." *Chile* 3 [?], No. 45 (November): 85, 87, 89.

Caldwell, Helen. (1977). *Michio Itō: The Dancer and His Dances.* Berkeley: University of California Press.

Campbell, Patrick, ed. (1996). *Analyzing Performance: A Critical Reader.* Manchester: Manchester University Press.

Carter, Alexandra. (1996). "Bodies of Knowledge: Dance and Feminist Analysis." In Campbell, 43–55.

———. (1998a). "Feminist Strategies for the Study of Dance." In Goodman, 247–50.

———, ed. (1998b). *The Routledge Dance Studies Reader.* London: Routledge.

Castro, Beth. (1984). "Dancer visits childhood home, remembers past." *The Ranger,* San Antonio, Texas (April 6).

Cherniavsky, Felix. (1991). *The Salome Dancer: The Life and Times of Maud Allan.* Toronto: McClelland and Steward.

Chowdhury, Bhaskar Roy. (1980). "La Meri: The High Priestess of Ethnic Dance." *New York Dancer: IN-STEP* 1/1 (March): 7–9, 13.

Chujoy, Anatole. (1943). "Dance in Review: La Meri." *Dance News* (March).

———(1944). "Dance in Review: Swan Lake in Hindu Idiom." *Dance News* 5 (March).

Chujoy, Anatole, and P. W. Manchester, eds. (1967). *The Dance Encyclopedia; Revised and Enlarged Edition.* New York: Simon and Schuster.

Cleve, Felix. (1934). "Dance Recital, La Meri," from *Neue Freie Presse,* Vienna, June 6 (JP).

———. (1942). "A Quarter-Century of Artistic Dance," unpublished speech given at EDC reunion October 15 (JP).

———. (1944) "'Swan Lake' in Hindu," from *Staats-Zeitung und Herold,* February 27 (JP).

———. (1945?). "The Significance of the Dancer La Meri," from *Staats-Zeitung und Herold,* May 20 (JP).

Code, Grant. (1940). "Reunion at New School of Natya." *Dance Observer* 7 (November): 33.

Coomaraswamy, Ananda K. (1924). *Dance of Shiva.* New York: Sunwise Turn.

Coomaraswamy, Ananda, and Duggirâla Gopâlakrishnâyya, trans. (1936). *The Mirror of Gesture—Being the Abhinaya Darpana of Nandikesvara.* New York: E. Weyhe (1st pub. 1917).

Coorlawala, Uttara Asha. (1992). "Ruth St. Denis and India's Dance Renaissance," *Dance Chronicle* 15 (2): 123–52. Reprinted in *Intersections: Dance, Place, and Identity,* ed. Ann Dils, Robin Gee, Matthew Brookoff. Dubuque, IA, 2006.

Cowell, Mary-Jean. (2001). "Michio Itō in Hollywood: Modes and Ironies of Ethnicity." *Dance Chronicle* 24 (3): 263–305.

Cunningham, Kitty. (1998). "Jacob's Pillow." *International Encyclopedia of Dance* 3: 571–72.

Current, Richard Nelson, and Marcia Ewing Current. (1997). *Loie Fuller: Goddess of Light.* Boston: Northeastern University Press.

Dallal, Alberto. (1995). *La Danza en México, Primera Parte: Panorama Crítico,* 2nd ed. México: Universidad Nacional Autónoma de México (UNAM), Instituto de Investigaciones Estéticas (1st ed. 1986).

———. (1997). *La danza en México en el siglo XX*. (Lecturas Mexicanas, Cuarta Serie). México: Consejo Nacional para la Cultura y las Artes (first published 1994).

Danitz, Marilynn. (2009). "Hadassah (Spira Epstein)." *Jewish Women: A Comprehensive Historical Encyclopedia*. March 1, 2009. Jewish Women's Archive Oct. 22, 2010. http://jwa.org/encyclopedia/archive/hadassah-spira-epstein.

Dempster, Elizabeth. (1998). "Women Writing the Body: Let's Watch a Little How She Dances." In Carter 1998b, 223–29.

Desmond, Jane. (1991). "Dancing Out the Difference: Cultural Imperialism and Ruth St. Denis's *Radha* of 1906." *Signs* 17 (Autumn): 28–49.

———, ed. (1997). *Meaning in Motion*. Durham, NC: Duke University Press.

Duncan, Isadora. (1928). *The Art of the Dance*. Edited and with introduction by Sheldon Cheney. New York: Theatre Arts.

Dzhermolinska, Helen. (1942). "A Gallery of American Dancers: La Meri" (No. 3 of a Series). *Dance* 15 (May): 10–11, 37.

Ellis, Havelock. (1923). *The Dance of Life*. Boston: Houghton Mifflin.

———. (1931). *The Soul of Spain*. Boston: Houghton Mifflin.

Erdman, Joan L. (1987). "Performance as Translation: Uday Shankar in the West." *The Drama Review* 31 (Spring): 64–88.

———. (1998). "Shankar, Uday." *International Encyclopedia of Dance* 5: 580–81.

Fay, Anthony. (1976). "The Festival of '42: A History-Making Summer at Jacob's Pillow." *Dancemagazine* 50 (July): 61–65.

Foster, Susan Leigh, ed. (2009). *Worlding Dance*. New York: Palgrave Macmillan.

Gainor, J. Ellen, ed. (1995). *Imperialism and Theatre: Essays on World Theatre, Drama and Performance*. London: Routledge.

Gallini, Giovanni-Andrea. (1770). *Critical Observations on the Art of Dancing, to Which Is Added a Collection of Cotillions or French Dances*. London: Printed by Dodsley, Becket, et al.

Garafola, Lynn, ed. (1997). *Rethinking the Sylph: New Perspectives on the Romantic Ballet*. Hanover, NH: Wesleyan University Press.

Garelick, Rhonda K. (1995). "Electric Salome: Loie Fuller at the Exposition Universelle of 1900." In Gainor, 85–103.

———. (2007). *Electric Salome: Loie Fuller's Performance of Modernism*. Princeton, NJ: Princeton University Press.

Goellner, Ellen W., and Jacqueline Shea Murphy, eds. (1994). *Bodies of the Text: Dance as Theory, Literature as Dance*. New Brunswick, NJ: Rutgers University Press.

Goodman, Lizbeth, with Jane de Gray, eds. (1998). *The Routledge Reader in Gender and Performance*. London: Routledge.

Gopal, Ram. (1962). "Eastern Dances for Western Dancers." *Dancing Times* (London) 52 (October): 16–17.

———. (1957). *Rhythm in the Heavens: An Autobiography*. London: Secker and Warburg.

Gopal, Ram, and Serozh Dadachanji. (1951). *Indian Dancing*. London: Phoenix House.

Grau, Andrée. (1992). "Intercultural Research in the Performing Arts." *Dance Research* 10 (Autumn): 3–29.

Guten, Keri. (1981) "Dancing her way around the world," *San Antonio Light* (November 11), M1 and 4.

Hanna, Judith Lynne. (1987). *Dance, Sex and Gender: Signs of Identity, Dominance, Defiance, and Desire*. Chicago: University of Chicago Press.

———. (1993). "Classical Indian Dance and Women's Status." In Thomas, 119–35.

Happel, Richard V. (1955). "La Meri Little Show Bridges Two Arts." *Berkshire Evening Eagle* (July 29).

Heredia Casanova, Marta. (2002). *El Legado del Maestro Marcelo Torreblanca; Padrede la Docencia de la Danza Mexicana*. Guadalajara, Mexico: Universidad Autónomo de Guadalajara.

Hering, Doris. (1956). "La Meri's 'Little Show.'" *Dance Magazine* 30 (February): 11.

———(1966). Review of *Dance Composition: The Basic Elements*. *Dance Magazine* 40 (March): 23–24.

Homenaje en su Centenario: Antonia Mercé "La Argentina" 1890–1990. (1990). Madrid: Ministerio de Cultura, Instituto Nacional de las Artes Escénicas y de la Música (INAEM).

Igo, John. (1984). "Theater Review: La Meri visits childhood home here." *North San Antonio Times* (May 10).

India League of America. (1941). "The League Presents La Meri, a Great Dancer." *India To-Day* 2 (October): 4.

International Encyclopedia of Dance (1998). Selma Jeanne Cohen, ed. 6 volumes. New York: Oxford University Press.

Jones, Clifford Reis. (1998). "Rao, Shanta." *International Encyclopedia of Dance* 5: 309.

Jowitt, Deborah. (1988). *Time and the Dancing Image*. Berkeley: University of California Press.

Kant, Marion, ed. (2007). *The Cambridge Companion to Ballet*. Cambridge: Cambridge University Press.

Katrak, Ketu H. (2011). *Contemporary Indian Dance: New Creative Choreography in India and the Diaspora*. New York: Palgrave Macmillan.

Kay, Joan. (1980). "An 'awkward' little girl became a premier star of the dance." *Courier-Journal* (Louisville, KY) (February 10), G2.

Kaye, Joseph Arnold. (1940). "Dance in Review." *Dance* 7 (April): 32–33.

Kealiinohomoku, Joann W. (1983). "An Anthropologist Looks at Ballet as a Form of Ethnic Dance." In Roger Copeland and Marshall Cohen, eds. *What Is Dance?* Oxford: Oxford University Press, 533–49. (First published *Impulse* 1969–70, 24–33).

Kingsley, Walter J. (1926). "La Meri" in his column "The Playboy of Broadway," *Vaudeville News and New York Star* (November 26): 7.

Kinney, Troy, and Margaret Kinney. (1936). *The Dance: Its Place in Art and Life*. New and rev. ed. New York: Tudor Publishing (First published 1914, New York: Frederick A. Stokes).

Korey, Ellen. (1979). "La Meri: 'The Undisputed Queen of Ethnic Dance.'" *Contemporary Dance News* (June–July), 1, 4–6. Interview.

Koritz, Amy. (1994). "Dancing the Orient for England: Maud Allan's *The Vision of Salome*." *Theatre Journal* 46 (March): 63–78. Reprint in Desmond 1997, 132–52.

Kotelawala, Sicille P. C. (1974). *The Classical Dance of Sri Lanka*. New York: Performing Arts Program of the Asia Society.

————. (1998). "Kandyan Dance." *International Encyclopedia of Dance* 3: 647–49.

Kothari, Sunil. (1998). "Gopal, Ram." *International Encyclopedia of Dance* 3: 199–200.

Krokover, Rosalyn. (1940). "St. Denis and La Meri in Joint Program." *Musical Courier* (August 15): 9.

Lahm, Adam. (1978, 1979). "Grand Lady of Ethnic Dance: La Meri." *Arabesqué* 4. Part I (November–December):8–9, 12; Part II (January–February): 7–9.

————. (1978). "Mariano Parra: Spanish Dance Innovator." *Arabesqué* 4 (November–December): 15, 17.

————. (1979). "La Meri: Backwards and Forwards." *Arabesqué* 5 (November–December): 12–13, 23.

————. (1982). "La Meri: Ethnic Dance's Living Legend." *Dance Teacher Now* 4 (November–December): 4, 7, 9–10.

"La Meri." (1940). *Women of Achievement,* Donald S. Rockwell, editor-in-chief. New York: House of Field, 107.

"La Meri—Versatile Artist: Highest Authority on Ethnological Dances." (1941). By L.M. (Lucille Marsh?) in *Dance* 8 (February): 16–17.

Landers, Sherwood. (1970). "Ethnic dance is visualized as embryo." *Sunday Cape Cod Standard-Times* (May 17).

Larsen, Evelyn. (1972). "Dance on Cape Cod: Cultural Asset." *Cape Cod Standard-Times* (October 15).

Lavalle, Josefina. (2002). "Anna Pavlova y el jarabe tapatío." In *La danza en México; Visiones de cinco siglos,* vol. I of *Ensayos Históricos y Analíticos,* ed. Maya Ramos Smith and Patricia Cardona Lang. México: Instituto Nacional de Bellas Artes/CENIDI-Danza, 635–50.

Lawson, Evelyn. (1972). "Dance on Cape: cultural asset." *Cape Cod Standard-Times* (October 15).

————. (1973). "Who Is La Meri?" *Cape Cod Illustrated* (September 20).

Lawton, Shailer Upton. (1945). "Dance and the New 'Education.'" *Dance News* 7 (November): 4.

Lazzarini, John, and Roberta Lazzarini. (1980). *Pavlova: Repertoire of a Legend.* New York: Schirmer Books.

Lazzarini, Roberta. (1998). "Pavlova, Anna." *International Encyclopedia of Dance* 5: 119–27.

LeClaire, Anne. (1976). "La Meri: Cape Cod's First Lady of Dance." *Cape Cod Illustrated* 14 (April 22): 16–17.

Lengel, Laura, ed. (2005). *Intercultural Communication and Creative Practice: Music, Dance, and Women's Cultural Identity.* Westport, CT: Praeger.

Lloyd, Margaret. (1941). "Dance Travelogue by La Meri." *Christian Science Monitor* (February 3).

————. (1941). "World Traveler of Dance." *Christian Science Monitor* (April 5).

————. (1943). "Theatre for Ethnologic Dance—I." *Christian Science Monitor* (August 28).

————. (1944). "Hindu Swan Queen." *Christian Science Monitor* (February 26).

————. (1946). "The Expanding Universe of Dance—Modern Music Session." *Christian Science Monitor* (August 3).

Loney, Glenn. (1998). "Cole, Jack." *International Encyclopedia of Dance* 2: 184–85.

MacCormack, John. (2016). "Igo was San Antonio's genial literary uncle." *San Antonio Express-News* (August 10).

Magri, Gennaro. (1779). *Trattato teorico-prattico di ballo.* Naples. Trans. as *Theoretical and Practical Treatise on Dancing* by Mary Skeaping. London: Dance Books, 1988.

Manning, Susan. (1997). "The Female Dancer and the Male Gaze: Feminist Critiques of Early Modern Dance." In Desmond 1997, 153–66.

María y Campos, Armando de. (1938a). "La aparición de La Meri en el Teatro de B. Artes fija una fecha excepcional en los anales coreográficos de México." *Suplemento Dominica de "Las Noticias."* (Guadalajara, April 17).

———. (1938b). "La Meri, Bailarina Múltiple." *El Mercurio* (Santiago de Chile, May 15).

———. (1939). "La Meri, Bailarina Múltiple." *El Universal* (Caracas, May 21).

Marranca, Bonnie, and Gautam Dasgupta, eds. (1991). *Interculturism and Performance.* New York: PAJ Publications.

Marsh, Lucile. (1943). "Touring the World with La Meri." *Dance* 17 (July): 10–11.

Martin, John. (1940). "La Meri Appears in Racial Dances." *New York Times* (April 1).

———. (1941). "La Meri Presents 3 Dances of India." *New York Times* (December 22).

———. (1944). "The Dance: 'Swan Lake' in Hindu." *New York Times* (March 5).

McGowan, Margaret M. (2008). *Dance in the Renaissance: European Fashion, French Obsession.* New Haven, CT: Yale University Press.

Money, Keith. (1982). *Pavlova: Her Art and Life.* New York: Knopf.

Morin, Raymond. (1971a). "La Meri Opens Fete at Quinsig College." *Worcester Sunday Telegram* (April 18).

———(1971b). "Dancers La Meri, Adams making Cape center for ethnic art." *Worcester Sunday Telegram* (August 1).

Mukerji, H. C. (1937). "L'Art de La Meri." *Orient Illustrated Weekly* (March 21): 6, 13.

Narghis, Shirada. (1945). "India's Dance in America." *Dance* 19 (August): 10–11.

Neal, Josie. (1985). "Tamburitzans, La Meri share love of dance." Unidentified San Antonio publication in San Antonio Public Library (May 19).

———. (1988). "La Meri: The grande dame of ethnic dance." *San Antonio Light* (January 24): J11, 14.

———. (1989). "La Meri's 'Drishyakava'—A Video Presentation." *Proceedings Society of Dance History Scholars.* Twelfth Annual Conference, Arizona State University, February 17–19, 1989. Published by Society of Dance History Scholars (SDHS), University of California, Riverside, 148–52.

Oberzaucher-Schüller, Gunhild. (1998). "Wiesenthal, Grete." *International Encyclopedia of Dance* 6: 386–88.

O'Donnell, May. (1991). "May O'Donnell" In Marian Horosko, comp. *Martha Graham: The Evolution of Her Dance Theory and Training 1926–1991.* Pennington, NJ: A Cappella Books, 57–63.

Orthwine, Rudolf. (1943). "A New Type of Intimate Dance Theatre." *Dance Magazine* 17 (November): 17.

O'Shea, Janet. (2007). *At Home in the World: Bharata Natyam on the Global Stage.* Middletown, CT: Wesleyan University Press.

Otero Aranda, José. (1912). *Tratado de bailes; De sociedad, regionales españoles, especialmente Andaluces, con su historia y modo de ejecutarlos.* Seville. Republished: Madrid: Asociación Manuel Pareja-Obregon, 1987.

Pavis, Patrice, ed. (1996). *The Intercultural Performance Reader.* London: Routledge.

Peters, Julie Stone. (1995). "Intercultural Performance, Theatre Anthropology, and the Imperialist Critique: Identities, Inheritances, and Neo-Orthodoxies." In Gainor, 199–213.

Polhemus, Ted. (1993). "Dance, Gender and Culture." In Thomas, 3–15.

Pohren, Donn E. (1962). *The Art of Flamenco.* Jerez de la Frontera: Editorial Jerez Industrial.

———. (1964). *Lives and Legends of Flamenco: A Biographical History.* Seville: Society of Spanish Studies. Revised edition, Madrid, 1988.

Prevots, Naima. (1987). *Dancing in the Sun: Hollywood Choreographers 1915–1937.* Ann Arbor: University of Michigan Research Press.

Prickett, Stacey. (2004). "Techniques and Institutions: The Transformation of British Dance Tradition through South Asian Dance." *Dance Research* 22 (Summer): 1–21.

Raffé, W. G. (1942). Review of *The Gesture Language of the Hindu Dance.* In *Indian Art and Letters* 16 (May–June).

Ramon, Florence. (1943). "La Meri of Louisville Joins East-West Twain: Outstanding Ethnological Dancer Brings Home Native Oriental Art." *Morning Telegraph* (New York) (January 14).

Renouf, Renée. (1979). "La Meri: A Life in Ethnic Dance" (review of her two 1977 publications). *Dance Chronicle* 3/1: 67–74.

Robinson, Jacqueline. (1997). *Modern Dance in France: An Adventure 1920–1970.* Trans. Catherine Dale. Amsterdam: Harwood Academic Publishers.

Roy, Basanta Koomar. (1940?). "La Meri Opens her School of Natya in New York," released by the International Literary Exchange in New York. Typed article in New York Public Library.

Rubidge, Sarah. (1996). "Does authenticity matter? The case for and against authenticity in the performing arts." In Campbell, 219–33.

Ruyter, Nancy Lee Chalfa. (1979). *Reformers and Visionaries: The Americanization of the Art of Dance.* New York: Dance Horizons.

———. (1996). "Satirical Dance Texts as Historical Sources: Two Examples from Spain." *Cairón* (Universidad de Alcalá de Henares, Spain) I (January): 73–84.

———. (1999a). *The Cultivation of Body and Mind in Nineteenth-Century American Delsartism.* Westport, CT: Greenwood Press.

———. (1999b). "La Meri." *American National Biography,* vol. 13, ed. John A. Garraty and Mark C. Carnes. New York: Oxford University Press, 85–86.

———. (2000a). "La Meri and the World of Dance." *Anales del Instituto de Investigaciones Estéticas.* Mexico City: Universidad Nacional Autónoma de México, num. 77: 169–88.

———. (2000b). "La Meri: Pionera en la globalización de la danza en el mundo pre-tecnológico." *Zona de Danza* (Mexico) 3/14 (September–October): 25–27.

Santos, John Phillip. (1984). "She's danced across the globe." *San Antonio Express* (April 15).

Schlundt, Christena L. (1962). *The Professional Appearances of Ruth St. Denis & Ted Shawn: A Chronology and an Index of Dances 1906–1932.* New York: New York Public Library.

———. (1978). *Dance Out the Answer* (review). *Dance Research Journal* 10 (Spring–Summer): 50–51.

Schwarz, Edith. (1950). "De ethnische dans." *Dans Kroniek* (Netherlands), no. 3 Vierde Jaargang [4th year] (January): 29–31.

Scott, A. C. (1958). *Introduction to Chinese Theatre.* Hong Kong: Donald Moore.

Selden, Elizabeth. (1930). *Elements of the Free Dance.* New York: A. S. Barnes.

Shah, Purnima. (2002). "State Patronage in India: Appropriation of the 'Regional' and 'National.'" *Dance Chronicle* 25/1: 125–41.

Shawn, Ted. (1940, 1950). *Dance We Must (The Peabody Lectures, Series 1).* Pittsfield, MA.

———. (1953). "The History of Jacob's Pillow." In *Jacob's Pillow Dance Festival Souvenir Program 1953,* 3–6, 11–14.

———. (1963). *Every Little Movement: A Book about François Delsarte.* New York: Dance Horizons. (Republication of 1963 2nd ed. 1st ed., 1954).

Shelton, Suzanne. (1981). *Divine Dancer: A Biography of Ruth St. Denis.* Garden City, NY: Doubleday.

Sherman, Jane. (1978). "La Meri. Part III. A Life in Ethnic Dance: Two Recent Publications of La Meri." *Dancemagazine* 52 (August): 66–69 (review of *Dance Out the Answer* and *Total Education in Ethnic Dance*).

Shipley, Jos. T. (1940). "There Is Still Dancing." *New Leader* (August 24).

Sorell, Walter, ed. (1951). *The Dance Has Many Faces.* Cleveland: World Publishing Co.

———. (1986). *Dance in its Time.* New York: Columbia University Press (first published 1981).

Taylor, Diana. (1991). "Transculturating TRANSCULTURATION." *Performing Arts Journal* (PAJ) 13 (May): 90–104.

Taylor, Patricia. (1997). "La Meri: A Life Dedicated to Ethnic Dance." *Habibi* 16 (Fall): 2–7.

Temin, Christine. (1979). "La Meri at 81." *Boston Sunday Globe* (July 1).

Terry, Walter. (1940). "To a Greater Dance." *New York Herald Tribune (NYHT)* (March 10).

———. (1944). "La Meri Shows Lore of India in Dance Program." *NYHT* (December 22).

———. (1945). "Notes on the Hindu Dance." *NYHT* (December 9).

———. (1946). "The Dance." *NYHT* (July 20, 27).

———. (1947). "The Dance." *NYHT* (December 29, 31).

———. (1953). "Dance: Jacob's Pillow Festival." *NYHT* (August 13).

———, ed. (1978). "La Meri. Part II. A Chronology of Learning, Labor, Life." *Dance Magazine* 52 (August): 62–65.

Thomas, Helen, ed. (1993). *Dance, Gender and Culture.* New York: St. Martin's Press.

Venkateswaran, Usha. (2005). *The Life and Times of La Meri: The Queen of Ethnic Dance.* New Delhi: Indira Gandhi National Centre for the Arts and Aryan Books International.

Wingfield, Valerie. (2013). "Bhaskar Roy Chowdhury, Prince among Dancers." Article in Manuscripts and Archives Division of NYPL (August 1).

Wright, Frances B. (1966). "La Meri. The gesture language of the hindu dance" (review). *Ethnomusicology* 10 (May): 232–33.

Index

Page numbers in *italics* indicate illustrations.

104–14; Los Angeles and New York City (1937–38), 115–17; Latin America (1938), 119–26; Italy (1938), 126–27; United States (1939), 128–29; Latin America (1939), 129–30; New York City and New Jersey (1939–44), 132, 133, 134, 137–38, 140–41
Carreras, Juana (or Joanna). *See* Jurgeas, Joanna
Carreras, Maria, 26
Carrick, Edward, 150
Cartagena, Roberto, 212, 216
Carter, Alexander, 266, 267
Casino de Paris Girls, 33
Cendalli, Ricardo, 48, 49, 50
Ceylon. *See* Sri Lanka
Charles Weidman Theatre Dance Company, 215
Charmer, The (film), 22–23
Chascomús, 125, 126
"Chethat-al-Maharma" (dance), 56, 225
"Chethat-al-Selah" (dance), 56, *158,* 225
Chile, 48–49, 121, 122–24, 240, 269, 270
Chitra (Tagore), 273
Chow, Alan, 213
Chowdhury, Bhaskar Roy, 213, 215, 216, 221, 226–27, 236, 287n8
Christian Science Monitor, 141
Chronology 1973 (La Meri), 204, 211, 213, 214, 215, 220
Chronology Notebook (La Meri), 152, 153, 205
"Chrysanthemum Dance" ("Kikuzukushi"), *166*
Chujoy, Anatole, 182, 184–85
Clarke, Catherine, 21, 23, 41
Clegg, Agnes Terrell, 49–50
Cleve, Felix, 57, 68, 139–40, 185, 282n4
Cole, Jack, 136, 150
College of Industrial Arts, 15
Colombia, 47, 216, 240, 269
Columbia Concerts, 116, 128, 284n2, 284n3
Columbia University, 16
Commission of Texas Arts and Humanities, 224
Contemporary Dance News, 225
Coomaraswamy, Ananda K., 63, 71, 140, 244–46, 261, 265
Coorlawala, Uttara Asha, 208, 217
Coppicus, Francis Charles, 116–17, 284n2
Costa Rica, 48, 49, 240, 269
Court of Birds, 20–21
Covarrubias, Miguel, 30
Craig, Edward Gordon, 150
Cressy, Richard, 174

Cruz, Roberto, 30
Cuba, 34–36, 38, 117, *159*
Cueca, 123–24, 284n5
"Curandero Swahili" (dance), 62
"Curly Headed Baby" (song), 46

Dadswell, Lyndon, *89*
Dallal, Alberto, 30
Dallapiccola, Luigi, 57
Damrosch Conservatory, 16
Dance, The (magazine), 49, 132
Dance as an Art Form: Its History and Development (La Meri), 65, 241–43, 260–61, 287n2
Dance Chronicle, 253, 254
Dance Composition: The Basic Elements (La Meri), 207, 241, 250–52, 260
Dance Critics Conference, 226
Dance education of La Meri: beginning in San Antonio, Texas, 12–14, *80–82;* training in Burma, 106–7; in Ceylon (Sri Lanka), 98; in Chile, 123–24; in Hawaii, 114; in India, 102, 105–6; in Japan, 111; in Java, 109; in Mexico, 29–30; in Morocco, 55–56; in New York City, 16, 24–26; in New Zealand, 95–96; in Philippines, 110; in Spain, 17, 53–55; with Michio Itō, 34; with Uday Shankar, 63
Dance Has Many Faces, The (Sorrell), 259
Dance Magazine or *Dancemagazine:* August 1978 section on La Meri, 206, 207, 225, 254–55, 258, 260; and the Ethnologic Dance Center, 141, 144; review of La Meri's *Dance Composition,* 251–52; reviews of La Meri performances and other events, 171–72, 178, 225
Dance News, 175, 182, 184, 185
Dance Observer, 173, 179, 185
"Dance of Salutation." *See* "Chethat-al-Selah"
"Dance of the Five Senses" (Ruth St. Denis), 14
"Dance of the Handkerchiefs," 55
"Dance of the Hours," 13
Dance of the Seven Veils (Loie Fuller), 4
"Dance of the Spanish Shawl," 32, 33, 35, *85*
Dance Out the Answer: An Autobiography (La Meri), 230, 252–55, 260, 280n1
Dance pedagogy: La Meri's concepts and approaches, 53, 252, 256–58; La Meri's work at the Accademia dei Fidenti, 65–66, 67; at Ethnic Dance Arts, 218–21; at Ethnologic Dance Center, 141–43; at School of Natya, 136, 138; in Tokyo, 112

NANCY LEE CHALFA RUYTER, professor emerita at University of California, Irvine, taught in the dance department at the UCI Claire Trevor School of the Arts for thirty-two years. She has choreographed in various genres and has reconstructed Spanish dance works. She is the author of *Reformers and Visionaries: The Americanization of the Art of Dance* and *The Cultivation of Body and Mind in Nineteenth Century American Delsartism*. Her articles have appeared in *Dance Chronicle, Choreography and Dance, Dance Research Journal,* and other publications.